THE CINEMATIC GRIOT

Jean Rouch in the courtyard of the Social Science Research Institute in
Niamey, Niger, 1977. Photo by Judith Gleason.

THE
CINEMATIC
GRIOT

The Ethnography
of Jean Rouch

Paul Stoller

The University of Chicago Press
Chicago & London

PAUL STOLLER is professor of anthropology at West Chester University. His books include *In Sorcery's Shadow* (with Cheryl Olkes) and *Fusion of the Worlds,* both published by the University of Chicago Press.

The University of Chicago Press, Chicago 60637
The University of Chicago Press, Ltd., London
© 1992 by The University of Chicago
All rights reserved. Published 1992
Printed in the United States of America
01 00 99 98 97 96 95 94 93 92   5 4 3 2 1

ISBN (cloth): 0–226–77546–1
ISBN (paper): 0–226–77548–8

Library of Congress Cataloging-in-Publication Data

Stoller, Paul.
  The cinematic griot : the ethnography of Jean Rouch /
Paul Stoller.
    p. cm.
  Includes bibliographical references and index.
    1. Rouch, Jean. 2. Ethnologists—France. 3. Ethnolo-
gists—Niger. 4. Motion pictures in ethnography.
5. Songhai (African people) 6. Cinematographers—
France. I. Title.
GN21.R63S76 1992
305.8′0092—dc20   91-36724
                                              CIP
⊗The paper used in this publication meets the minimum
requirements of the American National Standard for Infor-
mation Sciences—Permanence of Paper for Printed Library
Materials, ANSI Z39.48–1984.

Ce follo a si fonda hinka gana.

One foot cannot follow two paths.

—Songhay proverb

Criticism can exist only as a form of love.

—André Breton

CONTENTS

PART III
WHEN FILMS BECOME DREAMS
Introduction: Postpositions 199

ACKNOWLEDGMENTS

Writing is never an isolated task. As every writer knows, it takes considerable dedication and goodwill from family, friends, colleagues, and institutions to give life to a book. *The Cinematic Griot* is no exception.

I could not have written this work without a thorough ethnographic knowledge of the Songhay of Niger. Such knowledge, still far from complete, has been built over a twenty-two-year period, 1969–90. During that time I lived in Niger as a Peace Corps volunteer (1969–71) and as a field anthropologist (1976–77, 1979–80, 1981, 1982–83, 1984, 1985–86, 1987, 1988, 1989–90). My anthropological studies in Niger were funded by the following institutions: United States Department of Education (Fulbright-Hays Dissertation Fellowship); the Wenner-Gren Foundation (two grants); the National Science Foundation (NATO Postdoctoral Fellowship Program); the American Philosophical Society (two grants); West Chester University (three Faculty Development Grants); and the National Endowment for the Humanities (Fellowships for Independent Research). I am deeply grateful to these institutions—and to the helpful people associated with them—for supporting my long-term research among the Songhay. I am also grateful to the government of Niger for authorizing me to conduct ethnographic research in Songhay and to the Institut de Recherche en Sciences Sociales of the Université de Niamey for being a home away from home.

In Niger a great many people have helped me in my efforts to write about Rouch. In particular I am grateful to Boubé Gado, director of the Institut de Recherches en Sciences Humaines and to Diouldé Laya, director of the Centre d'Etudes Linguistiques et de la Tradition Historique et Orale. Diouldé Laya has been a source of great intellectual and moral support. For their gracious hospitality in Niamey, I thank Thomas Price and Hadiza Djibo as well as the entire Djibo family.

The republic of Niger was one of two field sites germane to *The Cinematic Griot;* the other, of course, was Paris. Many friends in Paris have welcomed me into their homes over the years. Many thanks go to Suzanne Lallemand and her son, Christoph Lallemand, for housing the peripatetic American as well as to the Bernus family for their kindness. Special thanks go to Jean-Marie Giball and Christine Bergé, both of whom took great interest in my work on Rouch.

The Cinematic Griot would have lacked much pertinent information without the contribution of Nicole Echard, who has done extensive ethnographic research among the Hausa of Niger. In July 1988 Nicole Echard was hired by Radio France Culture to interview Jean Rouch. The result was ten hours of broadcasting that focused not on Rouch's technological or film accomplishments, but on the story behind his story. With the help of Nicole Echard and Jean Rouch, both of whom agreed to let me use the interviews for the book, Radio France Culture granted me formal permission. This material proved invaluable. In short, without Nicole Echard's intervention, the project would not have come to this happy end.

Many friends and colleagues have made invaluable contributions to *The Cinematic Griot*. The idea for my first article on Rouch, "Son of Rouch: Portrait of the Anthropologist by the Other," came from Wendy Wilson when she told me that people in Simiri, Niger, referred to me as "the son of Rouch." On hearing about my "son of Rouch" status, Cheryl Olkes also urged me to write about him. And so I did, thanks to her encouragement. Her creative ideas, rhetorical suggestions, and skill as a writer have profoundly influenced the contours of this book. I am also indebted to John Homiak, Kathleen Kuehnast, Daniel Rose, Steven Feld, Nicole Echard, Smadar Lavie, and Thomas Hale for their perspicacious comments on various versions of the manuscript. Special thanks to Jane Smyth and Jacquelyn Carter, who drafted the maps and illustrations in the book as employees of West Chester University. I would also like to acknowledge Wendy Shay and Pamela Wintle of the Human Area Film Archives of the Smithsonian Institution for their hospitality and encouragement. I worked on much of the manuscript as a research associate in the Department of Anthropology of the Smithsonian. I thank Donald Ortner, chairman of the department, for his kind hospitality. Jay Ruby and Faye Ginsburg both read the entire manuscript, and their incisive and constructive comments on Rouch's cinematic practices greatly improved *The Cinematic Griot*. Jay Ruby also was kind enough to provide many of the photos that are reproduced here. John Chernoff read the manuscript with a drummer's special attention to history, and for that I am deeply grateful. During the stage of final revisions, extended discussions with Rosemary Coombe helped focus my critical eye. I thank her for her critical spirit, her intellectual curiosity, her generosity, and most important of all, her laughter.

Finally I must pay homage, as all griots must, to the elders, my initiators. For their contributions to my intellectual development I thank Joan Rubin, Roger Shuy, Annette Weiner, and Joel Sherzer. For teaching me an appreciation of the "old words," I acknowledge my Songhay teacher, Adamu Jenitongo. For teaching me the value of long-term, participatory, shared anthropology, I thank Jean Rouch, whose example, patience, and cooperation nurtured me both as an anthropologist and as a student of the Songhay.

Portions of this book have appeared in other forms as "Son of Rouch: Portrait of a Young Anthropologist by the Other," *Anthropology Quarterly* 60:114–24, and as "Jean Rouch's Ethnographic Path," *Visual Anthropology* 2 (3): 249–65.

Many of the Songhay proverbs used as chapter epigraphs are collected in Hama (1988).

PREFACE

Ndebbi gave us seven hatchets and seven picks.
He came and gave us speech, and
He took it back
—Songhay incantation.

In December 1986 and January 1987, the year Jean Rouch turned seventy, the government of Niger invited him to Niamey to celebrate his first retrospective in Niger: *Jean Rouch, Seventy Years/Seventy Films*. During many cool evenings in the amphitheater of the Centre Franco-Nigerien, Rouch discussed his films, old and new, with Nigerien audiences. University students discovered images of their own culture; old men rediscovered the religion of the people of the past.

On 27 December 1987 Rouch showed *Pam kuso kar*. Pam was one of the principal *zima* (possession priests) of Niamey, and he taught Rouch a great deal about Songhay possession. When a zima dies, his life and death are celebrated during a ceremony called *kuso kar*, "breaking the jars." During this ceremony, all the dead zima's initiates repair to the bush. Elders pour water and powdered tree bark into a large clay jar. They recite incantations over the jar, then give each of the initiates a portion of the mixture. In the privacy of the bush, mediums wash away the filth of their zima's death. When the mixture is completely distributed the elders break the jar, severing the dead zima's last connection to the living world. The period of mourning is over; the filth of death is washed away. Then the initiates return to the dead zima's compound, where his possession costumes and objects are gathered. Elders take fresh milk and spray it over the objects to cleanse them. So cleansed, the compound is ready to receive the dead zima's spirits, which will seek new mediums to house their power. The air fills with the wail of the monochord violin and the pulsing clacks of the gourd drum. When the spirits come, they may name a new zima to replace the one who had so carefully led them down the ancestors' path.

After a lively discussion of this film, a tall young man approached Rouch and shook his hand. "Thank you, Jean, I am Abdu Sambo Zima, Pam's son" (Rouch 1989, 351). He had been so moved that he could say nothing else, but the next morning he gave Rouch a poem he wrote that night.

> Niamey, 27 December 1987
> Oh haunted night!
> Oh haunted night!
> Such as the night of 24 December 1974,
> That night will stay engraved in my memory.
> That severe night took away my father.
> Oh death, mortal enemy of joy! that took away from me papa.
> And so papa is far from us, far from this region where he will never
>   return.
> Papa is far away from his friends and from these people who loved
>   him so
> Nothing but this memory of the old zima remains. . . .

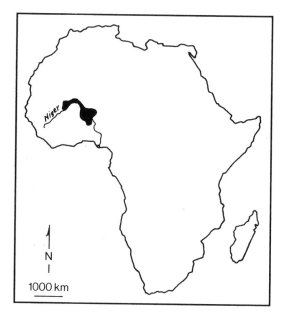

Songhay country.

I had this kind of nostalgia in my memories,

It is in this way that Jean Rouch enabled me to see my father again, smiling on a chair amid his friends in the Holey community; a rich and powerful community that this community sees again in the film, *Pam kuso kar!*

Jean opened for me the path of the past, a path that is filled with sadness.

I was so moved by this film that I don't know how to thank Jean, for this joyous gift he offered me.

But a little later my joy transformed itself.

I am becoming nervous before this impotence, this weakness . . . weakness because I could no longer relive that reality with papa. A few minutes later, I got a grip on myself, held back my tears, and listened to the music that Toukou, Garba, and Arba played on the gourd drums, this music to which the Old Man consecrated almost his entire life, which for me is an unforgettable memory. . . .

I thank you for this film, Jean, but mostly for having given me the will that night, 27 December, 1987, to taste my reality, that is to say, my

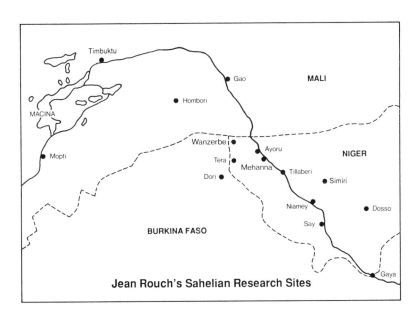

Jean Rouch's principal research sites.

heritage that I left due to modern influences, due to Western science that had demonstrated to me its power.

Abdu Sambo Zima (Rouch 1989, 351–52)

Abdu Sambo Zima, who holds an advanced degree in physics, has succeeded his father. He is a man who solves problems in two worlds.

When Rouch learned of Abdu Sambo Zima's immersion in the spirit community, he too was moved. He wrote: "Then I discovered that all my past work, all those rambles to Wanzerbe, those rides [on horseback] toward Hombori, those detailed visits to the archipelagoes to research the sorko, all those years had led to this future work. And the Niamey screenings seemed to me like an 'alternative' bullfight where I passed my cape and sword to ambitious and determined young matadors" (Rouch 1989, 352). As a griot (bard), Jean Rouch had fulfilled his greatest responsibility: to pass on his knowledge to the next generation.

The word *griot* might have been a Mande word that was Frenchified sometime during the French exploration of the western Sudan in the nineteenth century. According to some Mande specialists, the original Mandikan word *geeli* becomes *jeeli* in Bambara, the most widely spoken Mandikan language. In some Mandikan dialects *geeli* becomes *geri* or *gerio*. Linguists speculate that the early French explorers probably heard something like *gerio*, which became *griot*.[1]

No matter what one calls these men and women, they are considered "the masters of speech" in the western Sahel. The griot is above all a bard, a person who sings praises to the ancestors, to the life of the past. The griot is also the custodian of a society's traditions, the one who maintains and reinforces the links between present and past. "The griot is an artist, and music and oral art are his very definition" (Bird 1971, 17).

Griots are important personalities among the Wolof of Senegal, the

---

1. See Bird (1971, 15–22). There is quite a debate over the origin of the word *griot*. No one seems to know its "real" etymology. Mauny (1952) says it may have derived from Wolof, from Toucouleur, or perhaps from Portuguese. Camara (1976, 5) notes that the term first appears in seventeenth-century travel accounts and is spelled *guirot*. Watta suggests that griot is derived from the Fulfude term *gawlo*. In the end, the word "is a French rendering of a cluster of conceptual referents" (Watta 1985, 85). Hale (1990, 35) focuses on the verbal power of the griot: "The bard, then, is a master of the spoken word, a phenomenon that may be both ephemeral but also quite powerful. One reason for verbal power stems no doubt from the ancient Sahelian tradition that words, like many other materials worked by man, are endowed with an occult power, known as *nyama* among the Mande-speaking peoples."

various Mande groups of Mali, and the Songhay of Mali and Niger. As guardians of the power of "old words," the words of power, the griots practice an oral art highly venerated in West Africa.

Many Western scholars consider Jean Rouch a pathbreaking ethnographic filmmaker; he is the champion of *cinéma vérité,* a master of technical innovation in film. For the Songhay of Niger, however, who are the subjects of most of his films, Rouch is not a filmmaker, but a griot whose art is produced on a screen.

Just as Songhay griots share their knowledge with the descendants of the ancestors whose praises they sing, so Rouch shares his films with the people he has filmed. In 1954 Rouch shared his *Bataille sur le grand fleuve* with the hippopotamus hunters of Ayoru. Seeing their own images on the screen, they understood Rouch's work as that of a cinematic griot, for this film would become a record of the past, a record that could be "recited" in the future. Rouch and his camera became guardians of Songhay traditions. There are no more hippo hunts in Ayoru. Rouch's *The Lion Hunters* records the life of the hunters of Yatakala, men who tracked and killed lions with bows and arrows. Today the men of Yatakala no longer hunt lions, but the hunt lives on in the story recounted in Rouch's film. Although Hauka possession ceremonies are still staged in Niger, the Hauka cult that existed in the Gold Coast of 1954 is no longer. The film *Les maîtres fous* therefore conserves images of Songhay cultural resistance to the British colonialism of the 1950s. Rouch's films of the sixty-year cycle of Sigui ceremonies record the symbolic sophistication of Dogon cosmology. Embodied in these films are the images of the re-creation of the Dogon world. Although Rouch will not be among us when the next Sigui cycle begins in Yougou, Mali, in 2027, the Dogon, many of whom he has trained in filmmaking techniques, will use the Sigui films to ensure that the ceremonies are staged correctly.

This book is the story of Jean Rouch's story, the tale of a griot's tale.

CHAPTER ONE
In the Past, in the Present

Listen.
Listen and you shall learn, my son.
Listen to the old words of the past.
Listen to the voice of the ancestors.
Listen to the sounds of my father,
And my father's father.
Listen and know that my words are beyond their words.
Listen and know that my path is beyond their path.
Listen and know that what I know you shall know.
Listen and know that when I am gone, my son,
My words shall live on in your heart.
Listen and know, my son, that you too will pass
This knowledge on to your sons.

So it is that the word is passed from father to son among the griots, possession priests, and *sohanci* sorcerers of the Songhay of Niger.[1] So it is that the word images of Jean Rouch will be handed on to a new generation of scholars. So it is that Rouch will pass the camera to those who had always been in front of it (Rouch 1974).

This book is more of a griot's tale than a biography, for in it I shall present and assess the knowledge that Jean Rouch has offered to his sons and daughters. After more than fifty years of fieldwork among the Songhay of Niger and the Dogon of Mali, Rouch has produced an extensive body of ethnography in writing and in film, a body of knowledge that, like Songhay praise poems, preserves ethnographic traditions and challenges epistemological norms. Thus most of the book is not about Rouch's personal life or his technological innovations in

---

1. The epigraph is reconstructed from a variety of Songhay incantations known to me.

film, but about his ethnographic oeuvre. It does not address the entire corpus of Rouch's work in film but contemplates his major contributions to African ethnography in both prose and film. As a consequence, one of Rouch's most notable and most discussed films, *Chronique d'un été*, considered the first film of the *cinéma vérité* movement, is not treated here.[2]

Much time has passed. Many interviews, articles, and books have been published. Many films have been made and remade. And yet Rouch is an enigmatic figure. With one like Rouch, as the fathers say, the griot's task is difficult. Listen:

He is the most prolific ethnographic filmmaker in the world, yet only five of the more than one hundred films he has made are distributed in North America. He is a pioneering ethnographer of African societies, yet his ethnographic writings are largely unknown.

Jean Rouch is a controversial figure in the histories of anthropology and of film. His films, which are grounded in the ethnographic fieldwork he has conducted in West Africa from 1941 to the present, continue to prompt a torrent of negative commentary. It is said that Rouch's films are racist, that they reinforce a pernicious exoticism. It is said that Rouch fabricates stories and presents them as fact. Ousmane Sembène, a Senegalese author and filmmaker, once suggested that Rouch observed Africans as if they were insects (quoted in Predal 1982, 78). And yet Rouch's work is admired in Europe and Africa. He is a pioneer of *cinéma vérité* and is considered a cinematic innovator whose work influenced the likes of Jean-Luc Godard and François Truffaut.[3] He has helped train and support many African filmmakers,

2. Those who would like to read texts that discuss Rouch's cinematic practices more thoroughly are urged to consult the following works: J. DeBouzek, "The Ethnographic Surrealism of Jean Rouch," *Visual Anthropology* 2, 3–4 (1989): 301–17; B. Dornfeld, "Chronicle of a Summer and Editing of Cinéma-Vérité," *Visual Anthropology* 2, 3–4 (1989): 317–33; M. Eaton, ed. *Anthropology-Reality-Cinema* (London: British Film Institute, 1979); Steven Feld, ed., *Studies in the Anthropology of Visual Communication* (1974, first four issues); Steven Feld, "Themes in the Cinema of Jean Rouch," *Visual Anthropology* 2, 3–4 (1989): 223–49. See also Steven Feld, ed., special issue on *Chronicle of a Summer* in *Studies in Visual Communication* 11 (winter 1985). See also J. Ruby, ed., *The Cinema of Jean Rouch,* special issue of *Visual Anthropology* 2, 3–4 (1989): 233–367. For an extensive list of texts (in French) on Jean Rouch's work in film, see R. Predal, ed., *Jean Rouch, un griot gaulois,* special issue of *CinemAction* 17 (Paris: Harmattan, 1982).

3. The term *cinéma vérité* is often confused with *cinéma direct* and direct cinema. In this book *cinéma vérité* is used to mean filming that is both observational and participatory—the technique of Vertov and Rouch. Many film historians use the term direct cinema to characterize the observational style of Frederick Wiseman and Richard Leacock,

Jean Rouch filming the Dogon Sigui. Comité du Film Ethnographique.

including Moustafa Alhassane, Oumarou Ganda, and Inoussa Ouseini.

Despite Rouch's substantial contributions to both anthropology
and film, his work is only partly understood. Some of his most caustic
critics have seen only a few of his films, and some of his most faithful
admirers are unfamiliar with his ethnographic writing. The published

with synchronized sound and no narration. I am indebted to Jay Ruby and Faye Ginsburg, who pointed this out to me.

commentary on Rouch is therefore incomplete. Most of it considers his technical innovations or his narrative structures out of context—in isolation from Songhay and Dogon ethnography, in isolation from the ethnographic knowledge that Rouch, among others, has produced.[4]

In this book I choose the griot's path, for as a fellow recorder of Songhay social life, my primary concern is with Jean Rouch's ethnography. From his first foray into Niger in 1941 to the present, he has followed an ethnographic path that impelled him to participate in Songhay social life. His path led him onto the vast plain of Songhay history, political life, social change, sorcery, and possession. On that plain the elders spoke to him. He listened, he learned, he wrote, and he filmed. Starting in 1946, Rouch periodically left the Songhay plain to climb the Bandiagara cliffs of the Dogon. There too he listened, learned, wrote, and filmed.

I have followed Rouch's path in Songhay, visiting and living in many of the villages where he worked forty years ago. Having lived intermittently among the Songhay since 1969, I intend to show in this book that Rouch's cinematic vision has been profoundly influenced by his direct confrontations with the imponderables of the Songhay and Dogon worlds. These experiences compelled him to pick up pen and camera and become a griot, a man who, through his provocative words and evocative images, has told the story of a two peoples, the Songhay of the republic of Niger and the Dogon of the republic of Mali.

The Cinematic Griot is a broad and integrated analysis of Jean Rouch's ethnography of the Songhay as it is realized in his books and his films. It introduces English-speaking readers—this griot's audience—to the story of Rouch's ethnographic fieldwork and charts the ethnographic contexts of his most important films, whose powerful but often unexplicated images have sometimes provoked angry misunderstandings.

To comprehend Rouch's work, one must know something of the texture of life as it is lived along the Niger bend in Sahelian West Africa. Just as the epic of Askia Mohammed, the fifteenth-century Songhay king, considers both the man and the sociocultural and historical conditions in which he lived, so this book will not only discuss Rouch's life and work, but describe the historical, political, and sociocultural dimensions of the people he has described—the Songhay of Niger.

---

4. See Predal (1982, 62–77), in which several African filmmakers critical of Rouch admit they have seen only a few of his films. None of them mention reading his books or articles.

ROUCH'S ETHNOGRAPHY

In 1941 when he was a young engineer working for the French Travaux Publics in the colony of Niger, Jean Rouch had his first contact with the Songhay people in the Niamey region. With the aid of his mentors, Marcel Griaule and Théodore Monod, and his informant-friends, especially Damoré Zika, Rouch gathered information on Songhay mythology, history, and language. By 1942 he had amassed a collection of documentary photographs and ritual objects used in Songhay possession ceremonies. After the war Rouch returned to Songhay country, and in 1946–47 he, Jean Sauvy, and Pierre Ponty paddled a dugout the entire length of the Niger River. Back in Songhay in 1948, he toured the Tillaberi region, visiting the most culturally important cantons. In Sangara and Wanzerbe he met the famous sorcerers of Songhay, the *sohanci*, the direct patrilineal descendants of the great Songhay "magic" king Sonni Ali Ber. Rouch also conducted fieldwork among the Songhay in 1949 when he went to Aribinda and Dori (Burkina Faso) and to Hombori (Mali). This trip enabled him to complete his work on Songhay mythology. In 1950–51 he studied the Songhay populations living in what was then the Gold Coast, and he continued this work in 1953–54.

Rouch published his findings. One study appeared in 1953: *Contribution à l'histoire des Songhay,* which focused on Songhay archaeology, mythology, and history. *Les Songhay,* a classic ethnography, appeared in 1954, along with *Le Niger en pirogue,* the account of Rouch's descent of the Niger River in 1946–47. *Migrations au Ghana* (1956) is the result of his work among Songhay populations living in the colonial Gold Coast. In 1960 he published his *thèse d'état, La religion et la magie Songhay,* the culmination of almost twenty years of fieldwork. *Religion* is a comprehensive ethnography, covering in exhaustive detail Songhay mythology, possession, and sorcery.

His early years of research also resulted in some of Rouch's most memorable ethnographic films, *Initiation à la danse des possédés* (1948), *La circoncision* (1949), *Bataille sur le grand fleuve* (1953), *Les hommes qui font la pluie* (1951), and *Les magiciens de Wanzerbe* (1949). *Les magiciens de Wanzerbe* has a remarkable sequence of a sorcerer's dance (*sohanci hori*) during which a dancer vomits his magic chain and then swallows it again. Like many of Rouch's other films, *Magiciens* documents the horrors and delights of the Songhay worlds of sorcery and possession, worlds in which the inexplicable occurs with alarming frequency.

With the exception of a few articles, since 1960 Rouch has concentrated on filmmaking. Fieldwork in Ghana and the Ivory Coast resulted in the incomparable *Les maîtres fous* (1954), *Jaguar* (1954), and *Moi, un noir* (1957). Fieldwork in Niger between 1957 and 1964 culminated in his well-known *La chasse au lion à l'arc* (*The Lion Hunters*, English version). Rouch has also made several feature-length general-audience films based partly on his ethnographic experience (see *Petit à petit* [1969], *Babatu, les trois conseils* [1975], and *Cocorico, Monsieur Poulet* [1974]). The bulk of Rouch's film work, however, concentrates on Songhay possession. There are cinematic interviews with possession priests (*Daouda Sorko* [1967]) and a score of short films on Songhay *yenaandi* ceremonies, the possession rites during which spirits are asked to bring rain (see chap. 2 for more details on Rouch's fieldwork; see also Rouch's bibliography and filmography at the end of the book).[5]

While many Europeans applaud Jean Rouch as an artistic innovator, Songhay consider him in an altogether different light. Besides being thought a griot, he is also, to quote one of my teachers in Wanzerbe, Niger, "the European who follows the spirits." For many Songhay Rouch is the shrewd European who had the foresight to take seriously the Songhay world of power. "It is no mere coincidence," a spirit possession priest told me, "that Rouch is a big man; he has power. The spirits clear his path for him."

Early on his ethnographic path, Jean Rouch visited Wanzerbe, a Songhay village famous—and feared by most Songhay—for its sorcerers, where he penetrated into a world of great power. Word spread widely in Songhay: Rouch had been to Wanzerbe, had learned great secrets, and had eaten *kusu*, the substance of power. Rouch was a man to be feared and respected. Over time, many Songhay blended the notion of Rouch into the imagery of myth reminiscent of the epics retold by Songhay griots. He has become part of contemporary Songhay cosmology. When I returned from my initial trip to Wanzerbe thirty years after Jean Rouch's first visit there, the news of my travels spread widely as an instant legend in Songhay: Stoller had been to Wanzerbe, had learned great secrets, and had eaten kusu. Stoller was a man to be feared and respected. Stoller became the "son of Rouch."

5. My Filmography of Jean Rouch is adapted from Ruby's filmography of Rouch's work, annotated and published in *Visual Anthropology* 2, 3–4 (1989): 333–67. Readers seeking a fully annotated list are urged to consult Ruby's excellent work. Other annotated filmographies of Rouch appear in Eaton (1979) and in *Jean Rouch, une rétrospective* (1981), published by the French Ministry of Foreign Affairs.

SON OF ROUCH

It is only fitting for the "son" of the griot to tell the story of his father:

I suppose I was destined to meet Jean Rouch sooner or later. In 1969–71 I taught English at secondary schools in Tera and Tillaberi, two centers of Songhay culture in Niger. Between 1973 and 1976 I studied social anthropology, and in 1976 I won a fellowship to study the Songhay for my doctoral dissertation. My subject was the relation between language, religion, and Songhay politics.

I first encountered Rouch in Niamey, Niger, in August 1976. Having read his books and seen some of his films, I felt honored to make his acquaintance. As soon as we were introduced, he began to recount outrageously funny stories about his experiences in Niger and Mali. Having put me at ease, he confirmed that my ethnographic research was important.

I prepared to begin my fieldwork in Mehanna, a riverine village some 180 kilometers north of Niamey. My arrival there sparked a discussion about my lodgings.

"You could live in the *campement*," said Tondi Bello, the village chief.

"Yes," said his crony Saadu, "that's where Monsieur Rouch stayed when he came to Mehanna."

"Monsieur Rouch?" I wondered aloud.

"Yes," replied Tondi Bello. "Until you came, Monsieur Rouch was the only European to spend time here."

"When was that?"

"Oh, that was thirty years ago."

"Thirty years ago. I see."

"Do you want to stay in the *campement?*" Saadu asked.

"He doesn't want to stay there," interjected Boureima Boulhassane, who had shared the cab of the truck that transported me to Mehanna that morning. "He should stay in my family's compound; it's in the center of town."

"But Monsieur Rouch stayed in the *campement*," Saadu insisted.

"Monsieur Paul, where do you want to stay?" Tondi Bello asked.

"In town." I realized then that I needed to pursue an independent path.

My work proceeded smoothly, though it was disgusting when people categorized my efforts in terms of Monsieur Rouch. When I began to work with Zeinabou Djiketa, the possession troupe priestess in Mehanna, she told me that Monsieur Rouch had visited her compound thirty years before.

"Yes, Monsieur Rouch came here when my mother was the priestess. He asked us to take out all our possession objects [hatchets with bells, costumes, sabers, antelope horns]. We took them all out, and he took photographs of them. He paid us some money, and we gave him a few of our objects."

Seizing this opportunity, I asked her if I could do what Monsieur Rouch had done nearly thirty years before. She refused, claiming the possession objects had deteriorated; they were not fit to be photographed.

In March 1977 I decided to visit the fabled village of Wanzerbe, the center of unequaled Songhay sorcery. Romantic that I was, I decided to travel to Wanzerbe on horseback, a 120 kilometer trip. My guide was Idrissa Dembo, who was born in Wanzerbe. Idrissa was a felicitous choice as my guide, for his stepmother was the illustrious Kassey, the most powerful sorcerer in Wanzerbe. Working with Kassey would be a real ethnographic coup, since she had steadfastly refused to cooperate with researchers—Rouch, other Europeans, and Nigeriens alike—for thirty years. We spent two hot, dusty days in the saddle and at last arrived at the compound of Moussa Dembo, Idrissa's father. We were greeted warmly and fed well. In the evening men from the neighborhood came by to visit.

"You came here on horseback?" one asked.

"Yes."

"Monsieur Rouch used to come here on horseback. Do you know him?"

"I've met him," I responded.

"He used to ride in from Ayoru. Where did you come from?"

"Mehanna."

"Why didn't you come from Ayoru, like Monsieur Rouch? Mehanna is too far."

"Yes, it is," I agreed.

"Are you going to do what Monsieur Rouch did?"

"Not exactly."

Another man joined our discussion. He greeted me and then asked, "Do you know Monsieur Rouch?"

"Yes."

"Where is he?"

"I don't know."

"We haven't seen him in a long time."

"How long?"

"Many years. Say hello to him from us here in Wanzerbe, will you?"

"I'll be sure to do it," I told him.

The next morning I learned that Kassey had left town just before I arrived and would not return until after my departure. A wasted trip! Idrissa suggested we visit the hunters at Youmboum, a permanent water hole just north of the village of Yatakala. We mounted our horses and rode to Youmboum. There I was introduced to Monsieur Rouch's *godji* (monochord violinist) Issiakia, and his brother Wangari, two of the protagonists in Rouch's monumental *La chasse au lion à l'arc* (*The Lion Hunters*). Issiakia took me to an abandoned mud-brick house at the north end of the lake.

"This is where Monsieur Rouch stayed," he announced. We went inside, and I saw some electric wire attached to a closed window shutter.

"What's that?" I asked.

"Monsieur Rouch put it there. He had a machine that made light."

"I see."

"Do you know Monsieur Rouch?"

"Yes, I do."

"Do you know when he's coming back?"

"No, I don't."

We returned to Issiakia's house. "When Monsieur Rouch was here, I always played my violin for him. My brother Wangari sang praise songs. Shall we play for you?"

I took out my tape recorder, and Issiakia played his violin. Wangari sang about hunters' poison and the great hunters of the past. This musical poetry was familiar to me, for I had seen the same performance in a Jean Rouch film.

We returned to Wanzerbe and were on our way to the Dembo compound when we encountered the grandson of Mossi Bana, the sohanci who was Rouch's principal informant in the village of sorcerers.

"Are you French?" he asked, having never met me before.

"No, I'm American."

"Well, we don't want any more films. We are tired of your damn films. And if you want to talk with my father [Halidu Bana], you will have to pay him at least 50,000 francs CFA [about $200]."

This man was one of the people who felt Rouch's films did not portray Wanzerbe in a favorable light. (Six years later Kassey Sohanci told me: "We don't like films. We don't want strangers laughing at us.")

"I did not come here to make films" I told him. "I came to meet the people here. That's all. I'm not a filmmaker, and I don't take people's pictures unless they agree to it. I am not Monsieur Rouch, damn it."

"We don't want your films" he persisted.

For Mossi Bana's grandson, the legacy of Rouch was insurmountable. I left Wanzerbe completely frustrated.[5]

In 1979 I had a talk with Issaka Boulhassane, an elder living in Mehanna. A direct descendant of Askia Mohammed Toure, king of the Songhay empire from 1493 to 1527, Issaka Boulhassane has matrilineal ties to Wanzerbe. The famous Kassey is his maternal aunt. I described my work to him, and he complimented me on my command of the Songhay language. "The people have great confidence in you, Monsieur Paul," he told me. "They have opened themselves to you. I suppose it can be said that you are retracing the path of Rouch."

The greatest compliment one can receive from the older people in the Songhay countryside is to be compared to Rouch. But at the time I was a brash student of the Songhay, and I didn't want to be compared to anyone. How could I convince people like Issaka Boulhassane that I wasn't retracing Rouch's path? Would they ever understand that I had my own research agenda, which at the time was to study Songhay religion from a symbolic rather than a Griaulian perspective? I was interested in the interpretation of significant symbols, not in the exhaustive collection of data that had obsessed Marcel Griaule. I realize now that "retracing the path of Rouch" in Songhay put me on a trail leading to rich ethnographic rewards; it was part of my ethnographic initiation. (See Stoller and Olkes 1987; Stoller 1989a; Griaule 1956.)

Following Rouch's path, the path of the Songhay spirits, brought me to Adamu Jenitongo, the sorcerer and possession priest of Tillaberi, Niger, who became my teacher of things Songhay. In 1981 I saw Rouch and told him about being temporarily paralyzed by a sorcerer in Wanzerbe. "You're making progress," he told me. "You must continue year after year. You are following the right path."

In 1984 I learned fully what it meant to walk in the shadow cast by the reputation of Jean Rouch. A colleague of mine had been to Simiri, a village where Rouch had filmed many possession ceremonies over the years. I had not visited Simiri, but the people there, especially Daouda Sorko, the Simiri possession priest, knew I was following Rouch's path and that I had learned much about possession and magic from Adamu Jenitongo. My colleague was astounded that they knew so much about me.

"Do you know what they call you in Simiri?" she asked me.

"No."

"They call you Rouch'izo," which translates as "son of Rouch," "little Rouch," or "Rouch's seed."

HOW THE STORY IS TOLD

And so the griot's "son" intends to tell the tale of the griot. This is how the story will unfold. The chapters in Part 1, "Ethnographic Foundations," describe how, why, and where the cinematic griot conducted fieldwork between 1941 and 1974 and how that body of fieldwork is represented in his ethnographic writings and films. These chapters construct the social settings of Rouch's films. Chapter 2, "Rouch's Life in the Field," examines in detail the external events in France and West Africa that shaped Rouch's fieldwork—his research goals and field techniques—setting the methodological and epistemological context for chapters 3–5, which probe Rouch's ethnographic writings. Chapter 3, "Worlds of the Ancestors," considers Rouch's work on Songhay history and myth (*Contribution à l'histoire des Songhay*). Rouch's work on migration and social change (*Migrations au Ghana*) is recounted in chapter 4, "Migrations to New Worlds." Chapter 5, "People of Force, Spirits of Power," tells of Rouch's work on Songhay magic and possession (*La religion et la magie Songhay*).

In part 2, "Cinema Rouch," I delineate the connection between Rouch's ethnographic initiation—to borrow a term from Marcel Griaule—and the content of his films. In this section Rouch's major ethnographic films, including one film of "ethnofiction," are described and ethnographically contextualized. In chapter 6, *"Les Magiciens de Wanzerbe,"* I describe in some ethnographic detail sorcery among the Songhay. Chapter 7, *"The Lion Hunters,"* explores the relation of magic to hunting and of word to action. In both of these chapters I demonstrate how these films resulted from Rouch's ongoing participation in Songhay social life. In chapter 8, *"Jaguar,"* an analysis of an ethnofiction film about social change and displacement, I not only discuss the factors that impelled thousands of young Songhay men to migrate from Niger to southern Nigeria, Togo, Ghana, and the Ivory Coast—migratory voyages that Songhay men continue to undertake—but also compare their voyage to Lévi-Strauss's quest in *Tristes tropiques*. What does it mean to leave one's home to travel to "the Coast" and then return home? Chapter 9, *"Les Maîtres Fous,"* presents what the late Pierre Braunberger called Rouch's "masterwork," a film about Hauka spirit possession in Ghana. I provide a general description of the Hauka movement and how it is situated within the broader context of Songhay possession phenomena. *"Les Tambours d'Avant: Turu et Bitti"* is chapter 10, the analysis of an evocative ten-minute film of a Songhay possession ceremony. This film prompts a more general discussion on the phenomenology of possession and the cinematic innovation of Rouch's notion of ciné-transe. In chapter 11, "The Dogon Passion," I explore Rouch's series of films on the sixty-year cycle of Dogon Sigui ceremonies, which prompts a discussion of the relation between film and ethnography. This chapter demonstrates that film is more than a complement to ethnographic writing—that film can solve ethnographic mysteries.

In part 3, "When Films Become Dreams," I consider the theoretical and epistemological significance of Rouch's work. In chapter 12, "Rouch, Theory, and Ethnograhic Film," I describe how Rouch's prescient philosophical ideas on sociocultural fragmentation, academic imperialism, and implicated fieldwork are embedded in the narrative and structure of his films. Using Rouch's ethnographic practice as a model, I call for a more sensual and artistic ethnography, in which filmic and narrative ethnographies evoke other worlds and provoke our imaginations. Whereas in chapter 12 I consider Rouch's contributions to Euro-American intellectual life, in the Postface I take up his tangible contributions to the people he has portrayed in prose and film: the Songhay of Niger and the Dogon of Mali.

The Songhay say that the stranger is like the mist, which dissipates with the advance of day, but the son of the village is like the deep root of the dune palm. Although griots may leave their village, they always return home to the land of their forebears. Such is the wisdom of the ancestors.

Jean Rouch has returned to Songhay, to Niger, year in and year out for most of the past fifty years. Can such an investment of time, energy, and passion be reduced to field research? Can the people with whom he has continued to work so closely be categorized clinically as informants? Can Rouch's books and films be seen strictly as the impersonal product of his ethnographic research?

Jean Rouch is a cinematic griot, a person who has led his adult life in two places, France and Niger. Rouch the filmmaker is a Frenchman influenced by his rich intellectual life in France. Rouch the griot is a man profoundly influenced by the wisdom of men like the late Mossi Bana of Wanzerbe and Damoré Zika of Niamey. It is the compounding of this Nigerien-French experience that creates the stories projected in Jean Rouch's films, giving them a narrative immediacy and power rarely seen in documentary cinema. They are the stories told by a cinematic griot.

PART
I

Ethnographic Foundations

Baani fondo a si ku.
The sure path is never too long.
—Songhay proverb

INTRODUCTION
Son of Griaule

Boro baba haw ga no boro ga faawa dondon.
It it on his father's cow that a man learns
how to butcher.
—Songhay proverb

Imagine the following scene: jagged sandstone cliffs sweep up from a desiccated laterite plain baked brown by the sun. Dust hangs in the air like a thick mist filtering the intense Sahelian sunlight, which bleaches the cloudless sky. The stench of a rotting donkey carcass wafts over a village nestled against the base of an outcropping. It is 1969, some sixty years after the elders of Bongo performed the last Sigui ceremony, and Jean Rouch is there, camera attached to his shoulder—a natural extension of his body.

In 1969 Rouch and Germaine Dieterlen, Marcel Griaule's associate who began to study and write about the Dogon in the 1930s, were in Bongo to film *La caverne de Bongo,* the third of a series of seven films that follow the Sigui ceremonies of the Dogon people of Mali (see chap. 11). First described by Marcel Griaule, the Sigui cycle of seven yearly ceremonies is held every sixty years, moving each year from east to west, from village to village.

Bongo is the home of Anai, who in 1969 attended his third Sigui. For the Sigui of 1849, Anai was still in his mother's womb. In 1909 he was already an initiate, having drunk the ceremonial millet beer—of 1849—which had been saved for the newborns. Still alive and well in 1969, he prepared for his third Sigui, which made him 120 years old.

In Bongo the people considered Rouch an *olubaaru,* a Sigui initiate, for he had already drunk the ceremonial millet beer at ceremonies performed in Yougou in 1967 and in Tyogou in 1968. As an olubaaru Rouch was permitted to enter the sacred cave and film the initiates and their assistants as they made bull-roarers and prepared great Sigui masks to represent mythical serpents.

The initiates also prepared in Bongo's village square a mound of earth, the altar of Diounou Serou, the first ancestor, who died and was reincarnated as a serpent. The mound was covered with clay and spotted with red and white squares to represent the serpent's scales. Meanwhile other initiates painted a new mask, which they placed, along with three other tall, narrow masks, at the entrance of the Sigui initiates' cave. At sunset the bull-roarers whipped through the air, bringing to Bongo the voices of the past. The next day all the men of the village saw the four towering masks of Bongo: two painted black, red, and white to represent the dead mythical serpent, and two painted red and white to symbolize the serpent's rebirth. Wherever Rouch walked, he filmed.

The dancing began. The initiates sported their Sigui costumes: "Black trousers gathered at the ankles, cowrie-shell baldric earrings, rings and necklaces from their wives or sisters; in their right hands they hold a flyswatter, in the left a gourd with which they drink the Sigui beer and . . . hold . . . a cane seat" (Echard and Rouch 1988, interview 10).

Once the men of Bongo were dressed, they promenaded around the sacred square, sat down on their cane seats, then stood up and formed four lines—one line for each of the four sectors that compose Bongo. Millet beer was distributed, and beginning with the oldest person, all the men, in order of age, drank the tangy beverage. Singing the Sigui songs in Siguiso, the Sigui's ritual language, they marched around the sacred square, circling the mound representing their dead ancestor. The men danced until evening. At dusk the old men returned to their cave, and the older boys escorted the   rs around the mounc   they survive, would   initiates and filmed

In 1   m the fourth Sigui in   ned to Bongo to scree   old Anai was still aliv   Rouch fash- ioned a   s of the large baobab   on as he be- gan the   the calm of night o   ir lives, the

Funérailles à Bongo: Le vieil Anai. J. Rouch, Comité du Film Ethnographique.

people of Bongo had seen the faces of the dead (Rouch 1989, 348). They saw Anai's son, the chief. They were speechless when they saw a young boy who had died a mere two weeks before Rouch's return. They asked him to show the film time after time—he projected it five times. After the last showing, Bongo's new chief, Anai's younger son, spoke his pride at seeing the majesty of the Sigui for the first time. Others echoed his sentiment—they wanted to make sure the film would be available to their children, to ensure the purity of future Siguis. Having been introduced to the cinema, the people of Bongo immediately understood Rouch's long-term mission in Africa. As a griot, he had become part of their history, their tradition. That night in Bongo the reaction to the screening was "extraordinary; such pride, a sort of communion. The chief who had replaced his brother was there. At that moment I was truly the son of Griaule" (Echard and Rouch 1988, interview 10).

GRIAULE'S ETHNOGRAPHIC WORLD

To comprehend Jean Rouch's ethnography, one must know something of the ethnographic methods and orientations espoused by his professor and mentor Marcel Griaule, the first person in France to write a *doctorat d'état* in anthropology (Echard and Rouch 1988, interview 6). Most North American anthropologists are unfamiliar with Griaule's work and influence; only one of his many works has been translated into English: the incomparable *Conversations with Ogotemmêli* (1965), in which a wise elder of the Dogon people reveals to Griaule *la parole claire*, the secret key to the ever-complex Dogon cosmology.

Organizer of the Dakar-Djibouti mission (1931–33), Griaule was a meticulous field anthropologist who believed that the anthropologist's career should be devoted to studying one society over a long period. His ideas on data collection and interpretation are spelled out in a short monograph, *Méthode de l'ethnographie* (1957), which pulled together the threads of the course in ethnography he taught in Paris until his untimely death in 1956.

Méthode reads very much like a fieldwork manual. Throughout the dry text, Griaule describes how ethnographers should carry themselves in the field. He also calls for multidisciplinary research teams modeled after his Dakar-Djibouti group. These teams, he wrote, should include specialists in ethnomusicology, photography, film, linguistics, geography, and history. According to Griaule, the multidisciplinary field team ensures greater precision in documenting the other; it also provides a diversity of lenses on the other's complex universe. Eventually this diverse documentation could be fused into an ethnography of depth and breadth.[1]

Griaule advises his readers on the observation of "human facts,"

---

1. For his Dakar-Djibouti mission (1931–33) Marcel Griaule assembled a multidisciplinary team of ethnographers, writer-poets, linguists, geographers, and ethnomusicologists. See also Michel Leiris's *Afrique fantôme* (1981 [1934]) for a description of the mission.

proposing both "intensive" and "extensive" research, an early formulation of the -emic/-etic distinction. For Griaule, intensive research meant the long-term, ongoing study of one society. Extensive research, however, did not mean that one takes the results of intensive research and applies them to grand social theories; rather, one applies these results in a controlled comparative manner to shed light on cultural patterns in a region. As Griaule hypothesized, one cannot understand the significance of the Dogon Sigui without comparing the symbolic differences of the ceremonies in the seven villages where they are performed. Although Griaule never witnessed a Sigui, the Sigui films of Dieterlen and Rouch (see chap. 11) underscore the prescience of his hypothesis.

The hallmark of Griaule's method is intense documentation and long-term field research. For him ethnography is nothing less than a long apprenticeship during which the ethnographer collects material objects and rudimentary facts, "during ten years if necessary" (Griaule 1957, 36). It takes time, Griaule writes, to gain access to the more ontological aspects of a culture.

As part of his penchant for documentation, Griaule championed both the use of questionnaires and the direct observation of facts, though he was hesitant about the notion of "participant observation," believing that indigenous peoples during the colonial era wanted Europeans to act like Europeans. This view appears in a rather long section, which seems pernicious from our postcolonial vantage point, about the relation between ethnographer and informant. "The principal moral and intellectual qualities that should interest an ethnographer in an informant are memory and good faith. . . . The most dangerous informant is the forgetful one or the one who lies by leaving out details, one who produces a set of apparently sincere and coherent information that masks the principal essentials of the institution" (Griaule 1957, 56). Here Griaule does not speculate on why an informant might be motivated to produce what Marx might have called a localized fetishism.

Griaule also insists on linguistic, philological, and historical precision in ethnographic investigation. In passages reminiscent of Franz Boas, he calls again and again for massive multidisciplinary documentation and cautions against premature interpretations.

Given his penchant for documentation, it is not surprising that Griaule devotes an entire chapter of *Méthode* to field recording. He suggests that ethnographic data be documented with museological cards (*fiches muséographiques*), field drawings, maps, field photographs, including aerial photographs, and documentary films. These

data-collection techniques, according to Griaule, create an ethnographic archive, the foundation for precise descriptions and interpretations.

But collecting archival material does not an ethnography make.
One must always maintain, Griaule tells us, one's critical perspective.
One must cross-check informants' accounts and authenticate objects
that have been collected. Above all, one must be certain one's interpretations are carefully drawn from authenticated data.

In his essay "Power and Dialogue in Ethnography: Marcel Griaule's
Initiation," James Clifford (1988) underscores the methodological and
theoretical principles outlined in *Méthode*. Griaule's view of the
world, according to Clifford, was fundamentally theatrical; he considered fieldwork a long-term dramatic enterprise, like Rouch's experience in Bongo, in which the others "initiate" the ethnographer into the
mysteries of their social life and culture. Griaule's own fieldwork
among the Dogon spanned three decades. Early on, following his own
prescriptions, he collected as much low-level information as possible;
he documented the other by collecting artifacts, taking photographs,
and shooting documentary films.

Griaule's *Au pays des Dogon* (1938) and *Sous les masques noirs*
(1938) are testaments to his vision of documentary ethnography.
Griaule made these fifteen-minute documentary shorts, the first French
ethnographic films shot in the field, in 35 mm/16 mm black-and-white
and screened them in the film theater that he and his friends had built
in the Musée de l'Homme in 1938. Although in his writings Griaule
said that film was just another means of gathering ethnographic data,
the importance he accorded to the screening of documentaries may
have reflected the more theatrical dimension of his ethnographic vision
(see Homiak, n.d.; MacDougall 1975).

In the Griaulian scheme of ethnography, documentation—be it in
film, photographs, or transcribed texts—is the first stage of research.
For long-term fieldwork to yield deep knowledge (ontological and
metaphysical knowledge), there must be what Griaule called a break-
through. This event is essential for transforming one's external efforts
to document the other into an initiation into the deep secrets of a cosmology. For Griaule this change is embodied in the words of Ogotemmêli: the learned Dogon elder transformed Griaule from an arrogant
data collector into a more humble student who expressed respect for
the complexity of Dogon wisdom.[2]

---

2. See van Beek (1991) for a "field" evaluation of Griaule's work. In this restudy,
van Beek severely criticizes two of Griaule's most noteworthy publications, *Conversa-*

In summary, Griaulian ethnography consists of three major components: long-term fieldwork, a penchant for documentation, and initiation, which implies dialogue with wise teachers. As Clifford demonstrates (1988), the Griaulian orientation was very much the product of the political and social dynamics of French colonialism in Africa and the cultural revolution in France, especially Surrealism. To this I would add one other major factor—the impact of the Dogon themselves. Like that of other peoples in the Sahel, Dogon epistemology built on the gradual, cumulative development of knowledge—initiation. One cannot receive great wisdom, and the power and responsibility it entails, unless one's mind is seasoned.

GRIAULE AND ROUCH

Following his own methodological advice, Griaule filled most of his ethnographies with exhaustive ethnographic detail: local accounts of myth and history, lists of objects and their uses, maps of villages and clusters of villages, and photographs, including aerial shots of research sites and pictures of social activities, objects, and people. Almost Boasian in its scope, Griaule's *Masques dogons* (1938), for example, is a text in which ethnographic detail overwhelms modest interpretation.

Griaule's students usually followed his methodological lead. They scoured the Sahelian landscape for ethnographic data, which they faithfully reproduced in their published works. They attempted to limit their own Eurocentric interpretations as they highlighted local exegesis of ritual symbolism, myth, and cosmology.

In his fieldwork and writings, the subject of part 1, Jean Rouch is indeed the "son of Griaule." His written work on the Songhay of Niger has little literary character; it consists mostly of local texts and local explanations of historical events, of cosmology, spirit possession, and magic, as well as of the social and religious life of Songhay migrants to Ghana. His modest interpretations of the data are limited to brief pas-

---

tions with Ogotemmêli, and *Le renard pâle*, vol. 1, which Griaule wrote with Germaine Dieterlen. These later "interpretive" works, according to van Beek, should be distinguished from Griaule's earlier documentary works, like the exhaustive *Masques dogons*, which van Beek does not fault. Like all restudies of famous works, this one has sparked considerable controversy, especially with its claims that Griaule's and Griaule and Dieterlen's later works do not correspond to Dogon social reality as observed by van Beek and other researchers. Such claims have affinity with those suggested by Derek Freeman in his *Margaret Mead and Samoa* (1983) and recall Theodore Schwartz's apt article on the Mead controversy, "Anthropology: A Quaint Science" (1983).

sages that constitute the introductions and conclusions of the various works.

In part 1 I shall first explore the epistemological, political, and methodological foundation of Jean Rouch's ethnography. My intent is not only to demonstrate Rouch's descent from Griaule, but to stress his commitment and contribution to ethnographic scholarship, facts that are underappreciated by both his admirers and his critics. Accordingly, I consider his major written works in some detail—detail that demonstrates the depth of his knowledge and his attention to ethnographic nuance.

CHAPTER TWO
Rouch's Life in the Field

Zankey ga cehan; dortigiyan ga wani suuru.
Children know haste; elders know patience.
—Songhay saying

Songhay griots say that the sure path is never too long, for those who follow it know patience. Jean Rouch's path has been a long, circuitous one weaving its way through France, Morocco, Niger, Senegal, and Mali. At each stage on his route, Rouch opened his being to experiences that created the framework for his orientation to the world.

From early on Jean Rouch's life was molded by the felicitous marriage of science and art, the fusion of technology and imagination. For me this almost Nietzschean blending of Apollonian rigor and Dionysian intensity creates the unmistakable appeal of his ethnography—especially his films. In this chapter I recount how Rouch's long-term experience in the field—his patience—enabled him to blend observation and participation, science and art, constructing a provocative ethnographic oeuvre that challenges many of our provincial assumptions about Africa.

ROUCH'S EARLY YEARS

Rouch's formative years set the course for his ethnographic writings and his films—works that, as we shall see, fuse artfully structured narratives with scientifically grounded ethnography.[1] His father was an

1. Much of the material in this chapter is reconstructed from a ten-hour discussion between Jean Rouch and Nicole Echard, which was broadcast on France Culture in July 1988 ("Entretien avec Jean Rouch. A voix nu. Entretien d'hier à aujourd'hui"). This material is reconstructed here with the kind permission of Jean Rouch, Nicole Echard, and France Culture. The narrative is also reconstructed from several of Rouch's publications, including "Le renard fou et le maître pâle" (1978c), *Le Niger en pirogue* (1954a), and "Le 'dit' de Théodore Monod" (1990b).

explorer who sailed to the Antarctic with Captain Jean-Baptiste Char-
cot on the famous ship the *Pourquoi-Pas?* Rouch senior, a naval meteorologist, set a scientific model for Jean to follow. At the same time, he
had a deep appreciation for the arts and the cinema. Rouch's mother
came from a family of painters and poets who were active in the Parisian art scene between the wars.

Rouch was born in Paris on 31 May 1917. Mobility marked his
early years. He spent the first of part of his youth in Brest, the port city
of Brittany, where his father taught at the Ecole Normale. The family
also lived in Paris, Algeria, and Germany.

In 1928 the Rouch family set up housekeeping in Casablanca,
where the senior Rouch had been named *commandant de marine*. At
eleven years of age, Rouch found himself in the Magreb. In Morocco
he discovered the Arab world, befriending a young Berber boy through
whom he first encountered the other. Rouch often accompanied his
friend's father, a lawyer, on trips to see clients. In this way he visited
such places as Marrakech and met the people of the Moroccan countryside.

Sixty years later Rouch is still moved by his Moroccan memories,
which evoke for him the world of Delacroix. Rouch learned a great
deal in Casablanca. His Berber friend taught him to ride a horse and
to swim in Casablanca harbor, skills he would use in his early fieldwork in Niger. He also learned the importance of friendship in life:
that friendship can open doors to unimaginable worlds. Friendship is
a key component of Rouch's notion of participatory anthropology.

As Rouch says himself, his youth was "very beautiful." It was part
of his apprenticeship for the ethnographer's life (Echard and Rouch
1988, interview 1). The Moroccan interlude ended in 1930 when the
French government named Rouch's father *commandant de marine* for
the Balkans. The senior Rouch wanted his son to study for the baccalaureate in Paris, so Rouch moved in with his mother's sister and en-
rolled at the Lycée Saint-Louis.

In Paris Rouch came under the spell of the world of art. In the early
1930s Paris was the center of the avant-garde art world. André Breton
had published his *Second Surrealist Manifesto* in 1929. Louis Aragon
had published his *Challenge to Painting* in 1930. The Boulevard de
Montparnasse was awash with ideas, movements, and debates. This
exciting moment in intellectual history was to mark Rouch for the rest
of his life.

It was through the influence of his maternal kin that Rouch plunged
into the arts, especially painting and poetry. Like his mother, Rouch's
aunt was a painter. Rouch's cousin, also a painter, was on the fringe of

the Parisian avant-garde, and through him Rouch confronted the world of Parisian painters and poets. His cousin took him to the cafés and galleries of Montparnasse, where the young Rouch encountered Salvador Dali and confronted sculpture from Africa. He took him to the Louvre to see the paintings of Courbet and Delacroix. Rouch's uncle, a chemist who had traveled extensively, surrounded his nephew with photos he had taken in Afghanistan. The photos, the cafés, and the paintings inspired Rouch to write poetry and to paint.

But Rouch's father made sure his adolescent son did not ignore the elegance of the hard sciences. When he was sixteen, Rouch passed his baccalaureate exam. He and his father discussed Jean's next academic step. They both focused upon the *grandes écoles*, the most prestigious schools in France.

If Rouch graduated from a *grande école*, his father reasoned, his future livelihood would be guaranteed by the time he was twenty years old, for *grande école* graduates were assured high positions in the French civil service. Ever the scientist, Rouch's father wanted his son to prepare to enter the Ecole Polytechnique to study science and engineering. Ever the artist, Jean wanted to prepare for the Ecole Normale Supérieure to study art and philosophy.

Rouch studied for the highly competitive entrance exams to the *grandes écoles*. He failed in his attempt to enter the Ecole Normale Supérieure. He did well on the Ecole Polytechnique exam, but not well enough to be admitted. In the end he was admitted to Ponts et Chaussées, the *grande école* for civil engineering, and began his engineering studies in November 1937.

THE SCHOOL OF MAKE-BELIEVE

Rouch calls Ponts et Chaussées *l'école de l'imaginaire,* the School of Make-Believe. How could he or anyone else term an engineering school a school of make-believe? Ponts et Chaussées was a perfect choice for Rouch. First, he was pleased that classes there started later than those of the other grandes écoles. Second, he liked that the school was close to the Café Flore, his favorite. Above all, the professors at Ponts et Chaussées stressed what Rouch had known all along: that the construction of a bridge or road was a work of art. Guided by the stark images of De Chirico and the wild excesses of Dali, Rouch blended his artistic predispositions with the technological rigor of his engineering studies. He could not agree with the dehumanizing functional modernism of Le Corbusier.

The academic year 1937–38 was an exciting time in Paris. In 1937 the renegades of the Surrealist movement, Georges Bataille, Michel Leiris, and Roger Callois, formed the Collège de Sociologie. Tired of André Breton's psychologism, they sought to tie Surrealism to what Leiris referred to as "sacred sociology" (Richman 1990). In 1938 Paris was the site of the International Surrealist Exhibition. That same year the Musée de l'Homme was founded.

Rouch took advantage of these intellectual opportunities. In his free time he went to the Musée de l'Homme, where Marcel Griaule and his friends had installed a film theater, the first of its kind in a museum. Rouch writes: "And for me who then knew nothing other than the rapture of differential equations, I discovered at Trocadero [Musée de l'Homme] other equations in which three unknowns, red, black and white, represented in make-believe space fabulous and secret structures" (Rouch 1978c, 4). As he wandered along the Boulevard de Montparnasse, drank espresso at the Café Flore, and walked among the exhibits at the Musée de l'Homme, Rouch rediscovered the African masks he had first seen in Montparnasse in the early 1930s. These masks fired his imagination.

Although the Rouches feared war would break out in summer 1938, Hitler's Austrian Anschluss had not yet shattered the fragile peace. Rouch was therefore able to continue his studies at Ponts et Chaussées in the fall of 1938, a year that was an important milestone on his ethnographic-cinematic path. The cinema had mesmerized Rouch ever since his father took his young son to see *La crosière noire* and *The Blue Angel*. As an adolescent, Rouch went to the cinema whenever he could. He saw and appreciated the Marx brothers' films as well as those of Busby Berkeley. In 1938 Henri Langlois, who would have a profound influence on Rouch's cinematic practices, and Marie Merson, a beautiful Russian emigrée model who was the "queen of Montparnasse," founded the Cinémathèque Française. The Cinémathèque was housed at the newly founded Musée de l'Homme at the suggestion of Paul Rivet, the museum's director. The same year, Rivet invited Robert Flaherty to the museum to present two of his films, *Nanook of the North* and *Manoa*. Rouch attended the screening and saw his first ethnographic films, films that triggered his interest in anthropology.

By summer 1939 Rouch had successfully completed two of his three years of training at Ponts et Chaussées. He looked forward to constructing works of art—bridges—after his graduation in June 1940. But it was not to be. After the German invasion of Poland in September 1939, France declared war on Hitler's Germany. The French army, however, was too weak to repel the German blitzkrieg.

Then the war came. . . . With these years of retreat, I think that we had an insane opportunity to live through this insane epoch. All that we had learned in 20 years was revealed to be an illusion during the month of May in 1940: the army, Verdun, France, honor, dignity, money, the church, jobs, society, the family, *Homo economicus,* the libido, and historical materialism had been carried away in the winds of the sunniest spring in the world. And by a strange paradox, we began our Ponts et Chaussées engineering lives by blowing up the most prestigious bridges in France: the bridge of Château-Thierry that Jean de la Fontaine had known, or the bridge of the Briare canal, a stream of steel and water which runs below the Loire. (Rouch 1978c, 4)

Rouch and his Ponts et Chaussées friend Jean Sauvy spent much of 1939–40 riding their bicycles through the countryside of southwestern France, blowing up bridges—a veritable school of make-believe. Totally unrestrained, Rouch felt like he was on vacation. When the Germans occupied France, they asked him to rebuild bridges he had blown up. He refused.

In spring 1940 Rouch received a letter from the director of Ponts et Chaussées suggesting that the students in Rouch's class complete their final year's work. And so Rouch returned to occupied Paris in the fall to finish his engineering studies.

In 1940–41 Rouch spent a dark year in occupied Paris. Despite the German occupation, fires of resistance flickered in the shadowy corners of the city: "In this empty Paris of the German occupation, in 1940–41, the Musée de l'Homme was the only open door to the rest of the world. Once or twice a week, Jean Sauvy, Pierre Ponty and I left the Ponts et Chaussées of the rue des Saints-Pères and bicycled through silent and dead avenues to climb up Chaillot hill" (Rouch 1978c, 4). At the Musée de l'Homme, the Cinémathèque functioned; Henri Langlois, champion of the cinema and artistic freedom, showed a series of Soviet films that the Vichy government had banned. The Musée de l'Homme became a center of the French Resistance. Behind the screen of the museum's film theater, three men printed the first newspaper of the Resistance.

Even in occupied Paris, Ponts et Chaussées continued to be a school of make-believe, for its director allowed students to take electives no matter how far-fetched they might be. In 1940–41, Rouch took Marcel Griaule's course on Ethiopia.

I retained nothing of these austere seminars, but still hear certain mysterious phrases: In Peru, "the 'diabolo' creates and renews the sun . . . ," "there are three types of body decorations: deformities (head, trunk, skull), scars (to photograph them well on black skin, put some millet porridge on them), amputations (of a finger, for example)." . . . How to explain the fascination of being able to carry such strange notions while during the week we beat ourselves black and blue with the developments of the Fourier series, the problems of interior navigation, or precast concrete. However, the irrational human sciences were the indispensable counterpoint to the rationality of our engineering field. (Rouch 1978c, 4)

That same year he met Germaine Dieterlen. In the light of a magic lantern, she showed Rouch photographs of a "lost land," the Bandiagara cliffs of the Dogon.

Despite some flickers of Parisian light in 1940–41, the city was somber and sad: Rouch needed a change of scene. Why not return to Brest, the seaside town of his youth? For Easter 1941 Rouch, Pierre Ponty, and Jean Sauvy took a train to Brest in search of good beaches and seafood. In Brest they walked along the shore and talked to fishermen. As gulls squawked overhead and a stiff sea breeze chafed their faces, they breathed deeply and savored the fresh sea air. Their enjoyment was interrupted by a handful of German soldiers, who arrested them. At the local military headquarters, a German officer interrogated Rouch and his friends, suspecting them of being French officers trying to escape to Great Britain. Ponty intervened, saying they had come to Brittany to go swimming: "You can't swim to England, can you?"

The soldiers accompanied the trio to their hotel room and discovered that their luggage consisted solely of three swimsuits and some toothpaste. The German officer relented and sent them back to Paris. If they wanted to leave Paris in the future, he told them, they would have to get the authorization of the German army.

Disgruntled, they returned to Paris, having decided to leave France. As engineering graduates of Ponts et Chaussées, they realized, they could travel to the French colonies to work for the Travaux Publics, building rather than destroying roads and bridges. In this way Jean Rouch, engineer and artist, met his destiny, for in October 1941 the twenty-four-year-old graduate of the School of Make-Believe left France for Niger. He could not know that his first plunge into the Niger River would sweep him into the Songhay universe.

ROUCH IN NIGER, 1941–42

In 1941 Niamey was a large, isolated town without the usual amenities of a colonial capital. Although there were a few vehicles, there was no gasoline to fuel them. No stranger to two-wheeled conveyances, Rouch moved about on a bicycle. Mud-brick cubicles and straw huts housed most of Niamey's forty-thousand residents. For houses and offices, the French built colonial-style whitewashed cement structures with large rectangular windows, steel shutters, verandas, and balconies—all designed to catch the occasional breezes. But not even the most sophisticated architectural designs could bring relief from Niamey's blast-furnace heat.

Despite the heat and the lack of building materials, Rouch immediately felt welcome among his Travaux Publics colleagues. Like him, they were Gaullists—traitors to the Vichyist colonial government in Niamey. Their mission in Niger was to build two roads: one to connect Niamey and Gao, the other to join Niamey and Ouagadougou.

Rouch's superior assigned him to the Niamey-Gao detail. Given the harsh climatic conditions in Niger—blazing heat, choking dust, and malarial mosquitoes—the job of building roads, already a complex task, presented many difficulties. To add to the misery, Rouch's superiors asked him to build roads without cement, gas, trucks, picks, or pails—a perfect context for a graduate of the School of Make-Believe. A surfeit of laborers conscripted by the colonial government complemented the deficit in construction equipment and materials. The laborers feared the forced-labor details. In Tillaberi the workers referred to their French labor boss, a racist Norman, as "Kar ma bu" (Hit Until [He] Dies). Though other labor bosses were more sympathetic, Rouch found the racism of his compatriots despicable.

Without the necessary heavy equipment, Rouch had little to do. He began to take an interest in a few of the twenty-thousand men he was responsible for. In particular he befriended Damoré Zika, a literate Nigerien, who was a labor foreman. Damoré taught Rouch how to swim in the Niger's swift currents and how to steer a dugout to avoid sandbars (Echard and Rouch 1988, interview 4).

In July 1942, the rainy season in Niger, Rouch received a puzzling telegram from Pangnouf, a labor boss on the Niamey-to-Ouagadougou road. The telegram said that Dongo had killed ten laborers at the thirty-five kilometer road marker. Who was Dongo, and why had he killed ten laborers? Rouch called his Nigerien associates to a meeting in his office and asked for an explanation. Most of the Muslims there said this event was unimportant. Dongo, they explained, was the "devil" of thunder, and that the fate of the victims had nothing to do with Islam. Damoré Zika, however, spoke up and said that his grandmother Kalia could take care of the matter.

The port of Ayoru on market day. J. Rouch, Comité du Film Ethnographique.

Rouch and Damoré Zika informed Kalia of the laborers' death by lightning. Head priestess of the fishermen of Niamey, Kalia recruited an entourage of gourd drummers, a monochord violinist, and spirit mediums and left for Gangell. Damoré Zika and Rouch accompanied them. Kalia introduced Rouch to the astounding world of Songhay possession.

In Gangell, Rouch witnessed his first possession ceremony. He saw old Kalia pour fresh milk over the ten cadavers to purify them for burial. Then Rouch heard possession music: the piercing wail of the monochord violin and the clack-roll-clack of the gourd drums. Rouch was about to witness a *Dongo hori,* one of the more important ceremonies of Songhay religion. He had stumbled upon possession—a central element in Songhay sociocultural life.

Soon the accused murderer, Dongo, roared into the body of his medium, a frail old woman wrapped in indigo cloth woven from local cotton.

"Why have you killed these men?" Kalia asked the deity.

"The people here have cultivated my land," Dongo said defiantly.

To demonstrate his displeasure, the brutal Dongo took the lives of ten human beings.

The ceremony both terrified and attracted Rouch. The terror resulted from the otherworldliness of the ceremony, the presence of the corpses, the eerie sounds of the music, the physical violence of possession; the attraction stemmed from the ceremony's theatrical evocation. For Rouch, to enter into the possession compound was to cross the threshold into a world of unimaginable feats. The ceremony evoked for him the Surrealist poems of André Breton and Paul Eluard, both of whom composed in a trance state they called automatic writing. His introduction to Songhay possession was a fitting gift for his graduation from the School of Make-Believe; Rouch had entered a truly surreal world. Inspired by the magisterial presence of Dongo, Rouch dreamed of making films. At that moment Rouch may have realized, like the Surrealist poets and painters who had inspired him, that "film is the ideal medium in which to combine verbal and visual collage as in the films of Man Ray, Buñuel and Dali, or Desnos" (see Lippard 1970; Kuenzli 1987). At that moment Rouch may have realized that film was the best way to capture the dream he was living.

And the dream continued, for Kalia invited Rouch to other ceremonies. In Gamkalle, a fishing village now incorporated into greater Niamey, a fisherman had drowned in the waters of the Niger during a storm. Kalia asked Rouch to witness a possession ceremony. Sharp music cut through the air as spirited dancers kicked up a cloud of dust that hovered over the possession dance grounds. When Dongo took his medium's body, Kalia asked him and his "mother," Harakoy Dikko (goddess of the Niger River), to explain the tragedy. With Damoré Zika's aid, Rouch transcribed the texts that Kalia recited during the ceremonies. With Kalia's permission, Rouch took photos.

Days later Rouch sent his notes to Marcel Griaule in Paris. Rouch's data intrigued Griaule, who replied encouragingly and sent Rouch an ethnographic questionnaire, suggesting that he collect as many texts and ritual objects as possible. Stung by anthropology's magic arrow, Rouch began his research. At first he understood nothing (Echard and Rouch 1988, interview 4). He had brought only two books with him to Niger: Leiris's *Afrique fantôme,* most of which described *zar* possession in Ethiopia, and Hegel's *Phenomenology of Knowledge,* most of which explained nothing at all. Neither book helped him in his quest to comprehend Songhay possession.

Meanwhile, Rouch's ethnographic research boiled the local political pot. Rouch's first *chef de service,* a Gaullist, had been replaced by a Vichyist. This man had been unhappy in Chad, which was a Gaullist enclave, and was granted a transfer to Niger, which in 1942 was still a center of Vichy authority. There was immediate bad blood between Rouch and his new boss, who objected to his Gaullist sympathies and his increasing contact with the local population. In October 1942

Rouch's *chef de service* censured him, which at the time was a serious judgment. Vichy officials often executed censured traitors or banished them to a desert camp in Mauritania—a slower death.

Governor Toby of Niger decided to send Rouch to Dakar, where Governor-General Boisson would decide his fate. Théodore Monod, then director of the Institut Français d'Afrique Noire (IFAN), intervened to prevent Rouch's being sent to a work camp (Rouch 1990b). Monod had heard about Rouch's anthropological research and had already encouraged him to continue his ethnographic investigations. He arranged for Rouch to work on the preliminary construction of the Dakar airport at Yoff.

Monod also offered him a "welcome table" where he could organize his Niger data. During his stay in Dakar, Rouch spent his spare time reading West African ethnography in the IFAN library. During several months of study, he discovered that possession in Africa had been studied little, if at all. He read the reports of local colonial officials, especially those of Léca, who had been the commandant of Tillaberi.[2] He studied Depuis Yacouba (1911) on the Gow possession ceremonies of the Bara Issa in Mali. In 1943 Rouch presented his first paper at an IFAN seminar. That paper was eventually published in *Notes Africains*—Rouch's first article.

Dakar in 1943 was a strange crossroads. Rouch wrote: "What a strange period! The line of the ocean made us forget yesterday's shame and tomorrow's fear; the crunching beaches were only a stopover vacation where, given the example of the newly arrived Americans, Africa would never lose its colonial helmet, freeing her hair in the trade winds for an instant, before enclosing it in a steel helmet" (Rouch 1990b). In Dakar, Rouch met Paul Rivet for the first time. Rivet was in transit between Central America, where he had been in exile, and Algiers, the locus of the Provisional Free French Government. Rivet had stories to tell of Latin America, of the Musée de l'Or he had founded on the equator, of the Indians of the great South American rivers. Rouch talked of Niger, of possession ceremonies, and of his dream of descending the Niger in a dugout, which Rivet encouraged. They arranged to meet at the Musée de l'Homme after the war (Rouch 1990b, 1).

---

2. See Léca (n.d.). Nicholas Léca, the commandant of Tillaberi in the 1930s, had legendary knowledge of Songhay language and culture. People who knew him in Tillaberi call him a veritable *sorko*, praise singer to the spirits. So integrated was he in local affairs that he staged possession ceremonies behind the *sous-préfecture* (his administrative offices).

THE LAST YEARS OF THE WAR

In early 1943 Rouch was drafted into the Batallion de Génie (Corps of Engineers) of the Free French Army. His unit traveled north through Mauritania and Morocco (Port Lyautey, or Kenitra). They arrived in Oran, the port of embarkation for his battalion, which was part of the Primière Division Blindée (First Armored Division), headed for the Riviera. Rouch's division consisted of Corsicans, Berbers, and *pieds noirs*, as well as young Frenchmen who had traversed Spain and crossed the Mediterranean to join the Free French Army. They steamed across the Mediterranean to Marseilles, where the battalion's first war operation was to clear Marseilles's Catalan beach of land mines (Rouch 1990b, 6). From Marseilles they went by train to Lyons and eventually arrived at their destination in Alsace, where Rouch continued to build mines and blow up bridges.

Waiting for the Allied offensive that would free the rest of Alsace, Rouch returned to a liberated Paris in December 1944. While he was in West Africa the Vichy government had named Griaule a professor at the Sorbonne, which infuriated his Resistance-oriented colleagues at the Musée de l'Homme. Back from his exile, Paul Rivet summarily threw Griaule out of the Musée de l'Homme, where he had been the central personality in the Département de l'Afrique Noire.

Rouch nonetheless decided to continue his studies with Griaule. He liked Griaule's uproarious sense of humor, his love of fun, and his commitment to the Dogon. In his spare time he took Griaule's course at the Institut de Géographie. In June 1945 Rouch earned his certificate in anthropology, and in October 1945 he left the military and returned to Paris to complete his diploma in anthropology. He took certificates in psychology, sociology, and the history of art. Between November 1945 and February 1946, he earned six certificates.

Rouch found the Paris of 1945–46 a new and strange city. In music, bebop had replaced the jazz of the interwar years. In literature and philosophy, existentialism reigned over a *dépassé* Surrealism. André Breton had not returned from exile in the United States. The Germans had exterminated *all* of Rouch's Jewish friends from Saint-Germaine-des-Prés.

Alienated by the excesses of the world, Rouch and his friends Sauvy and Ponty dedicated themselves to at least one year of anarchic fun. They decided to go ahead with the Niger River descent from headwaters to delta—in a dugout. They had earned one year of vacation from the army, but they needed to supplement their meager vacation income. After studying philosophy and literature for several months, they collectively entered the world of journalism as "Jean Pierjean." Existential explorers, they wandered about France and published articles in newspapers, including *Le Monde*. Sauvy would conceive of the subject, Rouch would write a text, and Ponty would rework it in his fine handwriting. In response to the success of their "walk on the wild side" stories, Agence France Press (AFP), a syndicated wire service, hired them. When AFP wanted photographs, "Jean Pierjean" shot and developed them. In short order they had achieved their goal: they were free to do as they pleased.

VOYAGE ON THE NIGER, 1946–47

In 1946 Rouch received a letter from Damoré Zika wondering when he would return to Niger. Meanwhile, Marcel Griaule had agreed to supervise Rouch's doctoral thesis on Songhay religion. Sauvy was to prepare a thesis on economic change and development. "Jean Pierjean" was ready to descend the Niger. After buying a used sixteen-millimeter Bell and Howell camera in the Paris flea market, the adventurous journalists flew to Niamey in July 1946 to initiate "Project Niger," which would be financed mostly through the photojournalism of "Jean Pierjean."

Shortly after their arrival in Niger, Rouch, Ponty, and Sauvy left Niamey to spend a month in Ayoru, a village that hugs the east bank of the Niger near the Mali-Niger border. The Niger is usually wide and swift near Ayoru, but in July it dwindles to a web of sorry streams. Rouch knew people there, and it was a good place for them to "toughen up" for their arduous journey. They also needed a cheap place to stay while they waited for more financial backing.

In Ayoru they heard from Théodore Monod, who offered to pay their way from Niamey to Bamako, an offer they gladly accepted. In Bamako they encountered Griaule, who was about to return to Dogon country with Solonge de Ganay, his daughter Geneviève, and Germaine Dieterlen. This trip would be his first since the war and would result in his groundbreaking *Conversations with Ogotemmêli* (1965). Rouch, Ponty, and Sauvy promised to visit the group on the Bandiagara cliffs in three months' time.

And so some 150 years after the Scottish explorer Mungo Park set out on his ill-fated expedition to follow the Niger to its end, Rouch, Sauvy, and Ponty made their way to the Niger's headwaters. They took a truck to the last village on the road to Guinea and continued on foot with several porters, an interpreter, and a cook (Rouch 1954a, 6–7). It

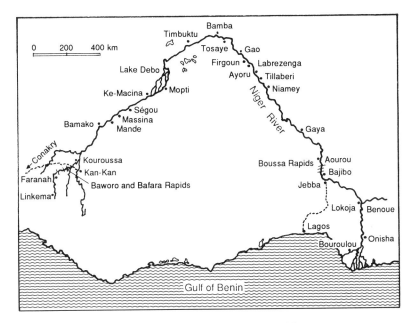

The descent of the Niger, 1946–47.

was August, the peak of the rainy season, which meant that runoff
from the mountains had filled the lowlands, swelling the tall grasses,
deepening the murky swamps, and increasing the infernal humidity.

Despite their faulty charts, they eventually stumbled on the source
of the Niger. In a humid, nondescript low-lying area shaded by trees,
they came upon a pond from which flowed a small stream. Their
guide, Soro, proclaimed this pond the source of the Niger. Inspired by
this moment, Rouch wrote:

> Under our feet was born this extravagant river, which turned its back
> squarely to the sea but closer [to us] pushed all its young strength to-
> ward the north, abandoning the forest and the savanna only to risk los-
> ing itself in Saharan sands before consenting to redirect itself toward the
> south in order to empty into the Gulf of Benin through a delta more
> than 330 kilometers wide: 4,200 kilometers of running water that
> trickles slowly under our feet. (Rouch 1954a, 7)

Using machetes to clear the thorny underbrush, they followed the narrow stream on foot until they reached Linkema, where they found no
dugouts to buy. Tired of walking and hacking their way upstream, the
creative engineers from Ponts et Chaussées, the School of Make-

Believe, built a raft from materials they gathered. The porters refused to float down the Niger on their makeshift raft; they carried the trio's cargo along the mountain paths that followed the course of the river.

The strong current carried them rapidly northward, but the waters were high. Thorny branches scratched their arms, faces, and legs. Army ants bit them incessantly. "It was hell" (Echard and Rouch 1988, interview 5).

After traveling three weeks and 150 kilometers through unknown stretches of the Upper Niger they reached Faranah, where they hired Moussa, a Niger River pilot, to maneuver them through a treacherous section of the river. They also bought a dugout in Faranah and built a catamaran. Pushing on to the north through uncharted sections of the river, they reached Kouroussa, where they greeted the local French administrator. They had mastered the Upper Niger. Swelled with confidence, they bought a second dugout and continued northward toward Bamako.

With the uncharted Upper Niger behind them, they no longer focused on the river's geography. As they sailed through Manding country, Rouch studied a fishing cult; Sauvy investigated the local markets. They took notes, shot photographs, and developed the film on board their dugout. When they reached Bamako, they sold their catamaran and gave a lecture at the Alliance Française, for which they received a much-needed honorarium. Intending to buy a better dugout in Mopti, they rented a canoe for the trip from Bamako to Mopti. In Ségou, the capital of Bambara country, one of their boatmen stole all their money.

To the resourceful "Jean Pierjean" the theft was but a minor setback. They lived off the river until they glided into Mopti completely broke. In Mopti, the great fishing center of the Niger, they wired the AFP, which was kind enough to send them 200,000 francs CFA—an enormous sum in 1946. They bought a large "riverworthy" dugout and readied it for the trip downstream.

Before resuming the river trip, they left Mopti to visit Marcel Griaule and company in the Dogon hill country. The jagged outcroppings and towering cliffs of Bandiagara charmed Rouch. He had entered a world of villages wedged into the nooks and crannies of towering sandstone cliffs. Above the villages Rouch, Sauvy, and Ponty explored tunnels that led to Dogon burial caves. "In a single blow, I found again the nostalgia of adolescence, the mineral countrysides of Dali, the perspectives and hard light of De Chirico, the odor of the old Trocadero" (Rouch 1978c, 10). Overwhelmed by this land of the Minotaur, Rouch vowed to return to the Dogon one day. He did so in 1951.

They spent one day with Griaule and wrote an article, "Griaule among the Cliffs." Back in Mopti, they outfitted their dugout and sailed north and east. Traversing Lake Debo, a veritable inland sea, they inched northeastward toward Timbuktu, leaving Sauvy's Manding world with its society of lineages and entering Rouch's Songhay world with its possession ceremonies.

Timbuktu was depressing. Its empty streets and decaying buildings symbolized a dead tradition, a town "lost in the sands" of the Sahara (Echard and Rouch 1988, interview 5). The river carried them ever eastward to Bamba, where Rouch collected stories about Faran Maka Bote, the ancestor of the Sorko—the ancestor of old Kalia and of Damoré Zika. Eventually they arrived in Gao, the former capital of the Songhay empire. Ponty, who had developed a serious abscess, returned to Paris. Rouch collected more historical material on the conquests of the Sorko, which would eventually be published in his *Contribution à l'histoire des Songhay* (1953).

Six months after they left Ayoru, Rouch and Sauvy docked at its shore. Yacouba, the local paramount chief, told them the Sorko of Firgoun were about to organize a hippo hunt. They wanted Rouch to film it.

This was a great opportunity. To shoot the film, Rouch had to get authorization from the regional environmental official in Niamey. They conceived their plan of action. Rouch and Sauvy would sail downstream to Niamey, make the necessary arrangements, and return to Ayoru by truck. Rouch's friend from the Travaux Publics suggested he make a courtesy call on Governor Toby, the same man who had expelled Rouch from Vichyist Niger in 1942. As Rouch said at the time: "Same man, different uniform" (Echard and Rouch 1988, interview 5). At their meeting Toby was all warmth and gratitude; Rouch hadn't bothered to testify against him at a reparations trial after the war.

Authorization in hand, they motored north to Ayoru, a trip of two hundred kilometers. Rouch didn't know how to film and clumsily broke the camera's tripod. Because of this mishap he was forced to hold the camera to shoot the footage that eventually became his first film. This was the earliest version of *cinéma vérité*, part of Rouch's *pourquoi pas* (why not) method.[3]

---

3. The term *pourquoi pas* method is my invention, not Rouch's. I use it to denote the improvisational character of Rouch's fieldwork and filmmaking and to evoke a genealogical connection to the *Pourquoi-Pas?* the ship on which Rouch's father sailed to the Antarctic.

Rouch and Sauvy returned to Niamey to attend Damoré Zika's second wedding; his first wife had died in childbirth. Damoré was so happy to see them that he insisted he and his new bride would sail down the Niger with his French friends—a Niger River honeymoon. Damoré and his bride accompanied Rouch and Sauvy to Kare Kaptu, the birthplace of Faran Maka Bote, ancestor of the Niger River Sorko and the first possession priest. At Damoré Zika's suggestion, Rouch hired Lam Ibrahim, a young Fulan who sought work in Nigeria. Rouch had met the second of his three lifelong Nigerien friends.

Days passed. The river carried the dugout party southward, ever closer to the famous Boussa rapids. As they approached the rapids they thought again of Mungo Park, who had perished in the whitewater there. Since then, people claimed that ghosts haunted Boussa. Field reports on the rapids cautioned extreme care; the slightest error could result in catastrophe. There are two main rapids at Boussa, but the second one at Aourou is the more famous. There the entire Niger narrows to ten meters, the width of the Boulevard Saint-Michel, and gushes through a gorge some three hundred meters long. There are submerged rocks, and the turbulence raises waves two to three meters high.

But Rouch's men were up to the test. They positioned the dugout perfectly for the descent through the first set of rapids. Over safely. For Aourou, they concentrated their strength. Again positioned perfectly, the dugout squeezed through the rapids at forty kilometers an hour. They passed through in thirty seconds. The passage through the Boussa rapids was not without some losses. When the force of the water dislodged the roof of the dugout, Sauvy lost his field notes.

South of Boussa, the Niger flowed lazily to the sea, as savanna gradually turned into thick forest. Slowly they made their way through the delta. In March 1947 their dugout slipped into the sea; they had spent nine months on the river and were exhausted.

RETURN TO FRANCE, 1947–48

Rouch and Sauvy prepared to return to France. They had no debts to repay; revenue from frequent articles about their adventures had paid all the expenses of the voyage. In Lagos they arranged to ship all their things to France: ritual objects, equipment, and the dugout.

When Rouch returned to the Musée de l'Homme, he found the dugout, cut in half, in the museum's parking lot. Everything else had been stolen. In 1947, as today, Lagos was known as a thieves' paradise. Rouch also discovered the disappointing results of his incipient filmmaking. There were several beautiful shots of Lake Debo, but those images and the footage on the Manding hunters would not make a film. The footage of the hippo hunt at Firgoun, however, had possibilities.

Rouch made a thirty-minute silent film on the hunt. At André Leroi-Gourhan's request Rouch screened the film at the Musée de l'Homme, to an audience of Leroi-Gourhan, Claude Lévi-Strauss—who was then deputy director of the museum—Marcel Griaule, Michel Leiris, and Germaine Dieterlen. They liked the film, and Leiris and Jacques Valcroz asked Rouch to project it at the Orienté, an avant-garde club. The pianist at the Orienté, Claude Azi, suggested that Rouch approach his father, who was head of a company that produced French newsreels. Soon thereafter the senior Azi saw the film and said that "it worked" (Echard and Rouch 1988, interview 6).

Rouch, Ponty, and Sauvy signed a contract with Azi, who agreed to enlarge the sixteen-millimeter film to thirty-five millimeters, add some "stock shots," and provide the sound and the title. The result was *Au pays des mages noirs*, which appeared in 1947. It was the first film in France ever enlarged that way. The end product was something quite different from what Rouch and his friends had shot, but the film did not embarrass Rouch, for it appealed not only to his anthropological colleagues, but to a wider public. Rouch had moved from painting and poetry to civil engineering, from civil engineering to anthropology and soldiering, and from anthropology and soldiering to film. But as the Songhay griots say, "the sure path is never too long."

BACK TO THE FIELD, 1947–48

In 1947 Théodore Monod proposed that Rouch become a researcher for the Centre National de Recherche Scientifique (CNRS), a French government agency that provides research funds and salaries to scholars. With Monod's backing, CNRS admitted Rouch as *attaché de recherche,* the lowest rank. Paul Rivet, chairman of the CNRS Commission, insisted that Rouch be given a temporary appointment; he had three years to complete his thesis.

Rouch returned to Niger and spent seven months conducting fieldwork with his Nigerien friends Damoré Zika and Lam Ibrahim. On horseback, they went from Ayoru to the Hombori Mountains in Mali by way of Dori and Aribinda in what is now Burkina Faso. They also spent time in the Tera region of Niger, staying a month in Wanzerbe, the home of the great sohanci sorcerers. This seven-month trip was a laboratory in "practical ethnography" (Echard and Rouch 1988, interview 6). Rouch had no program, no proposal, no questionnaire, no specific goals. As in his Niger descent, he practiced his *pourquoi pas* method. He went to villages and listened to the people. Following this improvisational trail, Rouch collected myths, transcribed many historical texts, and photographed the prehistoric gravures at Kourki. In this way he collected the bulk of the data for his encyclopedic thesis, *La religion et la magie Songhay.*

By 1947 Rouch refused to consider film apart from ethnography—still a revolutionary notion in today's world of ethnographic films (see Östör 1990; see also Rouch 1974; Ginsburg 1991). He discovered that the camera opened as many ethnographic doors as the notebook. Following as always the Surrealists, Rouch found that film not only captured the fragmentation of a hybrid reality of Songhay possession and sorcery, but also stimulated his comprehension of the Songhay world. And so he strapped his Bell and Howell to his horse and lugged it from village to village. Despite harsh conditions, Rouch shot three films in 1947–48: *Les magiciens de Wanzerbe* (see chap. 6), *La circoncision,* and *Initiation à la danse des possédés.* These seven months in the field convinced Rouch of the utility of "participatory ethnography." He traveled far and wide in Songhay country, lived among the people he visited, and demonstrated his respect for them. He would come to a village on horseback, which transformed him from a tourist to a traveler, an important distinction among the Songhay. Rouch had crossed the first of many ethnographic boundaries in Songhay and had recorded his impressions in prose and on film.

TO THE SAHEL AND BACK, 1948–52

In the fall of 1948 Rouch worked on his thesis and edited his three films. In 1949 Leroi-Gourhan asked him to present his films to the Société des Africanistes at the Musée de l'Homme. Griaule did not like Rouch's films on Songhay possession and magic, but he was thrilled with the short film (nine minutes) on circumcision rites in Hombori. This screening prompted Jacques Valcroz to invite Rouch to Jean Cocteau's avant-garde gathering, the Biarritz Film Festival (also called Festival Maudit or the Cursed Festival), in 1949. There Rouch was well received by Jean Cocteau, Henri Langlois, and Pierre Braunberger. At the festival Rouch presented his *Initiation à la dance des possédés,* which won the festival's grand prize. Rouch had become part of the avant-garde French film scene; Braunberger proposed to produce his future films.

Early in 1951 the Commission of the CNRS met and decided that

Cimetière dans la falaise. J. Rouch, Comité du Film Ethnographique.

Rouch had not fulfilled his contract. Because three years had elapsed since his initial appointment and Rouch had not yet completed his thesis, the Commission dismissed him from CNRS. During this difficult moment Rouch's faithful protector, Théodore Monod, intervened, providing him a scholarship from the Ecole Française de l'Afrique. Though it paid a paltry stipend, this small sum would put food on Rouch's table until he completed his thesis.

Also in 1951, Griaule proposed to Rouch a film project on the Dogon. He wanted Rouch to make a film that would pay particular attention to sound. With a linguist friend Roger Rosfelder, who also was one of Griaule's students, Rouch made *Cimetière dans la falaise,* a film shot in color in which Rosfelder recorded authentic sounds. Between 1951 and 1952 Rouch and Rosfelder worked on two other films: *Bataille sur le grand fleuve*, a reprise of Rouch's first film, *Au pays des mages noirs*, and *Yenaandi, ou Les hommes qui font la pluie*, a film about a Songhay possession ceremony in Simiri during which the people ask their divinities to bring rain. Rosfelder and Rouch also spent several months in the Gold Coast making arrangements for future field projects among migrant laborers from the Sahel.

Rouch returned to France and received his doctorate. Accordingly Théodore Monod asked the CNRS Commission to reinstate him. In 1953 Rouch was named *chargé de recherche*. He had joined a select group of scholars in France who had written theses in anthropology: Griaule, Leroi-Gourhan, Lévi-Strauss, and Dieterlen. Rouch brought out his historical study of Songhay ethnographies, *Contribution à l'histoire des Songhay*, in 1953. In 1954 he published his ethnography, *Les Songhay*, and a photo essay on his descent of the Niger River, *Le Niger en pirogue*.

Secure in his post at CNRS, Rouch prepared his next mission to Africa. Anthropology was changing in France. The earliest French anthropologists had migrated to the field from other disciplines. Paul Rivet had been a veterinarian. Griaule had sold cloth in the Marais of Paris, trained as a pilot, then gravitated to literature. As we know from *Tristes topiques*, Lévi-Strauss first studied philosophy. Leiris was a poet and writer. André Schaeffner arranged Stravinsky's symphonies. In the early 1950s, however, CNRS began to recruit professionally trained anthropologists. An era had passed. No longer could a civil engineer from the School of Make-Believe wander into anthropology.

PARTICIPATORY CINEMA

In 1954 Rouch, who had since married, left for Niger with the express purpose of screening *Bataille sur le grand fleuve* in Ayoru. Having given a series of "Explorer of the World" lectures in Belgium, Rouch earned in one month a sum that equaled his yearly CNRS salary. He bought a Land Rover and crossed the desert with his new bride, Jane. After a series of adventures in the Sahara, the Rouches arrived in Niamey and soon went up to Ayoru (Echard and Rouch 1988, interview 7; see also Jane Rouch 1981). They waited until nightfall, hung a white sheet on a mud-brick wall, and projected the color film. At first the projector itself attracted the curiosity of the people in Ayoru; but as soon as the images appeared on the makeshift screen, the people understood the meaning of the cinema. They quickly recognized themselves. They cried when they saw the "phantoms" of people who had died since the initial filming in 1951, for it was as if the departed souls of the dead (*bia* in Songhay) had magically materialized. "They learned the language of the cinema," Rouch remarked, "in less than ten minutes" (Echard and Rouch 1988, interview 7).

Members of the audience asked Rouch to show the film again and again—he ran it five times that night. About midnight, the people began to comment on Rouch's film. It was the first time Songhay had criticized his work. They said the film was not good; it needed more hippos and less music. Rouch asked for an explanation. He had added a traditional hunting air, *gowey-gowey,* to dramatize the hunt, but the people explained that a hippo hunt requires silence—noise would chase away the hippos.

In 1947–48 Rouch had lived among the Songhay in Wanzerbe and Hombori, listening to their tales of the past and observing their rituals of the present, but they had not understood his mission. In Wanzerbe the people saw him as a strange, persistent white man who asked tiresome questions, wrote in a notebook, and walked around the village with a camera perched on his shoulder. In 1954 an audience of Songhay fishermen grasped what the people of Wanzerbe had missed—the essentials of Rouch's work. They also corrected important errors in the film. That night Rouch and the people of Ayoru witnessed the birth of "participatory cinema" in Africa, and ethnography became, for Rouch, a shared enterprise. He removed the music from the sound track of *Bataille sur le grand fleuve.*

That first night of participatory cinema produced other unexpected results. Tahiru Koro, a Songhay hunter from Wezebangu, some eighty kilometers west of Ayoru, happened to be in the audience. In response to the film screening, he asked Rouch to make a film about men hunting lions with bows and arrows. In this way, Rouch says, "one film gave birth to another [*The Lion Hunters*]" (Echard and Rouch 1988, interview 8). The screening that night led to yet another film, for Damoré Zika and Illo Goudel'ize, both of whom appeared in *Bataille,* saw themselves "on screen" for the first time. Damoré said, "On va jouer [We are going to play]." And so, under the large *farrey* tree that still shades the port in Ayoru, Damoré, Illo, and Rouch decided to make a film of ethnofiction—*Jaguar*—about the adventures of young Nigeriens, who migrate to the Gold Coast (see chaps. 4 and 8).

STUDIES OF MIGRATION

In 1953–54 Rouch began his full-fledged study of the Songhay migrations. He found a Gold Coast in the throes of change. Kwame Nkrumah campaigned for election; political demonstrators paraded in the street; political prisoners languished in jail. Concerned about the prison conditions of the "politicals," Jane Rouch, a journalist, wanted to observe firsthand the Accra jail. The Rouches unexpectedly discovered many Nigerien prisoners. Rouch asked the warden if he could show them *Bataille sur le grand fleuve,* a film that would remind them of their homeland and improve their morale. The warden gave his consent, and Rouch screened *Bataille* at the jail. The film filled the Nigerien prisoners with pride. Among them were Hauka mediums—mediums of the spirits of force, the spirits of colonialism. Show this film to our brothers and sisters, they told Rouch. Show it to the Hauka.

Rouch had come to the Gold Coast to study the Hauka. He wanted to learn how life there had changed this "family" of Songhay possession spirits. Did they still handle fire? Did they still foam at the mouth like rabid dogs and eat poisonous plants? Were there new deities? Rouch had come to the "Mecca" of the Hauka to find out.

Rouch showed *Bataille* to a group of one hundred or so Hauka mediums. The Hauka scenes at the end of the film moved them to appeal to their high priest, Mounkaiba, who eventually invited Rouch to film the annual ritual of the Gold Coast Hauka. When Rouch went to Mounkaiba's compound, he walked into the inner sanctum, the Kaaba of the Hauka's Mecca. Participatory cinema had given birth to another film, *Les maîtres fous* (see chap. 9).

Rouch remained in the Gold Coast almost a year. He filmed *Les maîtres fous* and shot three-quarters of *Jaguar.* Meanwhile, he employed a team of researchers. Through a battery of questionnaires and a series of group discussions, the team gathered data on the social structure economic activities, and religious life of the migrant communities in the Gold Coast.

A generous grant from the British Commission for Technical Cooperation in Africa South of the Sahara and the Scientific Council for Africa South of the Sahara (CCTA/CSA) enabled Rouch to extend his studies of migration to the Ivory Coast, focusing most of his attention on the migrant workers in Abidjan. Using survey research instruments similar to those of his Gold Coast project, his team went to work gathering data on the sociology of migration. Meanwhile, he started filming *The Lion Hunters* in and around Yatakala in Niger (see chap. 7). The same year, Kwame Nkrumah invited Rouch to the Ghanaian in-

Bataille sur le grand fleuve. J. Rouch, Comité du Film Ethnographique.

dependence celebration, which Rouch recorded in a short film, *Baby Ghana*. While Rouch was in Ghana, the director of the Ghanaian Film Unit lent him a sound studio to record the narrative of *Jaguar*. As they viewed three hours of footage, Damoré Zika and Lam Ibrahim started to talk, and talk, and talk, producing finally, in the words of Rouch, "a magnificent commentary" (Echard and Rouch 1988, interview 8).

When Oumarou Ganda, one of Rouch's research assistants in Abidjan, saw the *Jaguar* footage for the first time, he asked Rouch to make a film based on the life of someone like him, who had actually lived the life of a migrant. They came up with a provisional title, *Le Zouzou-man de Treicheville*, which eventually became the ethnofiction film *Moi, un noir*. Still working in Abidjan in the summer of 1958, Rouch filmed *La pyramide humaine*, which depicted the strained relations between Europeans and Africans at an Abidjan high school.

Rouch's long-term study of West African migration dropped him into the arena of West African politics, increasing his awareness of the complex relations between migrants and autochthonous populations. This phase of Rouch's ethnographic research also yielded several of his most memorable and controversial films, as well as a series of monographs by Rouch and others on West African migration and urbanization.

PARTICIPATORY ANTHROPOLOGY

Following his studies of West African migration, Rouch continued fieldwork in Niger and Mali but concentrated on ethnographic filmmaking. Since 1960 he has made scores of films but has not published other ethnographic monographs, although he has continued to write articles for scholarly journals and has updated and expanded his previously published work.[4] Since 1960 his ideas on ethnography—Songhay or otherwise—have been articulated indirectly in his films, in several articles, and in a series of interviews.

From 1960 to the present Jean Rouch has been a champion of ethnographic film. He has trained scores of African filmmakers and has showcased their work in catalogs published by UNESCO. He continues to inspire young filmmakers at his Saturday-morning film seminar. Rouch is currently president of the Cinémathèque Française (museum of the cinema), which affords him the opportunity to fuse art and science in events like Ciné-Danse/Ciné-Transe. In a recent article De-Bouzek (1989, 313) describes one of the entr'actes of this event. "Perhaps the most 'surrealist' of all was the *intervention choréographique,* in which a live dancer performed in front of a screen while an excerpt from Rouch's *Yenendi de Yantalla* [1969] was screened. The audience was an eclectic blend of artists, filmmakers, and anthropologists, who seemed to be enjoying the 'spectacle' with equal enthusiasm."

---

4. I am weary of hearing people suggest that Rouch has given up ethnography since 1960. He has not. He continues to research Songhay history and possession, and he continues to write, revising and updating his earlier texts as well as writing new ones. In this sense Rouch has not left ethnography for filmmaking, and this continuity underscores one of the major premises of this book: that for Rouch ethnographic and cinematic practices are dialectically linked—even after 1960.

What can we say about the fieldwork that produced Rouch's ethnographies and his major films? From the beginning of his field experience in Niger and Mali, Rouch realized that "doing" ethnography
and ethnographic film—which are interpenetrating rather than separate domains for him—is a profoundly human endeavor. While his
fieldwork is based on scientific principles and intellectual problems, it
is also founded on the principle of long-term friendship and mutual
respect. By way of his immersion in things Songhay, Rouch respected
"his others" and earned their respect.

Rouch's field methods are implicated ones in which the investigator
participates actively—and over a long period—in the lives of the
people being investigated. During his seven months of horseback fieldwork in 1947–48, Rouch's implicated orientation moved him to share
with his subjects the fruits of his cinematic labor.

The story of Jean Rouch is that of an anthropologist who participates in the lives of the people he portrays, which means that among
the Songhay—just like a griot—he has foes as well as friends. Rare in
anthropology, Rouch's entanglement in Songhay social life—his long-
standing friendships—accounts for the narrative force of his oeuvre.
Rouch's ethnography carries on the tradition of Ponts and Chaussées,
the School of Make-Believe in which art and science, real and imaginary, are fused. Rouch's ethnography also carries on the griot's tradition in which the expression of words and the creation of images enable the dead to live again.

CHAPTER THREE
Worlds of the Ancestors

Boro kan dirgan bi, a si hunkuna guna.
One who has forgotten the past will not grasp the present.
—Songhay proverb

The griot's primary task is to recount history—to chant the glories of past kingdoms, past kings, past battles. In Songhay, griots perform history during major Muslim celebrations: the end of the one-month Ramadan fast, the Tabaski, which commemorates Abraham's willingness to slaughter his son at God's behest, and the birthday of Muhammad the Prophet. During these ceremonies griots remind the Songhay of their glorious past, of their courage, of their deeply rooted culture.

Just as history is the passion of Songhay griots, so it is the passion of Jean Rouch, the cinematic griot. It is with a deep appreciation of history that Rouch made such memorable films as *The Lion Hunters, Jaguar,* and *Les magiciens de Wanzerbe,* as well as the series of Sigui films on the Dogon. The corpus of Rouch's films on Songhay possession—the bulk of his work in film—is also tied to Songhay history, for possession ceremonies are recreations of Songhay historical experience. In this chapter I describe the historical foundation of Rouch's ethnography, for one cannot fully appreciate Rouch's oeuvre without some knowledge of the Songhay past.

In the previous chapter I set the context for the analysis of Rouch's three written ethnographies: *Contribution à l'histoire des Songhay, Migrations au Ghana,* and *La religion et la magie Songhay.* In the next three chapters I discuss these works in some detail—for several reasons. First, they were published in French and are difficult to find. Second, they describe ceremonies that are no longer performed. Third, they provide material that contextualizes some of Rouch's more controversial films. Fourth, they demonstrate Rouch's descent from Mar-

Jean Rouch filming history: *Babatu, les trois conseils*. J. Rouch,
Comité du Film Ethnographique.

cel Griaule. Finally, these works reveal the depth and breadth of Rouch's ethnographic knowledge.

THE SONGHAY PAST

As any griot's performance demonstrates, history is a living reality for most Songhay. In *Contribution à l'histoire des Songhay*, Rouch completes a historical fresco in which background fuses with foreground, in which the past blends into the present. For the Songhay, history is indeed a living tradition. Battles waged centuries ago have contemporary importance. During possession ceremonies, spirits from the distant past return to advise their descendants. On ceremonial occasions praise singers chant "old words" to remind their audiences of Songhay's glorious imperial past. This part of Rouch's tale comprises a detailed presentation of *Contribution*. It is a work that Songhay specialists return to time after time, for it contains material—the stories of the past—that modern Songhay have long since forgotten.

In *Contribution* there emerges a textual pattern that Rouch uses in his other ethnographic writings: a limited amount of anthropological—that is, theoretical—interpretation. From the beginning of *Contribution* it is clear that Rouch has no intention of using the rich historical data he collected to refine the social theory of his day or to promote a particular brand of historiography. The book's textual form is no doubt influenced by the Griaulian attention to documentation; it also stems from the legacy of the griot who chants stories but refrains from extratextual interpretation. This fusion of perspectives demonstrates Rouch's thoroughness as a scholar of African history.

The penchant for documentation can be grasped in a simple perusal of the text. Rouch's introduction, only two pages long, spells out the underlying theme of his text: that for the Songhay history is a living, ever-present tradition. He does not review the literatures of historiographers, anthropologists of religion, or British structural functionalists. He does not cite his mentor, Marcel Griaule. His intent in this short introduction is to outline his ideas about the Songhay's conception of history as it relates to their cosmology.

The introduction is followed by two chapters that set the framework of Rouch's study. The first is a brief description of climate and ecology. One expects this kind of introductory material in a traditional ethnography; indeed, there is just such a chapter in Rouch's slim volume *Les Songhay*. Why devote several pages to ecology in a historical work? The reason is simple and paramount: the climate and the land are major characters in the Songhay story. The Niger River, rocky, dry terrain, and drought have all played major roles in Songhay history.

The second chapter, "The Men of Before," is a brief discussion of Songhay prehistory. In the 1950s little was known about the "men of the past." Here Rouch makes no leaps of interpretation; rather, he lists the various archaeological sites in Songhay country that provide clues about prehistory: lithic monuments, rock engravings, the remains of fortifications, rock shelters, grave sites, sites of ancient villages, ancient waterworks (cisterns), and examples of pottery.

Rouch admits that the men of the past left a great many material remains, but they are scattered. With Griaulian caution, he warns readers that without systematic archaeological study there can be no scientific assessment of the ancient populations. With the verve of the griot, he weaves a cloak of mystery around the men of the past, who he says were *laabu koy,* or "proprietors of the earth," the first people to establish contact with the earth spirits of what is today Songhay country. The ancestors maintained their contact with the supernatural by making periodic offerings to the spirits of the soil. These ritual traditions are attributed to the Kurmey, probably the ancestors of the Gurmantche and Kurumba, Voltaic-language speakers who today live in Burkina Faso. They are peoples whose oral tradition indicates that their ancestors long ago lived in what is today Niger.

The remaining two parts of *Contribution* are "The Songhay Empire" and "The Invasions." The chapters in "The Songhay Empire" describe in concrete detail and concise language the transformation of a small state into a powerful and important medieval West African empire.

The origin of the Songhay is shrouded in mystery. Various historians have their own theories. Songhay griots say the Songhay came from either Mali (sometimes it is Mande, sometimes it is Gao) or Yemen. Rouch is far more interested in the traditions of the First Men, populations that left archaeological remains that can be analyzed to reconstruct the past.

From these remains and from gleanings from the symbolic repertoire of important Songhay ceremonies (possession and sacrificial offerings to land spirits), Rouch concludes that the Songhay people were fashioned from contact among four groups: the Do, the Gow, the Sorko, and migrating Berbers, probably from the Gharmantes in southern Libya. The Do were the "masters of the water," the first inhabitants of various sections of the Niger River. The Gow were the "masters of the bush," hunters of wild game. The Sorko were fishermen; their mythic ancestor, Faran Maka Bote, mastered the river spirits and became the first possession priest. The descendants of all these groups live today in Niger, where a select few continue their ancestors' ancient practices. Although Rouch writes dispassionately about these groups, they come alive in his films on Songhay magic and possession.

Rouch discusses at some length the origin of the Sorko, who he thinks developed the market at Koukya, which attracted hunters, cultivators, and fishermen as well as blacksmiths and weavers. And from this mélange of peoples there emerged the early Songhay population, of which a *sorko,* doubtless a descendant of Faran Maka Bote's clan, was the chief. Sorko, of course, figure prominently in Rouch's work. Kalia introduced Rouch to the Songhay world of possession, and her grandson Damoré Zika was Rouch's guide on the various paths of Songhay religion. And like the sorko, Rouch considers himself a "son of the water." His father was, after all, a naval meteorologist who sailed on the *Pourquoi-Pas?*

The Sorko, to return to the Songhay past, established themselves in Koukya. This social situation set the stage for the coming of the Za, probably sometime in the latter part of the eighth century. Rouch says the Za were Christian Lempta Berbers from the Tripoli region of Libya. Once received by the Songhay of Koukya, they quickly became a clan of rulers. The Za are never mentioned in the oral traditions but are described extensively by such medieval Timbuktu historians as Kati and es-Saadi.

The Za rapidly integrated themselves. They married Koukya women and quickly forgot their Christian practices. Apart from several obscure myths and the Timbuktu chronicles, little is known about this early epoch of the Songhay. Still less is known about the social, political, and religious practices of the Songhay in this period. Rouch suggests that between the seventh and twelfth centuries the political dominance of the Za compelled the Sorko, who had once been masters of the region, to migrate up the Niger to the west. The migrations of the Sorko notwithstanding, Rouch describes ancient Koukya as a center of magic and the arts of war, the foundation for Songhay expansion centuries later. Here then is the historical foundation of the Songhay religious practices that were to figure prominently in his later writings and in his films (*Les magiciens de Wanzerbe, Jaguar, The Lion Hunters,* and *Les tambours d'avant: Turu et bitti*).

About the eleventh century, Islam spread widely into the Sudan. At the instigation of the Almoravids in Morocco, hundreds of marabouts (Muslim teachers and missionaries) roamed the Sahel in search of converts. Simultaneously Gao, founded by migrating Sorko about 690, became an important commercial center. To promote commerce, the Gao merchants asked Za Kosoy to establish his capital there. And so he did in 1010. Henceforward Koukya became a religious capital to which the Za traveled to fortify themselves and their legitimacy through magic. Muslim clerics converted Za Kosoy to Islam soon after his arrival in Gao. Remarkably, Rouch tells us, this conversion had no impact at the beginning: none of Za Kosoy's successors carried an Islamic name. All of his successors were master magicians; they all knew the *gind'ize gina,* "the first incantation," which gave them the supernatural force to kill people with their words.

During the time of Za Assibai (He who doesn't know), Songhay came under the suzerainty of the empire of Mali, but the domination of Mali over Songhay, Rouch suggests, lacked stability, though it lasted much of the fourteenth century. In the fifteenth century the power and prestige of Mali waned. The Tuareg sacked Timbuktu in 1431, and in 1463 Sonni Ali Ber became the Songhay leader. His armies would establish the Songhay empire.

Za Assibai was the last Songhay ruler to carry the title *za.* One of his two sons, Ali Kolen, who was conscripted by Mali as a military officer, but he escaped from the army, gathered arms he had hidden along the route to Gao, and returned to the Songhay capital. He overthrew Za Bada and became the Songhay chief, taking the title *si* or *sonni.* Reaffirming the scholarship of Delafosse, Rouch states that this was not a new chiefdom but merely a change in title from za to sonni (see Rouch 1953).

In the first half of the fifteenth century Songhay grew in prestige and power, while Mali was moribund. According to the *Tarikh es-Soudan,* Sonni Souleyman Dandi conquered the village of Mema in the northeast of Macina (the inner delta of the Niger River), which brought the end of Mali: "Songhay was ripe for Sonni Ali's great adventure" (es-Saadi 1900, 180, 181).

And so it was. Rouch writes of Sonni Ali with the unequivocal admiration of a griot. Sonni Ali was the founder of the Songhay empire, a great warrior and an even greater magician. He used supernatural powers to render his armies invincible and to legitimize his rule. From his father, Sonni Ali received the gind'ize gina, the master word of magic, the key to the power of the Za. From his mother, who was of the Faru (she was probably from near Sokoto, Nigeria), he learned the magic of statuettes fashioned from wood and stone. In time of war he would consult these objects. "When Sonni Ali took power in Songhay, he was the most powerful magician that the Sudan had ever known," wrote es-Saadi (1900, 181).

During his reign, Sonni Ali Ber engaged in continual warfare. He took Timbuktu from the Tuareg. He fought a campaign against the Bariba of the Bourgu (in the north of present-day Benin). He conquered Djenne. He battled the Mossi, Dogon, and Kurumba. The conquering Songhay armies took thousands of captives, who became Songhay slaves. Ali Ber also established a navy and formed a political structure with regional governors and military commanders.

Rouch describes the military strategies and tactics of Sonni Ali Ber. His campaigns against the mountain peoples and the Tuareg enabled him to capture brave soldiers, whom he then used in his own army. Rouch knows less about how Sonni Ali's army fought. The sohanci of the twentieth century say, however, that Sonni Ali Ber gave his soldiers amulets that rendered them invisible, enabling them to fly or to change themselves into serpents. Legend has it that Sonni Ali Ber could transform himself and his magnificent horse, Zinzinbadou, into vultures. These images are reflected in the design of rings a few sohanci possess: a vulture-horse mounted by a vulture-man. It is said of Sonni Ali Ber:

> Si flies in the night
> Si flies at the cock's first crow
> Si takes all the souls
> Si kills a man between his hat and his head
> Si kills a man between his shoe and his foot
> Si kills a man between his shirt and his neck.
> (es-Saadi 1900, 184)

Ostensibly Sonni Ali Ber, like his predecessors, was a Muslim, a member of the Kharedjite sect. To the dismay of the Timbuktu scribes, the holiest and "wisest" men in the Songhay empire, Sonni Ali Ber refused to eschew his magical powers. Accordingly, these scribes, on whom Rouch and others have relied for firsthand historical accounts of imperial Songhay, took a dim view of Sonni Ali. Mahmoud Kati considered him no better than a heathen who delighted in using a pestle to pound the heads of pious Muslims into pulp (Kati 1911, 104).

A shrewd politician, Sonni Ali Ber took on the Timbuktu scribes. Rouch writes (1953, 185): "Thus, even if the magician is hostile to Islam, he is nonetheless ready to take advantage of its opportunities. Sonni Ali, who massacred the sages of Timbuktu, whose growing influence seemed dangerous to him, thought highly of their science; he eliminated his enemies, saving only those who could teach him something." Despite the negative portraits painted by the Timbuktu historians, Rouch believes that Sonni Ali Ber is the dominant personage of Songhay history and Songhay experience. Ali Ber, according to Rouch, died like a true magician—in mysterious circumstances. Returning from a military campaign in the East, he allegedly drowned during a flash flood. His soldiers embalmed his body and buried him, but no one, says Rouch, knows the location of his grave. "I willingly believe that Sonni Ali died as a true magician, his body disappearing in the bush, but his spirit remaining present, nourished by the good graces of his sons, and then by their descendants, and continuing always to guide their works" (Rouch 1953, 186). It is said that Sonni Ali's head is buried in Wanzerbe, the center of Songhay magical power and the site of Rouch's remarkable film *Les magiciens de Wanzerbe* (chap. 6).

Rouch writes (1953, 186): "Such was Sonni Ali. His terrible and troubling personality dominates all of Songhay history, of which he is the very pure and very cruel hero. The twenty-seven years of the reign of Si, the conquerer, the engineer, the organizer, the master magician, represent the brief summit of Songhay civilization." This is perhaps why Songhay have immortalized him as the first magician and the father of the genie of water, *za beri wandu,* "the great and dangerous za."

With Sonni Ali Ber's death in 1491 Songhay slips into a brief period of civil war. The armies of Si Baru, Sonni Ali's son, and Mohammed Touré, one of Sonni Ali's generals, challenged one another for power. Si Baru renounced Islam and embraced fully the magic-sorcery of his father. Mohammed Touré embraced Islam and became the champion of the Timbuktu scribes. What was at first a power struggle quickly became a battle for religious domination. For Rouch the turning point of Songhay history was the battle of Anfao, 12 April 1493, when the armies of Islam defeated those of the "infidel" Si Baru, who escaped to the south, to the archipelago of Tillaberi. "The 'victory' of Anfao," Rouch writes, "is in fact the first [Songhay] defeat and the sign of future catastrophes" (1953, 187).

In the third chapter of this part of the text, Rouch writes about the Songhay empire under the Askia, the successors to Sonni Ali Ber. In this chapter and in the chapters of the remainder of *Contribution,* he relies heavily on documents written by Songhay historians Mahmoud Kati (*Tarikh al Fattach*) and Abdoulrahamane es-Saadi (*Tarikh es-Soudan*). Kati, a Timbuktu scribe, was a firsthand observer of the Askiad. As Askia Mohammed's official historian, he accompanied the first king of the Askiad on his illustrious pilgrimage to Mecca. So began a political transformation from magicians to Muslim kings.

From the outset of his reign (1493) Askia Mohammed impressed his followers with his organizational ability. Improving on Sonni Ali's foundation, he built a powerful and efficient government structure, making sure to choose his brothers and sons for key government posts. Rouch (1953, 192) outlines the most important government positions under Askia:

First are the provincial chiefs:
1. *Kourmina fari:* the chief of Kourmina and the first dignitary of Askia's court;
2. *Bara koy,* the governor of Bara province, who was called *mansa,* the title of the kings of Mali. Alone among the officials, he could veto an imperial decision;
3. *Dendi fari,* the governor of Dendi (southern) province, who gave Askia frank advice;
4. *Dirma koy,* the governor of Dirma province;
5. *Bangu farma,* the governor of lakes;
6. *Hombori koy,* the governor of Hombori province;
7. *Aribinda farma,* the governor of Aribinda, the province of the Kurumba people, masters of farming magic;

Second are the military chiefs:
1. *Balama,* the chief of staff and the only man who could sit during an imperial audience;
2. *Hi koy,* the boat chief or admiral of the fleet;
3. *Tara farma,* the general of the cavalry; and
4. *Hari farma,* the chief of commercial navigation.

Third is the council of ministers:
1. *Barey koy,* minister of protocol, who was assisted by two managers;
2. *Kalisi farma,* the finance minister, assisted by the supervisor of assets, the supervisor of salaries, and a chief buyer;
3. *Fari moundio,* the minister of agriculture;
4. *Asara moundi,* the justice minister, assisted by a sentencing judge.
5. *Sao farma,* the minister of forestry;
6. *Hou kokorey koy,* the chief of the palace eunuchs; and
7. *Kore farma,* the minister of "whites" (Tuareg and Moors) affairs.

Some years after consolidating his local authority, Askia Mohammed sought to legitimize his rule through a pilgrimage to Mecca in 1497–98. Rouch is quick to point out the divergences between Kati's official account of this historic adventure and the oral tradition of Askia's pilgrimage. Kati describes Askia as a strict Muslim who goes to Mecca to receive the assurances of the holy city's great *sherif* (descendant of the Prophet Mohammed). He returns to Gao as *khalif* of the Sudan. In the oral traditions of Wanzerbe, however, Askia goes to Mecca as a Songhay pagan (Rouch 1953, 194; see also Stoller's interview with Kassey of Wanzerbe in chap. 6). In the words of Kassey of Wanzerbe, he went to Mecca full of iron—rings that had "drunk" sacrificial blood and had "eaten" the powerful powders made from pulverized tree barks and plants (interview, 5 July 1984).

According to the oral tradition, "Mohammed would have started by basing his authority on the magic powers of Si (spirits, the insignias of command like the lance of a very particular form . . .); but Sonni's sons, having dug up his magic (seven drums buried on an island) incited Mohammed to look for other foundations of authority, to rely on Islam" (Rouch 1953, 194). Rouch suggests that the oral version of Askia Mohammed's pilgrimage is closer to the way events actually occurred at the end of the fifteenth century.

Upon his return from Mecca, Askia Mohammed mounted a series of military campaigns to extend his empire—for Islam. He launched a holy war against the "pagan" Mossi of Yatenga in 1498–99. In 1499–1500 he fought the Baagana, west of the Macina in contemporary Mali. In 1501–2 he fought in Diara, a Malian province, supplying himself with slaves. From 1502 to 1504 Askia remained at court in Gao, but in 1505–6 he began his ill-fated campaign against Bourgou (Bariba) in present-day northern Benin, where many soldiers died. No wars were fought in 1506–7, but the following year Askia Mohammed engaged the remnants of Mali. In 1512–13 he fought against the non-Muslim Fulan Tenguella, and in 1513–14 against the Hausa state of Katsina. Askia Mohammed continued to deploy his armies against Agadez and against rebelling populations in Kebbi (northwestern Nigeria) and Bagana (Mali).

The year 1519 marked the beginning of Askia Mohammed's decline. His brother the Kanfari Omar died, and Askia Mohammed began to go blind. His son Moussa, minister of agriculture, began to plot against his father. Finally, in 1528 Moussa killed the Kanfari Yaya, the dedicated assistant to Askia Mohammed, and deposed his father (Rouch 1953, 197).

In this chapter, as in those on Sonni Ali and the Za, Rouch evaluates his source material, contrasting the Islamic and oral versions of Askia Mohammed, known through the oral tradition as Mamar. Whereas the Islamic version of Askia Mohammed's reign credits his success to the *baraka* (divine grace of Allah) the Sahelian monarch obtained in Mecca, the oral tradition suggests that magic charms played the decisive role in his bureaucratic and military victories. They are also seen as major factors in his defeat in his campaign against Kebbi. Rouch, in fact, suggests that Askia Mohammed's endorsement of Islam marked the beginning of the end of the Songhay empire.

In the end his sons rendered Askia Mohammed powerless; they banished him to a desolate island infested with mosquitoes and toads.

> This terrible end is very different from the mysterious disappearance of Sonni Ali at the peak of his power. During these ten miserable years, Askia Mohammed, without doubt, would have realized the vanity of his work. From a Songhay reunited around the never-vanquished magic king Sonni Ali, a Songhay cemented by an authority rendered indisputable by purely black beliefs, Askia Mohammed, apostle of Islam, had certainly enlarged a better-administered state, a state in which his authority, based on an undoubtedly prestigious religion, which was nonetheless external and limited, lacked the power to mold his empire. The first defeats were a signal of the [coming] debacle. (Rouch 1953, 199)

Rouch completes his sad chapter on the Askiad by recounting briefly the rapid decline of the empire. Apart from the rule of Askia Daoud (1549–82), Songhay was governed by a succession of madmen, simpletons, or cruel despots, all coveting the emperor's chair. The scene at the Songhay court was one of intense jealously, corruption, and deadly plots. This internecine conflict considerably weakened the Songhay state, making possible the Moroccan defeat of the Songhay army at Tondibi in 1591, which marked the end of the Songhay empire.

Rouch also describes as best he can the quality of social life during the Askiad: the easy relationship of nobles and soldiers; the relative economic prosperity of the Sahel; the high social position achieved by certain imperial slaves who bought their freedom. He also writes of the seventeenth-century Zerma migration from Mali to Niger, a reconstruction based on scraps of historical texts and the oral tradition of the epic *Mali Bero*.

In the end Djouder, commander of the El Mansur's Andalusian army, conquered Songhay. For Rouch, however, the Askiad was some kind of aberration: "Even before Djouder and his Andalusians had arrived along the banks of the Niger, the true Songhay, the partisans of the old Sonni, or the infidel Zerma still faithful to the ancient cults, had already withdrawn to the south, and it was around this group that there was organized a resistance movement" (Rouch 1953, 209).

In the final part of *Contribution* Rouch describes in detail the Moroccan invasion, the battle of Tondibi (1591), and the negotiations between Djouder and the last Askia. The defeat of Songhay cut the empire into two parts. In the North, Djouder and his Moroccans governed Gao and Timbuktu. In the South, the Dendi, the Askia maintained their authority, and Askia Nouhou led a resistance movement. The open war between independent Songhay and the Moroccans began soon after the initial Songhay defeat in 1591 and continued until 1598. When Gao "cracked," as the defeat of Tondibi is described in the oral tradition, neighboring states asserted their independence (interview with Kassey of Wanzerbe, 5 July 1984). The Fulan of the Macina plundered the countryside. The Tuareg raided sedentary villages. In 1591 Tuareg attacked Timbuktu, setting fire to the city. These attacks complicated the military and political situation of the Moroccans, who faced resistance movements from all fronts. Internal conflict among the princes sapped the Songhay resistance from the south. From 1635 to roughly 1660, some of the princes seceded from Songhay and established their own states. By 1660 the princes in the South had balkanized their state into the small principalities of Kokoro, Garuol, Ayoru, Tera, Dargol, and Namaro. There were also states in Hombori in the North and in Loulami in the South (Rouch 1953, 213–20).

After 1660 not much is directly known about Songhay until the French conquest of the western Sudan. "In this way the true Songhay, after the seventeenth century, is no longer the one of Timbuktu or Gao, but the one farther south near the Anzuru, the Garuol, on the islands of the river surrounded by rapids" (Rouch 1953, 224). These regions are, ironically, the centers of Songhay magic and spirit possession.

During the eighteenth and nineteenth centuries the Fulan and the Tuareg terrorized Songhay. The Fulan states of Sheiku Amadu in the Macina of Mali and Ousmane dan Fodio in northern Nigeria extended their power and influence in Songhay. More important than their military power, however, was their mission to Islamize "heathen" peoples. Before the Fulan states, Muslims in the Sahel lived mostly in large towns, but with the advent of these states Islam spread far and wide in the western Sudan.

The small Songhay states were more directly menaced by the small Fulan state in Say, forty-five kilometers south of present-day Niamey on the west bank of the Niger River. The Tuareg invasion from the north further complicated the Songhay political situation. Tuareg claimed suzerainty over large tracts of formerly Songhay and Zerma land. Periodically the various Songhay states would ally themselves against the Tuareg, who had joined with other Songhay principalities. The Say Fulan might ally themselves with Dendi against Tera. These forged and broken alliances, according to Rouch, led to a series of "guerres intestins" that continued up to the last invasion: that of the

French in 1898, which resulted in colonization and ultimately in 1960 in the birth of the state of Niger.

HISTORY, ANTHROPOLOGY, AND THE SONGHAY

A tension runs through *Contribution:* the conflict between Muslim and non-Muslim Songhay. Rouch's reconstruction of the distant and non-Muslim Songhay past depends heavily on the Timbuktu chroniclers Kadi and es-Saadi, both of whom were pious Muslims bent on leaving certain impressions of Songhay for posterity. Rouch probes the *Tarikh al Fattach* (Kati) and the *Tarikh es-Soudan* (es-Saadi), attempting to sort historical observation from religious bias. It is a daunting task, for he must rely on the uncertainties of the oral tradition to support his frequently non-Muslim positions on Songhay history and experience (see Vansina 1985).

Despite these historiographic difficulties, Rouch suggests time and again that the Muslim version of Songhay history is flawed. He claims the oral tradition of Wanzerbe presents a better picture of Askia Mohammed's pilgrimage to Mecca. He is highly critical of the Muslim portrait of Sonni Ali Ber, whom he considers the central personality of Songhay history and cultural experience. Between the lines of *Contribution* one gets the impression that Rouch favors the practices of the sohanci and zima, which are faithful to the past glories of Songhay. To him Islam is an external source of Songhay destabilization. Ultimately Askia Mohammed, the "apostle of Islam" in the Sahel, is defeated by his religious fervor. He goes blind and is banished to a pest-infested island by his scheming, power-hungry sons. Rouch also writes that by the time the Moroccans conquered Songhay, the true Songhay—the descendants of Sonni Ali Ber—and the Zerma migrants who practiced the ancient cults lived in the South. In Rouch's scheme of Songhay, Askia Mohammed and his descendants are little more than foreign usurpers of power; they introduce an alien and ultimately destructive religion to Songhay.

Rouch is an ethnohistorian whose perspective on Songhay history is no doubt influenced by his field experience among the sohanci of Wanzerbe and the Zerma possession priests of Simiri. His is the griot's perspective on the Songhay past, a perspective that permeates his films. Other scholars present a very different picture of Songhay history. Urvoy and Delafosse rely almost exclusively on the original source material found in the Timbuktu chronicles. More recent historical work by Kaba (1984), Hunwick (1985), Saad (1983), and Abitbol (1977) also relies on written source materials, mainly the Timbuktu chronicles. In their requisite discussion of sources, these historians pay scant attention to the oral tradition.

In contrast to the historiography of imperial Songhay, there are several works of Songhay ethnohistory that like Rouch's, take a more anthropological perspective. Adam Konaré Ba's study of Sonni Ali Ber (1977) judiciously combines the written records of the historiographer and the oral tradition of the ethnographer. The resulting monograph is a balanced and fair portrait of Sonni Ali Ber, one that describes his administrative and political skills as well as his personal cruelty. Sonni Ali Ber, as the Songhay griots say, was the epitome of a hard man, a man who was brave and unyielding. Hard men have earned the respect of their peers. In the same vein, Jean-Pierre Olivier de Sardan's historical studies have relied heavily on the oral tradition. Some of his accounts, most notably *Quand nos pères étaient captifs,* could be called history "from below" in that they describe the experience of Songhay captives and other marginal social groups. His gaze is directed primarily at the nineteenth century, for which there are few if any written records germane to Songhay (see Olivier de Sardan 1976). He has also written extensively on the sociopolitical dynamics of nineteenth-century Songhay-Zerma society, using oral accounts to flesh out cultural concepts, many of which derive from the historical memory (see Olivier de Sardan 1982, 1984).

The most recent project in Songhay history is that of Thomas Hale, who has recorded, transcribed, and translated the epic of Askia Mohammed. In Hale's *Scribe, Griot, and Novelist: Narrative Interpreters of the Songhay Empire* (1990), the epic is the foundation for a hermeneutic analysis of Songhay history and experience. Here is a book that combines the best historiographical scholarship with a meticulous reading of an epic text. The outcome is a culturally sensitive account of Songhay imperial history.

FROM A SONGHAY PERSPECTIVE

In *Contribution* Rouch depicts Songhay society and culture from—as much as possible—a Songhay perspective. For Muslims the hero of Songhay experience is undoubtedly Askia Mohammed Touré, who transformed the imperial court from a center of paganism to one of pious devotion to Allah. For many Songhay Askia Mohammed remains a hero, a figure of unquestioned historical importance, a man whose renown has spread far and wide—even in our day. For Rouch, however, the central figure of Songhay experience is Sonni Ali Ber. Ali Ber and his descendants are "true" Songhay, practitioners of the rites of the Za and the Sonni. Like their famous ancestor, these are men whose limitless capacities defy death itself, for the nourished spirit of Sonni Ali Ber lives and guides them along their paths.

In Rouch's view Songhay history is a series of events that have created social disequilibrium, a fundamental instability that allows the world to arrange itself in its final and stable order. In Songhay, the life that has been led is but a game:

> And this God, *iri koy,* "our master," aided by all of his secondary divinities, conducts this game without pity. What men do, be they simple humans or heroes, derives from their attitude toward these rules. Some of them fearfully avoid subverting the order, but others do not hesitate to give way to more dangerous acts. With a certain prudence, priests go through the secondary intermediaries, attempting to render them favorably [disposed]. The magicians, on the contrary, personally take all risks, provoking God himself while knowing full well the consequences. This is the way of their ancestor, the one who dominated the entire history of the Songhay, Sonni Ali. (Rouch 1953, 245)

For Rouch, then, the importance of Songhay history is not the sequence of events that led to the establishment of the Askiad; it is not the economic forces that enabled Sonni Ali to become a great monarch. It is clear from a reading of *Contribution* that the importance of Songhay history, from a Songhay perspective, is symbolic. History creates for Songhay a symbolic foundation, an anchor in a world of turbulent crosscurrents.

In the end Songhay history lives not in or between the lines of some dusty book, but in experience. It lives on in the theatrics of possession ceremonies, in the "old words" of a magical incantation, in the smell of incense used to beckon the spirits. As such, Songhay history becomes the framework for the cinematic griot's major ethnographic films. In Rouch's films the mists of Songhay history are not dissipated by the technological reproduction of contemporary social life.

Rouch's historical studies eventually led him to study the Songhay migrations to the Gold Coast. Rouch had learned about the Zerma-Songhay mercenaries who went to the Gold Coast in the middle of the nineteenth century—early military migrants who blazed a trail that other Zerma and Songhay followed. In the next chapter I shall describe in detail Rouch's pioneering sociological study of labor migrations, a study that provided the ethnographic foundation for two of his greatest films, *Les maîtres fous* and *Jaguar.*

CHAPTER FOUR
Migrations to New Worlds

Boro kon mana naaru, nga no mana laakal.
The person who hasn't traveled can never be wise.
—Songhay saying

Since the nineteenth century, when the lure of the cities, war, and ready cash drew young men from the Sahel to the Guinea coast, young men have sought their fortunes as migrant laborers. Drawn sometimes by adventure, more often by economic necessity, significant numbers of foreign workers were common in the bustling ports and teeming cities. When Rouch became interested, Ghana (then known as the Gold Coast) was a frequent destination; a generation later the favored destination has shifted to Togo, the Ivory Coast, or Nigeria, depending on the politics of the moment. By definition poor, most of the migrants accepted that their trip would be neither comfortable nor particularly easy. Most took trucks or bush taxis to their destination and carried the scantiest baggage. Most knew the rigors and rules of border crossings. "Are you carrying arms, contraband?" "Let's look at your luggage!" "You'll have to stay here until everything is in order. How long? Who knows, it could be until. . . ." the poor migrant paid his bribe. And once in Lome or Abidjan, the taxis still deposited them in the Muslim quarter, where they searched for their countrymen. Some things had changed; many things remained the same.

With its aura of romance and reality, "the road" captured Jean Rouch's attention in the 1950s—for two reasons. First, he sensed a historical pattern to the migration, a pattern he traced to the mid-nineteenth century. Second, he wanted to visit the Mecca of the Hauka, the Songhay spirits of colonial force in the Gold Coast. In 1953 he began the second phase of his fieldwork (1953–60), funded in part by the British Commission for Technical Cooperation in Africa South of the Sahara and the Scientific Council for Africa South of the

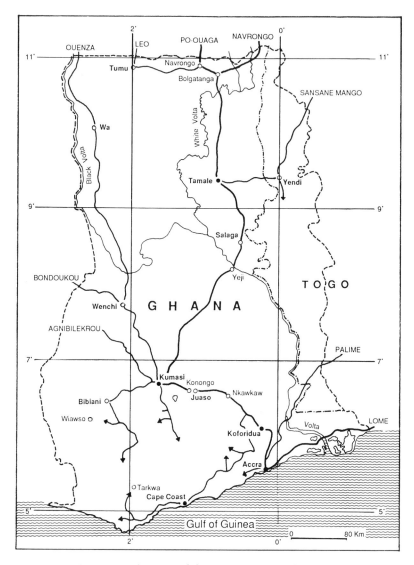

Principal routes of the immigrants to Ghana.

Sahara (CCTA/CSA). This well-financed research project resulted in extensive multidisciplinary fieldwork in Ghana and the Ivory Coast; it also resulted in Rouch's *Migrations au Ghana* in 1956, as well as a series of other migration studies written by Panofsky (1958, 1960), Prothero (1962), Bernus (1960), and Dupire (1960) (see also Rouch

1960; Schildkrout 1978). Rouch's pioneering work in Ghana set the framework for other significant studies of migration in West Africa (Painter 1988).

Rouch's entry into Ghana made him an eyewitness to the clash of two worlds: that of "traditional" Africa with its kinship practices and its rites of magic and possession, and that of Europe with its ethos of social dislocation and its industrial factories. The climate of change in Ghana inspired Rouch to make sense of a world without boundaries, a fuzzy netherworld in which the frontiers between fact and fiction, text and story, determinate and indeterminate had been obliterated. During this period of sociological research, Rouch crafted two of his most notable films, *Jaguar* and *Les maîtres fous,* films that confront directly the imponderables of a world fraught with tension created by European colonial domination.

But we move too quickly, for to comprehend these masterly films from the griot's perspective, we need to return to the beginning, to the cinematic griot's research and writing on West African migration.

True to his Griaulian heritage, *Migrations au Ghana,* like *Contribution à l'histoire des Songhay,* is a weighty but drab text; it presents the results of what Thomas Painter (1988) has called the largest study ever undertaken of West African migration. Despite the massive amounts of data Rouch and company collected, Rouch's interpretations, some of which have been criticized recently, are modest. *Migrations* reads more like the "final report" of a consulting sociologist than an ethnographic monograph. The text is divided into seven chapters dealing with the historical, geographical, structural, economic, political, social-organizational, and religious dimensions of the migrations to Ghana. The data-rich bulk of the study is sandwiched between the two-page *avant-propos* and four-page introduction and the five-page conclusion, the same textual structure found in *Contribution* as well as in *La religion et la magie Songhay* (chap. 5).

SOCIOLOGICAL METHODS

Rouch's first experience in the Gold Coast dates to 1950–51, when he and Roger Rosfelder spent two and a half months there. Initially Rouch wanted to study the new Songhay divinities, the Hauka. Since most of the Hauka mediums were migrants, Rouch decided to follow them to the Gold Coast. But his initial experience convinced him to broaden the scope of his study.

In 1947–48 Rouch used a rather unstructured method. With his companions Damoré Zika and Lam Ibrahim, he traveled from one ghay village to another on horseback in pursuit of a very loose survey. If their "respondents" suggested they visit a specific site or village, they mounted their horses and went there. But the complex study of the sociology of migration forced Rouch to abandon the *pourquoi pas* research strategy that had worked so well in Niger. In its place he constructed a method Marcel Griaule would have been proud of. But Rouch was no votary of quantitative sociology; he hated administering surveys. As in Niger, he preferred to attend rituals and talk to individuals informally (Echard and Rouch 1988, interview 7). Rouch's distaste for the dehumanizing methods of quantitative sociology is perhaps one reason the research project was never completed. The CCTA/CSA expected Rouch to study how the migrants reintegrated themselves into Songhay society. This phase of the project was never initiated.

Despite his methodological preferences, Rouch recruited a team of specialists to explore the various aspects of what he recognized as the complex matter of migration. This team of five Africans, including Damoré Zika and Lam Ibrahim, introduced Rouch to the world of the migrants: prosperous beef and fish merchants, Muslim and traditional priests, laborers, the unemployed—a stew of sociocultural diversity.

Rouch gathered data on migrant society in three ways. First, his team interviewed the migrants as they worked. Second, he organized large group meetings with such migrant laborers as dock workers, miners, and merchants. Third, he circulated a questionnaire. The team administered five hundred individual questionnaires and surveyed another thousand migrants in groups of twenty to thirty (Rouch 1956, 42–44). Rouch was aware of the pitfalls of the research methods and evaluated the results accordingly. Although written questionnaires intimidated respondents and produced uncertain information, the need for statistics obliged the team to use these formal techniques. Group discussions produced better results. The meetings, which were recorded, provided a forum for expressing feelings, frustrations, and sociopolitical sentiments. Individual interviews produced data that added depth to the study (Rouch 1956, 42–44). Demonstrating Griaulian caution, Rouch reminds readers that the data are not exhaustive and that to fully comprehend the social dynamics of migration to the Gold Coast, one would have to conduct systematic studies of other migrant communities as well.

HISTORY OF MIGRATIONS

Like all griots, Rouch is empassioned by history. Accordingly, he devotes inordinate space in *Migrations* to the history of "the road." He dwells on the arrival of various populations on the Gold Coast. Before the coming of the Akan peoples from the North, the Gold Coast was populated by *lamlam*, little people who wore no clothing (Rouch 1956, 46). The first Akan populations arrived in the twelfth century. There followed successive migrations of Adansi, Twi, Ga, and Fanti. Osei Tutu founded the Ashanti federation in the seventeenth century, a time when Wangara influence from Mali propelled a wave of Islamizing in what was to become Ghana.

In 1471 the Portuguese landed at Shama and ushered in a new era in Gold Coast history. Besides bringing European goods, language, and culture, they introduced Western chattel slavery, which became an important economic factor in the development of Ashanti and Dagbamba. Most of the slaves hailed from the North (Basari, Gurunsi). Competition for them precipitated conflicts between Ashanti and Dagbamba. In 1735, firearms helped Ashanti defeat Dagbamba. Unable to pay the victors a tribute of two thousand slaves, Dagbamba was forced to pay Ashanti an annual tax of two hundred slaves, a practice that continued until 1874 (Rouch 1956, 51). This annual burden obliged Dagbamba to raid the villages of northern peoples (Gurunsi), for which it engaged first Mossi and then Zerma mercenaries. These Zerma soldiers were the first people from Niger to migrate to the Gold Coast.

Incessant war during much of the nineteenth century had laid waste the sociopolitical landscape of Songhay and Zerma (Painter 1988). After the devastation of the Fulan wars of 1850, two Zerma soldiers, Alfa Hano and Gazari, journeyed to Dagbamba to sell horses. They were well received in Karaga, and so their compatriots soon joined them, becoming a small cavalry force of fifteen soldiers. In 1856 the small contingent of Zerma mercenaries accompanied the Dagbamba to Gurunsi on a slave-raising mission. The raid was a failure and the Zerma, under the command of Alfa Hano, remained in the North. Between 1856 and 1862 these Zerma plundered Gurunsi villages and built an army by forcibly drafting young Gurunsi men as foot soldiers. Gazari succeeded Alfa Hano in 1863. A remarkable administrator and negotiator, Gazari forged alliances with other Gurunsi groups and repulsed a Dagbamba war party. In Kasana, a village near the present-day Ghana-Burkina Faso border, Gazari established his headquarters: "Composed of Zerma cavalry and Gurunsi foot soldiers, [it] was divided into eight companies, each headed by a Zerma chief. Tribal markings were invented by these chiefs to avoid mixing slaves with the troops of each company, and many of these marks are still found today among the Gurunsi. Prisoners not destined for the army were sent from Kasana either toward Mossi in exchange for horses, or toward Zerma to farm there, or toward Salga, to be sold there" (Rouch 1956, 54). Gazari led his soldiers until his untimely death in 1872. Now commanded by Babatu, the protagonist in one of Rouch's fiction films (*Babatu, les trois conseils*), the Zerma army quickly lost its organizational efficiency and its political dexterity. In 1875 Babatu ravaged Dagati and Lobi. He wanted to attack the Wangara but could not. In 1877 Babatu suffered tremendous losses at the hands of the Dagbamba. Between 1878 and 1890 his Zerma army reached the zenith of its power; he conquered the Wa and the Gonja, becoming master of the Ghanaian North.

European occupation soon put an end to Babatu's military adventures. With his power reduced by the French and the British, Babatu lost his military edge. At San, Dr. Hans Rigler's German expeditionary force defeated Babatu's army and deported his warriors to Konkomba. Babatu continued to raid villages, though, and captured slaves in Konkomba. In response the Germans sent his army to Yendi, where "Babatu and his principal chiefs remained . . . but their lieutenants either scattered throughout the Gold coast or returned to Zerma. The Zerma warriors had become migrants" (Rouch 1956, 56).

Between 1900 and 1910 European domination transformed the old slave routes between the Sahel and the Guinea coast into commercial passageways. Hausa merchants increased their trading in salt and kola; Fulan and Manding-speaking peoples marched cattle to the coast. Songhay and Zerma, "unemployed soldiers," went south "to see" (Rouch 1956, 57). In the beginning they sold magic charms. As their numbers swelled, they labored for Europeans. The "South" also attracted huge numbers of former slaves from the Sahel. By 1911, perhaps one-third of all the precolonial slaves had left for the Gold Coast to seek independence and their fortunes (Roberts and Klein 1980, 363). The fervor for the Gold Coast spread through Songhay during the first decade of the twentieth century. Niamey people left for the South in 1903; in 1905 people from Dargol, Wanzerbe, and Sakoire trekked south. In 1909 people from Ayoru, Zermaganda, and the general region of Garuol departed, and in 1910 Gao people followed "the road" (Rouch 1956, 58).

For these early and later migrants, the trip to the Gold Coast was, according to Rouch, a great adventure, a rite of passage:

The trip to the Gold Coast was, however, a very great adventure. The roads were "open" but they were not without difficulties. Armed with spears and clubs, bows and arrows, the emigrants left ready for war; they formed groups of twenty to sixty; they carried magic charms to protect them from arrows and bullets. Most often they took with them several animals, some tobacco, and salt, which they sold on the road to buy food. Their itinerary followed the old slave routes and the trip lasted one and a half months. (Rouch 1956, 57)

After World War I, migrations became routine. Between 1920 and 1939 the Gold Coast boomed economically. Industrialists opened mines and factories; the British built roads and constructed a deepwater port at Takoradi. This development exponentially increased the need for labor. By 1931, 200,000 people had migrated to the Gold Coast from the French colonies (Rouch 1956, 59).

Before World War II the great majority of "the men from the North" were seasonal laborers. Leaving Niger for the Gold Coast after the harvest in October, they would return home in May to plant millet. During and after World War II, many of the migrants settled in the Gold Coast, especially in Accra and Kumasi, married local women, and raised families. They learned Ewe, Twi, and Ga as well as English, and some became civil servants. After Ghanaian independence in 1956, the Zabrama—as the Songhay and Zerma from the North were called in Ghana—remained in Kwame Nkrumah's nation. They bought and sold merchandise in the market; they labored in the ports and the mines. Some became policemen; others volunteered for the Ghanaian military. In Niger the people called these veterans of Ghana *Zerma zena* (old Zerma). But the Zabrama paradise in Ghana could not last forever. Invoking the theme of Ghana for Ghanaians, President K. A. Busia expelled foreign laborers from his country in 1969. Thousands of Zerma zena returned to Niger that year, leaving behind jobs and families. But Busia's edict did not end the migrations; it merely changed the ultimate destination to Lomé, Abidjan, and Lagos.

In this sense the history of migrations provided the framework for *Jaguar* and *Les maîtres fous*. In *Jaguar* Rouch refers to the great migrants of the past—the first men, like Alfa Hano and Gazari, who as warriors had traveled to Ghana. In *Jaguar* Rouch likens the modern-day migrants to the heroes of the previous century. Likewise, in *Les maîtres fous* historical themes are indexed in the depicted possession ceremonies. The sacrifices, the music of the monochord violin, the "old words" of the incantations all evoke the historical experience of the Songhay.

THE ROAD

For Rouch "the road" was part of the adventurous world of Songhay and Zerma migrants. This world of adventure-seeking travelers so fascinated him that it became a major theme of *Jaguar*.

When they were in the North, migrants made ethnic and even subethnic distinctions (see Olivier de Sardan 1982, 1984). In the Gold Coast these distinctions disappeared. Songhay, Zerma, Kurtey, Dendi, Wogo, and Bella from Niger, for example, became "Zabrama"; they also called themselves *kurm'ize* (children from afar). Songhay, Arma, Bella, and Tuareg from Mali were called "Gao." Migrants from northern Dahomey were called "Zugu"; peoples from the north of Togo were "Kotokoli"; and so on. In this sense "the road," for Rouch, entailed the creation of "supertribal" categories of people based not on ethnicity but on geography.

No matter their ethnicity, "the road" obliged migrants to follow certain time-honored routes to the Gold Coast, one of which is followed by the protagonists in *Jaguar*. According to Rouch, early voyagers walked most of the way. Having crossed the border into the Gold Coast, migrants continued to Accra or Kumasi by train or truck. After 1945 the general development of the West African infrastructure prompted the transformation of travel, so most migrants could travel to the Gold Coast in automobiles or trucks.

Coming from Songhay, one could follow several routes to Accra and Kumasi, making sure to cross borders at the "easiest" checkpoints. Fulan shepherds would cross the Burkina Faso–Ghana border at Bawku and continue to Gambaga and then Patenga, and Salaga, another important crossroads. From Salaga they made their way to Yeji and Prang and would then choose to take their herds to Kumasi or Accra.

From Niamey one could take a truck or taxi to Accra following two itineraries, the choice depending on relative cost and the reputed toughness of the various customs agents at border crossings. Beginning in Niamey, some migrants traveled to Fada N'Gourma (in Burkina Faso) and ventured south to Sansane Mongo in northern Togo. From Sansane Mango they crossed the border into the Gold Coast and headed to Yendi, capital of Dagbamba. From Yendi they trucked to Tamale. From Tamale they could go to Kumasi. If Kumasi was not their final destination, they could take the train to Accra. The other possibility was to travel from Niamey to Dosso, continuing south to Mallenville, Parakou, and finally Cotonou (all in present-day Benin) on the Guinea coast. From Cotonou one turned west to Grand Popo (in Togo) and arrived in Lome. From Lome the trucks entered the Gold Coast at Aflao and continued to Accra by the Tefle ferry.

Rouch's team investigated why migrants chose a given route. For us the best itinerary is one that economizes on time, distance, and money. For the Zabrama, Rouch discovered, choice was based on the reputation of the customs stations (Rouch 1956, 81).

Once in the Gold Coast, most of the migrants headed for either Kumasi, Accra, or Takoradi. A smaller percentage ended up in gold, diamond, or manganese mining areas. Other migrants worked on cocoa plantations or in the forests cutting trees.

SOCIOECONOMIC ASPECTS OF MIGRATION

Rouch devotes 56 pages of his 163 page monograph to two chapters on the socioeconomic aspects of the migrations. These data, one assumes, were generated through the individual and group questionnaires Rouch's team administered. Rouch also perused archival records (specifically census materials) to complement his data. Although this information is dry, it is the raw material from which Rouch molded *Jaguar, Les maîtres fous,* and *Moi, un noir,* about the life of migrants in Abidjan in the Ivory Coast.

We discover information on the length of the migrants' stay in the Gold Coast as well as their average age, their sex (predominantly male), and the frequency of their voyages. Rouch estimates the number of migrants and cross-references them by their Nigerien district, canton, and ethnicity. He is also able to determine their destinations. Almost all the travelers from Tillaberi migrated to the Gold Coast; by contrast, 50 percent of migrants from Niamey went to Nigeria. Rouch also presents estimates of the number of migrants in Accra and Kumasi by geographically categorized ethnic groups (Zabrama, Wangara, Mossi, etc.).

Rouch divides migrant occupations into salaried and merchant jobs and lists the kinds of wage-paying positions migrants held, which range from agriculture (cacao plantations) and fishing to mining, construction, the army, and the police. For each occupation Rouch provides a breakdown of the number of workers cross-referenced by ethnicity. Through these data, Rouch concludes that ethnic groups specialized in certain occupations. For example, the Zabrama worked in diamond mines and in commerce.

Commercial activities were divided into several categories: transport (foot transport [carriers]; truck transporters [truck "boys," loaders], automobile transport [drivers, apprentices, bookers]); livestock

(cattle, sheep, and goats driven down from the Sahel); cloth and clothing (clothes merchants, tailors, used-clothes merchants). Rouch also
includes the *nyama nyama* (children of disorder), merchants who establish small shops or wander the streets carrying their merchandise
on tables on their heads. Much of this information is brought to life at
the beginning of *Les maîtres fous* and throughout *Jaguar.*

Most of the migrants in Rouch's sample either are wage earners or
make their living through commerce. Some defy this categorization;
they are griots, priests and magicians, smugglers and thieves.

Rouch's presentation of migrant society in the Gold Coast now
takes a more economic turn. Having established the range of occupations, he lists the various wages or profits a migrant might earn and
measures these earnings against the cost of living in places like Accra,
Kumasi, Takoradi, and other commercial centers. Rouch even attempts to estimate the average budget of the migrants. Most attempted
to economize as much as possible, for they all wanted to send money
home to help their families and make names for themselves—a major
premise of Rouch's film *Jaguar.* In the nineteenth century travelers won
recognition through military exploits; in the twentieth century Gold
Coast migrants made their reputations through economic success, ex-
emplified by lavish gift giving upon their return to Niger—the theme
of the *Jaguar*'s last scenes: "The Gold Coasters created for themselves
the obligation to send money [home]: since they were forced to speak
upon their return home about the opulent life they led in the Gold
Coast, their audience was persuaded that it was easy for them to send
money home" (Rouch 1956, 144). The migrants thus spent much of
their accumulated savings on "magnificent gifts" from the Gold Coast.
By the time they had paid their transport and the various customs
taxes, they returned home with only the gifts they had purchased.
These they gave away in one day—the Songhay version of the potlatch.

SOCIAL LIFE

In his chapter on the social life of the Zabrama in the Gold Coast,
Rouch once again underscores the historical continuity of the migrations—one of the reasons he was drawn to Ghana in the first place.
From the beginning of migration in West Africa, Hausa migrants had
traveled with their families to the Gold Coast and other locales to establish small sedentary communities (Cohen 1969). Rouch contrasts
this practice with that of the Zabrama: "Having come to fight wars

during the time of Babatu until about 1939, in groups of semiwarriors, they were alone. They found women among the captives of their combat and later among the villagers they lived with. Even today the voyage to the Gold Coast, for the Zabrama, has preserved this characteristic of the voyage: to [not] hamper oneself with a woman" (Rouch 1956, 154). In the absence of women, many Zabrama took up relations with local women; some became their concubines, some were simply prostitutes. Here Rouch discusses the structure of prostitution in the Gold Coast of the 1950s. He distinguishes three types: *tutu*, mostly divorced Ewe women; *jaguar*, unmarried women from the coast who engaged in occasional prostitution (mostly with Europeans and Levantines) and who dressed *jaguar*—short skirts and European shoes; and *karua*, prostitutes from Niger, all of whom were divorcées. At the beginning of *Les maîtres fous*, the viewer sees a procession of Hausa prostitutes protesting low wages.

The Zabrama population of the Gold Coast consisted mainly of young adult men—between twenty and twenty-five. Each community, as in Songhay and Zerma areas, appointed two chiefs of the young, one for the young men and one for small groups of unmarried young women. Occasionally these groups met to discuss their common problems. Sometimes they sponsored dances.

In other domains, the Zabrama community in the Gold Coast adopted traditional political and social structures to organize its social activities in a foreign land. People from the same Songhay villages, for example, clustered in Accra. Men from Gotheye, a Songhay village on the Niger's west bank in Niger, organized the Accra timber market. In this way new migrants from Gotheye knew they should report to the timber market upon their arrival, where their fellow villagers provided them with work, housing, food, and other social necessities. These practices are also referenced in *Jaguar*.

In the political domain, twenty to thirty elders represented the community to outside groups, but this hierarchy did not mitigate the rivalry among "village" groups. Like the other migrant populations in the Gold Coast, the Zabrama appointed one chief, who assumed many of the rights and responsibilities of a canton chief in his own land.

Relations between the Zabrama community and the autochthonous populations, Rouch suggests, were limited by language, though many of the Zabrama learned Pidgin English, the local lingua franca. Given these limitations, Rouch reports cordial but formal relations between the Zabrama and indigenous groups. Initially the southerners thought of the northerners as savage brutes—bushcats. In time they came to respect the commercial successes of the Zabrama (Rouch 1956, 154). In *Jaguar* Damoré Zika works for a wealthy, car-owning Zabrama who owns a lumberyard.

RELIGIOUS LIFE

Rouch's initial interest in the migrations to the Guinea coast stemmed from his fascination with the Hauka spirits; in the 1950s they had an important presence in the Gold Coast, which Rouch called the "Mecca of the Hauka." The Gold Coast had become the center of the Hauka spirit movement, which featured the violent fire-handling antics of the spirits of colonial force. Rouch had already encountered the Hauka in Niger and had filmed sequences of Hauka possession in his *Au pays des mages noirs* as well as in *Bataille sur le grand fleuve*. In 1954 he wanted to investigate the Hauka in the Gold Coast.

Surprisingly, Rouch devotes relatively little space in his monograph to the religious life of the migrants—only 16 pages out of 163. Of those 16 pages, only 5 describe the non-Islamic religions of the migrants. Perhaps Rouch thought a dry sociological discourse did not lend itself to descriptions of the dynamics of religious life—the Hauka cult, for instance—that derived from the explosive confrontation of the traditional and the modern in the Gold Coast.

Rouch focuses most of his attention on the religious life of the autochthonous populations in relation to Islam. As in his other writings, his comments on Islam are fascinating. In *Contribution à l'histoire des Songhay* he suggests that the emergence of Islam in Songhay corresponds to the decline and fall of the Songhay empire. In *Migrations* he confines himself to placing the migrant Muslims in two categories: real and superficial. He considers the migrant Fulan and the Hausa real (zealous) Muslims.[1] He finds the Zabrama, Gao, and Kotokoli to be superficially Muslim; they recite their prayers some of the time, but their profound religious beliefs lie elsewhere. In the case of the Zabrama, Rouch contends, the real religion stems from pre-Islamic beliefs: possession, magic, witchcraft, the ancestors.

Rouch shows his cards quite clearly in the following passage: "Under the veneer of an Islam more or less fragile, there appear the ancient cults of veritable black Africa. What happened to them in the Gold Coast?" (Rouch 1956, 185). He goes on to describe the Songhay

---

1. Many Hausa specialists would disagree with this overgeneralized assertion (see Nicolas 1978; Schmoll 1991).

possession cult and the Hauka cult as manifested there. The traditional possession cult did not flourish in the Gold Coast for the simple reason that most of its mediums were women who did not accompany their men.

As a consequence, the Gold Coast provided the perfect context for the flowering of the mostly male Hauka movement. Eventually Rouch made contact with the Hauka community and was able to attend numerous ceremonies, including the yearly ritual that he immortalized in *Les maîtres fous* (see chaps. 1, 9). In a few highly condensed pages, he presents the stories surrounding the origin of the Hauka movement in Niger as well as accounts of its growth through the years in Ghana.

The Hauka arrived in the Gold Coast about 1929 and became important there after 1935 (for a more detailed historical account of the Hauka movement, see chap. 9). As the power of the movement grew in the Gold Coast, so did the prestige of the Hauka mediums among the Zabrama, a prestige that escaped them in Niger, where possession priests frowned on the brutish antics of the Hauka spirits.

MIGRATORY POLITICS

Rouch's study of the migrant community of the Gold Coast would have been incomplete without a chapter on the politics of independence. He sets the stage for Nkrumah with discussions of the history of British colonization and the policy of indirect rule. He follows the development of the Ghanaian independence movement, beginning in 1947 when Joseph Danquah's United Gold Coast Convention demanded independence and continuing in 1950 with the founding of Nkrumah's Convention People's party (CPP), which was victorious in the legislative elections held in 1951. By the time of Rouch's research in 1953–54, several political parties were challenging Nkrumah's CPP. These political developments are also reflected in *Jaguar*, where Rouch includes scenes of CPP political rallies as well as Moslem Association party activities.

The migrant communities played roles in the evolution of Ghanaian independence politics. The CPP and the Moslem Association party competed for Zabrama adherents. After several recruiting efforts, Rouch reports, the CPP seemed to win the confidence of the Zabrama elders: "When we arrived in March 1954, the position of the Zabrama was clear. They wore all the emblems of the CPP, attended their meetings, voiced their slogans glorying the party and sang praise to Kwame Nkrumah: in the entire southern Gold Coast it was the same" (Rouch 1956, 192).

MIGRATIONS RECONSIDERED

Migrations is structured like *Contribution à l'histoire des Songhay*. Rouch presents an overwhelming array of statistical data, from which he draws conservative inferences. In this text he makes no attempt to use social theory to interpret his findings. The most consistent interpretation in *Migrations* is Rouch's insistence on the historical continuity of the "adventurous" voyages from Niger to the Gold Coast.

The historical romance of migrating mercenaries—Alfa Hano, Gazari, and Babatu and their warriors—is maintained in studies of Songhay and Zerma history and migration by a later generation of scholars. These writers also consider adventure to be *the* factor explaining the Songhay-Zerma "rush to the South" (see Diarra 1974; Fugelstad 1983).

Fugelstad writes (1983, 87):

> The young Zerma/Songhay began to go as seasonal labourers to the Gold Coast, mainly to the Kumasi region, following in the footsteps, as it were [but pushing farther to the south than], of their nineteenth-century warrior ancestors, who had conquered the Mamprussi-Dagomba region. . . . It is probable therefore that there occurred among the "adventurous" Zerma/Songhay a form of culture transfer in favour of migrant labour. In particular, the long and at times perilous journey to the Gold Coast became part of a "modernized" initiation ritual.

Here Fugelstad misappropriates some of Rouch's material. The Zerma mercenaries, according to Rouch, did not conquer Mamprussi-Dagomba but became masters of Gurunsi—after years of incessant raiding. Incontestably, the journey to the Gold Coast was perilous between 1900 and 1910, but it became much less so as the Ghanaian economy and infrastructure developed. By the 1930s greedy customs agents posed more danger than hostile "natives."

In a recent study Thomas Painter argues that the urge to migrate to the Gold Coast sprang not so much from the sense of adventure as from French colonial policies. Painter does not deny the importance of the precolonial link between Zerma-Songhay and the Gold Coast, but he criticizes Rouch for not delving into the socioeconomic and political basis for migration:

> Characterizations of early Zarma migrants suggest that, in addition to defunct warriors, the overwhelming majority of early migrants quickly included commoner, freemen peasant cultivators and freed slaves who were not given to wandering, mercenary ways. If this is so, and it seems

to be, how do we explain the growing and, on the face of it, surprising mobility among peasant cultivators from southwestern Niger to distant areas of the Guinea Coast? What was happening in western Niger? (Painter 1988, 92)

Toward the end of the nineteenth century social life in Niger was miserable. In the 1890s western Niger suffered from persistent drought and from locust plagues, which caused widespread famine. In 1898 the French military took Niger. In 1899 the infamous Voulet-Chanoine mission passed through Niger, leaving death and destruction in its wake. Once established in Niger, the French army built military garrisons, collected taxes, and recruited able-bodied men for forced work details. By 1909 the colonial administration in Niger insisted that taxes be paid in French currency. The same administration had officially abolished slavery in 1905, which enabled "former" slaves to leave their masters' lands—and they did in great numbers between 1900 and 1910 (Painter 1988, 93).

For Painter, most Zabrama migrants did not seek adventure; they sought relief from French economic exploitation. Migrants "were *forced* to do so *whatever* the initial linkage role of displaced warriors during the period of transition from warriors to migrants" (Painter 1988, 93; see also Roberts and Klein 1980).

Although the current government of Niger has reduced the pernicious colonial head tax, large numbers of young men continue to migrate to the Guinea coast. Colonial policies linked the peoples of western Niger to world markets and introduced taxes that increased the need for currency, so rural peasants in Niger left the countryside in search of wage labor, at first traveling to the Gold Coast. Postcolonial policies in Niger have aggravated the economic situation of rural peasants, who continue to be cash poor. Today they travel to the Guinea coast to seek relief from the exigencies of the government of Niger. As one Songhay peasant told me in Mehanna: "The more things change, the more they remain the same."

Despite his perspicacious criticisms, Painter, a sociologist, finds Rouch's *Migrations au Ghana* a "pathbreaking work" (Painter 1988, 94). Rouch's own opinion of the work is more problematic. At one point he claimed that no Songhay migrant would ever read it. During the filming of *Jaguar* he hung the book from the rearview mirror of his car—a symbolic execution? (See Collet 1967.)

Rouch's research on migrations was the first and most ambitious of its kind in West Africa. Subsequent studies of migration have been nar-

rowly focused. The multidisciplinary research design of Rouch's project—derived from Griaule's methods—generated extensive and illu-
minating sociological data, some of which are not used in *Migrations*.

Why would Rouch disdain the written account of his research in
Ghana? Consider first the contrast of field methods. In Niger Rouch
used two techniques: improvisation and shared anthropology. In the
Gold Coast he replaced these techniques with systematic research instruments that yielded quantitative data—techniques he personally
disliked. Consider also that Rouch's films of this era resulted from
shared cinema and participatory anthropology. Although *Migrations*
is a "pathbreaking work," Rouch has suggested in several interviews
that his films about the migrants (*Jaguar, Les maîtres fous,* and *Moi,
un noir*) truly evoke the texture and nature of social life on the coast
(Collet 1967; see also Rouch 1978c). As was the case with *Bataille sur
le grand fleuve* in Ayoru, Niger, the migrants in Ghana and the Ivory
Coast saw and criticized these films; few if any migrants read *Migrations au Ghana*.

Referring to *Migrations*, Rouch said: "It was a very serious book on
the migrations to Ghana, full of statistics and numbers. Today when I
compare this book with *Jaguar*, I notice that *Jaguar* provides the best
representation" (Collet 1967). Rouch's denigration of *Migrations* does
him a disservice. In his interviews Rouch often privileges the cinema
over written ethnographies—even his own written work—and these
comments give readers the impression that Rouch's perspective ex-
cludes serious ethnographic investigation. My own observations suggest otherwise: Rouch remains a serious ethnographer. He continues
to read African ethnography and to write ethnographic and ethnohis-
torical texts.[2] His interest in Songhay history and prehistory has not
waned with the years. I see a dialectical relation between Rouch's ethnographies and his films. When he was in the Gold Coast, Rouch did
not first gather sociological data and then make films. As was true in
Niger during the late 1940s, films played a central role in his research.
It is Rouch's ethnographic depth, developed dialectically, that sensi-
tizes his filmic eye in *Les maîtres fous* and *Jaguar,* giving these films an
evocative power rarely seen on the screen.

In the next chapter I look at the dialectic relation between Rouch's

2. Rouch (1990a). This article, "Les cavaliers aux vautours," a historical text about
the nineteenth-century exploits of Alfa Hano, Gazari, and Babatu, was published in the
Journal de la Société des Africanistes 60 (2): 5–37.

texts and films on Songhay religion. Accordingly, I extend the analysis of Rouch's written ethnographies to his masterwork, *La religion et la magie Songhay,* a text in which one finds the ethnographic references for all his films on magic and possession—the bulk of his cinematic oeuvre.

CHAPTER FIVE
People of Force, Spirits of Power

Zanka kan mana lamba dottiijey ga si du ndunnya bayrey.
The child who doesn't frequent the elders will never obtain knowledge.
—Songhay proverb

As the Songhay griots tell us, knowledge is the property of the elders. Through their experience in life, the elders develop wisdom as they learn the lessons of the past and present. They prepare the young for the future. As a young man, Jean Rouch fully understood this Songhay proverb. Throughout his travels he frequented Songhay elders and revered their wisdom. Old sorcerers spoke to him of the wisdom of Sonni Ali Ber; old zima revealed the path of the spirits. Rouch listened and learned from these wise men and women, and like a good griot he preserved this knowledge in his encyclopedic *La religion et la magie Songhay*.

When Jean Rouch first went to Wanzerbe in 1947–48, it was a small village of straw huts. Today Wanzerbe is a town of mud-brick houses. When Rouch first went there, he had to ride at least one hundred kilometers on horseback to reach his destination; today trucks and taxis go there once a week. But much remains the same in Wanzerbe. Sargumey mountain still looms over the village like a medieval European castle. Karia and Sohanci remain Wanzerbe's two main neighborhoods, and strangers continue to live in a quarter called Zongo at the southern edge of the village. And in this desiccated space one still feels the undeniable presence of people of force and spirits of power. Just as the past reverberates through the present in Wanzerbe, so Rouch's representation of the past in *La religion et la magie Songhay* reminds us of the present in Niger—the task of the griot.

I have already considered the Griaulian framework within which Rouch conducted his fieldwork and then produced his studies on Songhay history, myths, and migration. To reiterate briefly, Marcel

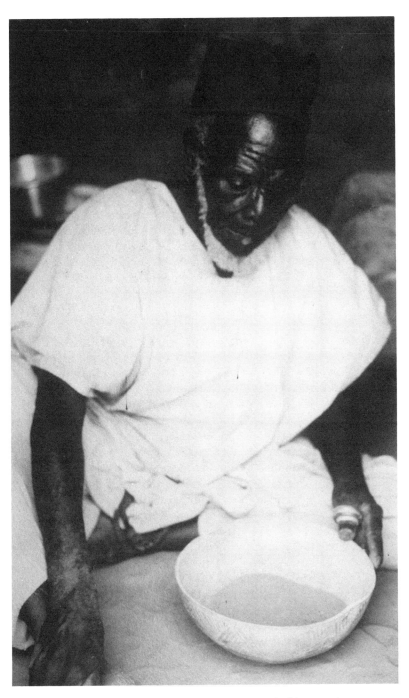

Sohanci Adamu Jenitongo reciting a magical incantation.

Griaule taught his students to collect exhaustive amounts of data: photographs, objects, and most important, the testimony of informants. For him, collection was the first stage of the anthropologist's initiation. And once these data were collected, following Griaule's phenomenological prescription, they should be presented with as little European interpretation as possible. *Contribution à l'histoire des Songhay*, the monograph considered in chapter 3, weaves information from archaeology, Muslim manuscripts, and myths into a comprehensive history. *Migrations au Ghana* presents a wide array of sociological data on the Songhay-Zerma migrant community of the Gold Coast. But it is in the pages of *La religion et la magie Songhay*, the topic of this chapter, that Rouch fully reveals how Griaule and his own Songhay friends shaped his textual presentation and his orientation to the Songhay world. In this chapter I analyze *Religion* to demonstrate the care and respect with which Rouch conducted his ethnographic research.

TEXTUAL CONTOURS

La religion and la magie Songhay, published in 1960 as Rouch's *doctorat d'état*, is dedicated to the memory of Marcel Griaule, "without whom this work would have never been undertaken." In the preface of the book Rouch describes the conditions under which the work was done (see chap. 2). Briefly, he went with Damoré Zika and other Songhay friends to diverse field sites, where he took many photographs and collected ethnographic objects. He recorded myths and ritual incantations, and he filmed magic rites as well as possession ceremonies.

Religion is a tribute to Griaulian documentation—an exhaustive compendium of Songhay religious beliefs and practices. It is a griot's text. Rouch opens the book with the general principles of Songhay religion and guides readers along the sandy paths of the Songhay world. There are thickly described chapters on myth, ritual incantations, the identities of the spirit cult, possession dance, and magic. In "Les mythes," Rouch presents myths about genies, the ancestors, and the spirits (*holle*). In "Les objets rituels" there are comprehensive descriptions of sacred musical instruments, altars, costumes, sacred stones, hatchets, and staffs. For each of these objects, moreover, Rouch describes origin, fabrication (where relevant), and consecration. In the chapters on spirit possession, Rouch introduces readers to *all* the personalities of the possession cult and *all* of the more than 150 spirits of the Songhay pantheon.

As a text, *Religion*'s ethnographic description is reminiscent of Boasian ethnography. Following the textual prescriptions of *Contribu-*

tion and *Migrations,* Rouch limits his interpretive speculations to a four-page preface and a five-page general conclusion. As in his most important films, his prescient theoretical contributions are implicit in the text.

Perhaps the most significant textual feature of *Religion* is Rouch's acknowledgment of informants. Each myth in the book is "signed" by the informant who recited it. These "signatures" appear throughout *Religion.* For every ethnographic element Rouch introduces, there is a relevant and signed definition, observation, or explanation. Rouch lists the names, specializations, and villages of the sixty-seven informants whose knowledge is represented in their own words. In this way his major work on Songhay ethnography features the voices and visions of many "authors." Although some contemporary critics would say the presence of these attributions presages the postmodern "death of the author," I say the inclusion of other voices and visions is a thoughtful portrayal of Songhay wisdom.

But how did Jean Rouch cross the Songhay boundary so quickly, so deeply? Why would the great sorcerers of Wanzerbe, men capable of killing others with their words, take Rouch, a European neophyte, into their confidence? A facile answer would be that Rouch's success devolved from the power dynamics of colonialism. No informant, one would think, could refuse to speak to the powerful white man in colonial Niger. Although it is true that being a European in colonial times gave Rouch unobstructed access to Songhay populations, that access did not guarantee cooperation. Songhay resisted the military and cultural politics of colonialism throughout the colonial era (see Kimba 1981; Olivier de Sardan 1984; Stoller 1989a). One might also suggest that Rouch's friendship with Damoré Zika, a sorko, opened the closed doors of the Songhay world of power. But Damoré Zika's sorko status would not have aided Rouch's approach to the sohanci sorcerers living in the shadow of Sargumey. The best explanation for Rouch's phenomenal field success credits his open reverence for the Songhay and their wisdom. He knew how "to sit" with the elders.

Readers can gauge Rouch's admiration for Songhay in the preface to *Religion,* in which the author ruminates about his ethnographic approach and the nature of ethnographic observation. He writes the following passage about his entry into the world of Songhay possession: "But when the moment comes that the observer becomes a simple spectator among other spectators, when the moment comes that he speaks and understands the language sufficiently to know what is being said and to respond to it sometimes, he *participates* just like his neighbors. And so it follows that at each possession dance that I witnessed, the deities came to greet me as well as my neighbors, and spoke at length with me" (Rouch 1989, 17; my emphasis). Rouch also comments on his entry into the world of Songhay sorcery:

> The penetration of more private domains, like the magician's milieu, posed other problems. After a slow and gradual approach, contact could be established (with the aid of the intervention of the deities in the course of a possession dance). Slowly I entered the game, but as soon as certain doors opened before me, they would close immediately behind me, prohibiting all retreat and cutting all ties with the outside. The observer was completely overwhelmed by what he observed. Was this still a matter of observation? The assurances I gave these men that nothing could be repeated or published without their agreement enabled me to learn many things, but it also limited what could be revealed. It is without doubt that the world of initiation carries with it not only certain conditions of silence, but also a respect, which appeared evident, for those who welcomed me and treated me as a friend. The ethnographer is not a policeman who extorts what one does not want to say or to reveal, and his elementary honesty consists exactly of respecting those he learns to know better, which is to say to love better. (Rouch 1989, 17)

Religion, in sum, is a relatively selfless text that reflects Rouch's debt to Marcel Griaule and his admiration of Songhay knowledge.

RELIGION IN *RELIGION*

In Rouch's view, Songhay religion is an open system. Songhay populations, he suggests, tend to maintain old traditions as they assimilate new religious elements introduced by strangers. The Songhay appear to be completely Islamized. Most of them pray five times a day and attend Jumma services at the Friday mosque. Most of them observe the fasting of Ramadan. In their births, marriages, and mortuary ceremonies, Songhay follow Muslim practices. And yet, as Rouch puts it, every Sunday in Niamey or Gao groups of Songhay gather for possession dances. In the compounds of the great sohanci sorcerers not far from Friday mosques, men perform rites that make them stronger than God.

Songhay consider their religion to be a series of meandering paths fraught with danger, "for the Songhay religion is *fondo,* 'the path,' which consists of many tangled trails on which men lose their way and their courage; but the most patient and sensitive come through test after test, without stopping at levels on which others would be satisfied, to reach a dangerous footpath that brushes against the Supreme

Master's domain and permits several among them to become superior to him" (Rouch 1989, 20).

The paths that form Songhay religion are not divergent; they are a network of traditions that coexist in Songhay experience. These religious paths comprise the following, according to Rouch:

1. masters of the soil
2. masters of the waters
3. sorko, or masters of the river
4. gow, or masters of the bush
5. the Koukya Berbers
6. the Mali empire
7. Islam, and other influences. (Rouch 1989, 22–24)

The masters of the soil are most likely a collection of Gurmantche, Mossi, and Kurumba. These peoples are Voltaic-language speakers who live today in Burkina Faso. In the past they performed fertility rites, some linked to local genies, as in the sacrifice to the genie of Wanzerbe's Sargumey that is depicted in Rouch's film *Les magiciens de Wanzerbe* (chap. 6). Some of the rites have been incorporated into Songhay possession as the Genji Bi, the Black Spirits or masters of the soil, the very spirits Rouch brings to the screen in *Les tambours d'avant: Turu et bitti* (see chap. 10). The masters of the water are called the Do; they control certain parts of the river and must grant fishermen permission to harvest fish from the master Do's waters. Sorko, descendants of Faran Maka Bote, are masters of the river, praise singers to the spirits and priests and priestesses of the Tooru spirits, especially Dongo, the thunder deity. The Gow are master hunters whose relationship with the Atakurma, the elves of the bush, provides them the power to "work" in the bush (Rouch 1989, 23). They are featured in Rouch's *The Lion Hunters*. From the Berbers of Koukya (the Za) comes the path of magic; from the influence of the Mali empire come the powerful stone cults. And there is of course Islam, which became a strong force in Songhay during the reign of Askia Mohammed Touré (1493–1528).

These diverse influences, which recreate Songhay experience in the world, provide the framework for a Songhay metaphysics. Rouch's elders say the Songhay world is a flat disk divided into villages and uninhabited land (or bush) through which flows the river. The sky consists of seven heavens. God (Iri Koy) lives in the most distant heaven; he is the creator of the world. Secondary divinities live in other heavens. Ndebbi (God's messenger) lives in the sixth heaven, while angels live between the second and sixth heavens. The *holle* (spirits) live in

A medium possessed by a Doguwa spirit.

the first heaven. There is also Iblis (Seytan), who lives in a kind of hell, as well as the *zin*, powerful creatures that live in mountains, trees, rivers, or the bush.

The Songhay elders say that a human being consists of flesh (*ga*), the life force (*hundi*), and the double (*bia*). Dreams result from the double's nocturnal adventures. Given the general powerlessness of the self, Songhay have engaged in, to use Rouch's terminology, a variety of "cults." Rouch lists seven of them. First is the cult of God, which is Islam. Second is the devil's cult, about which Rouch obtained no data. Third is the cult of the angels, which is familial. In certain families of magicians a sheep is "fed" and then slaughtered on Tabaski, the Muslim holiday commemorating Abraham's willingness to sacrifice his son Isaac to God, to satisfy the desires of a protector angel. Fourth is the cult of genies, which is local. Here villages organize rites, usually including a major animal sacrifice to appease the local genie that protects the village. Fifth is the ancestor cult, also local and limited to families of magicians. Sixth is the spirit possession cult, which is widespread in Songhay. Spirit possession is Rouch's true area of ethnographic expertise, and most of the subsequent pages of *Religion* are devoted to describing it. Seventh is the magic cult, in which the most powerful practitioners, the sohanci, attempt to accumulate more power than God.

SPIRIT POSSESSION IN *RELIGION*

Myths underscore the major themes of Songhay religion. There are myths for local genies, for the origin of certain ponds, forests, and villages, and for ancestors, especially the ancestors of the sohanci, the great Songhay magicians. Myths also constitute the charter of the Songhay spirit possession cult. In *Religion* Rouch recounts the myths about the origin of the various families of holle, or spirits. In presenting the spirit myths, Rouch retraces their genealogy, providing names and ethnic origins for all the families of the Songhay pantheon, including those spirits that never possess the bodies of mediums.

He also examines the myths concerning Faran Maka Bote, the ancestor of the sorko (fisherman) who was the first master of the spirits. Faran's father was an ordinary fisherman, but his mother, Maka, was a river genie. Using her supernatural prowess, Maka transformed a nasty crocodile-genie, Zirbin Sanghay Moyo, into an iron harpoon, which she gave to her son. Thus armed, Faran glided up and down the Niger without fear or equal.

Faran's rule of the river was soon challenged by Zinkibaru, a river genie whose sweet lute controlled the river spirits, which were ruining Faran's rice fields and chasing away game and fish. Faran confronted Zinkibaru, but Zinkibaru, whose knowledge of magical incantations surpassed Faran's, emerged victorious from their first encounter. In defeat, Faran slunk home to Kare Kaptu. Though Maka complained that Faran was empty-headed, she taught him an incantation to overpower Zinkibaru, and he set out to find his peripatetic nemesis.

They confronted one another at last. Zinkibaru led with the same incantation that had already bested Faran, but this time Faran riposted with Maka's counterspell, which dropped Zinkibaru to his knees defeated. Faran seized Zinkibaru's mesmerizing guitar and took captive the river spirits with their monochord violins and gourd drums.

Faran completely controlled the spirits for one year. But Dongo, deity of thunder, grew restless. Along with his older brother Cirey and Moussa Nyori, Dongo left the river. They became masters of the skies.

Busy with his hunting and fishing, Faran paid scant attention to Dongo. Offended, Dongo struck a fishing village, burning it to the ground. Corpses littered the earth. When Faran was called to the disaster scene, Dongo put him in his mortal place and insisted he pay homage to him and the other spirits. Dongo taught Faran spirit praise poetry and spat on the dead to transform them into the living. He said that from that day forward the spirits would be invisible to human beings. Dongo told Faran to wait one year to stage the ceremony. Musicians would play drums and the monochord violin; men and women would dance—only then would Dongo and his brothers come to earth and possess the bodies of the dancers. Faran promised to obey Dongo's commands.

One year later, Faran staged the ceremony he called the *yene*, the first possession ceremony (Rouch 1989, 72–74). From past to present, this ceremony is held every year at the peak of the hot season (between 1 and 15 May), and today it is called the *yenaandi*, "the act of cooling off." During this ceremony Songhay ask their spirits for rains that will ensure a bountiful millet harvest. One of Rouch's earlier films, *Yenaandi, ou Les hommes qui font la pluie,* is the story of the yenaandi held in Simiri in 1951.

As Rouch suggests, Songhay myths reflect the continuous fusion of the spirit and social worlds. Human beings are never far from the domain of the spirits, and the spirits often intervene in the social affairs of human beings. Spirits sometimes kill their mediums. Human beings and spirits are sometimes married to one another, as in the case of Sina, the spirit priest of Tollo Zermagunda, who married a male spirit, dressed as woman and had no other sexual relations (Rouch 1989, 86).

The proximity of the spirit and social worlds is signaled by the ritual incantations that specialists recite when human beings ask a spirit or, in the case of magicians, command the distant God to "work" for them. In *Religion* Rouch offers a wide variety of ritual incantations. There are incantations related to local genies, incantations that invoke the ancestors (especially in the case of the sohanci magicians), and of course incantations associated with the spirits.

Spirit incantations take the form of praise poems in which the sorko, the bard of the spirits, first indirectly declares his powerlessness—a kind of prostration before the spirit world—and then sings about the great exploits of the spirits. The most important set of praise songs is called *Tooru che,* and Rouch presents variant versions of them. He also considers the praise poems for the other spirit families, Genji Kwaari, Genji Bi, Hargay, Doguwa, and Hauka. These are much less elaborate than those recited for the Tooru, the nobles of the Songhay spirit world. In sum, Rouch offers fifty French translations of distinct spirit praise poems in *Religion.* No incantation or praise poem is reproduced in the original Songhay.

Through the good offices of Damoré Zika, Rouch was able to transcribe and translate all the texts presented to him. First he recorded the text, then he and Damoré Zika asked the informant questions about some of the more obscure passages or terms, some of which are not in Songhay. Each incantation in *Religion* is "signed" by the person who recited it. Viewers of Rouch's possession films, including *Les maîtres fous,* see and hear the recitation of several of these incantations.

Objects of the Possession Cult

Like any good Griaulian, Rouch collected material objects associated with the Songhay possession cult. But "object" for Rouch takes on the larger sense of ritual elements that are "material." He therefore considers as "objects" music and dance as well as costumes, altars, stones, hatchets, antelope horns, and dolls.

In his writing on the music of possession, Rouch stresses the importance of sound in Songhay possession, then goes on to describe the music, the instruments that create it, and the origin and consecration of the instruments. His attention to the instruments, their origin, and their consecration is not unusual for the ethnographic writing of his time, but what he writes about the cultural importance of the *godji,* the monochord violin, is worth repeating here: "This [musical] air, in the end, can replace the text of the praise song. In hearing it, men and the gods also hear words it carries [musically]. The Songhay say that the violin [or the drum] carries the words. Ritual music is therefore a veritable support for the phrases of the praise poem. It aids the memory to find difficult words again" (Rouch 1989, 146). Rouch then speculates about whether the music preceded the myths and the praise poetry of the Songhay spirits, but he does not go further in exploring the power of sound in spirit possession (see Stoller 1984, 1989a, b).

Rouch also writes about the dance movements of possession ceremonies, which he considers "inseparable from the music" (Rouch 1989, 145). He distinguishes three movements: the *windi,* in which the dancers sway to a slow, melodic rhythm as they move counterclockwise in a circle; the *gani,* in which one dancer, facing the musicians, moves toward them driven by a more rapid rhythm; and the *fimbi,* in which the dancer, directly in front of the musicians, moves head and arms to the rhythm, which begins slowly and gradually increases in tempo until the onset of the possession. Here Rouch also describes how the various spirits carry themselves in the bodies of their mediums, but he does not analyze movements or connect their symbolism to references concerning the mythology of the spirits (see Gleason 1982).

The chapter on ritual objects terminates with an exhaustive inventory of the objects associated with the spirit possession cult. Rouch writes about cult altars and about the highly sacred spirit houses (and their guardians, *kumbaw*) in Simiri, Begorou-Tondo, and Wanzerbe. In Songhay villages like Simiri and Wanzerbe sacred stones are found in sacred clay vases (*hampi*). There are also thunderstones—Neolithic ax heads—that Dongo, in fits of rage, threw to the earth. Inside the spirit huts of possession priests there are also vast arrays of scarves, bonnets and hats, belts, and jewelry—objects the spirits wear during ceremonies.

Sacred objects are dangerous, however. When an article is transformed from an everyday object to a sacred one, no one can know the extent of its power; one cannot know how one will be affected. In one case a sacred stone in Gotheye became what Rouch called a *porte-malheur,* or carrier of bad luck. "The one who possesses it dies quickly" (Rouch 1989, 181). The deeds of human beings sometimes unleash unimaginable forces; inert everyday objects become infused with live power.

Organization of the Cult

In *Religion* Rouch calls the possession troupe *une société religieuse.* For him this society creates specific roles that are hierarchized. Although the possession cult is not a church with an organized clergy governed by an absolute and distant authority, he does extend the religious society comparison, suggesting that possession societies reflect the organization of Songhay society: "In this way the religious society is a bit like contemporary Songhay society, a grouping of distinct chapels connected to each other by the same traditions and preoccupations, sometimes rivals, but always knowing one another quite well and considering one another with solidarity" (Rouch 1989, 192). Rouch says that the *société religieuse* has categories of participating members:

1. *The faithful:* men and women who are tied to possession directly or indirectly. As Rouch suggests, just about all the Songhay can fit into this category, except for several Muslim clerics. When push comes to shove, most Songhay will make an offering to the spirits (Rouch 1989, 192).

2. *Minstrels.* The minstrels may be griots who play either the *dondon* (the double-headed talking drum that looks like an hourglass) or the *ganga,* a cylindrical double-headed drum. According to Rouch, many of these griots trace their descent from Santama, the captive of Faran Maka Bote. The griots are usually not associated with possession troupes. By contrast, the possession musicians are either monochord violinists or gourd drummers, professional musicians who tour the Songhay countryside looking for work (Rouch 1989, 195–97).

3. *The possession dancers.* These men and women are spirit mediums who have been initiated into a spirit possession troupe. In a given Songhay locality only a small percentage of the inhabitants are spirit mediums, although I suspect the percentage has grown since Rouch's initial fieldwork (Rouch 1989, 197–203).

4. *The "tranquil" women.* These are women who, though never possessed, are ardent followers of spirit possession ceremonies. They help organize festivals and are asked to prepare food for the spirits. They also protect mediums during particularly violent possession episodes when they could easily injure themselves.

5. *The zima.* These are the priests of the possession troupe. They are usually spirit mediums who, through their great knowledge and organizational capacities, become established impressarios. In large towns like Niamey and Ayoru there are possession ceremonies once, if not twice, a week (Thursdays or Sundays or both) (Rouch 1989, 204–9).

6. The *kumbaw.* These men and women are the guardians of sacred spirit houses that existed in Begoro Tondo and still exist in Wanzerbe and Simiri. The origins of the kumbaw are obscure, but the position is nonetheless hereditary.

7. *The sorko.* The sorko, patrilineal descendants of Faran Maka Bote, are praise singers to the spirits as well as the specialized priests of the Tooru spirits.

The people living in what Rouch calls the *société religieuse* exist in a world where relations between humans and spirit fuse. Mediums are always conscious of the spirits they carry; spirits make ceaseless demands on their mediums. The people in the possession cult, Rouch argues, have a common purpose—they follow the path of the spirits— which means that if there is more than one possession cult in a larger town like Niamey, there would be no rivalry among the cults. Such harmony may have existed some years ago, but the thirst for money and what it can buy has made murderous rivalry a fact of life for spirit possession troupes throughout Songhay (see Stoller 1989a).

Possession in Practice

Rouch describes possession ceremonies in the same way he writes about myth and the organization of the cult: he lists the kinds of ceremonies that are staged and then describes in terse journalistic style the ceremonies he observed. Although Rouch's prose is flat here, the content is significant not only for Africanists but for scholars of religion. In these dry pages, Rouch provides a detailed record of Songhay possession as it was practiced in Niger in the 1940s and 1950s. Many of the ceremonies Rouch portrays are no longer performed there. More remarkable still is the way these data are shocked into life in Rouch's films on Songhay possession.[1]

MAGIC IN *RELIGION*

When ordinary Songhay address the spirits, they recite humble prayers: May you bring us rain; may you wash the filth from the sky; may you spare my husband, my child. By contrast, when the great Songhay sorcerers (sohanci) address themselves to the deities, they bark out *or-*

---

1. See also Stoller and Olkes (1987), Stoller (1989a). Notice the contrast of these books. Stoller and Olkes (1987) is essentially a memoir, a private textual strategy to describe the private world of sorcery. Stoller (1989a), by contrast, is a multigenre experiment written to capture the polyvocal, topsy-turvy world of Songhay spirit possession.

ders. Rouch says that the humble prayers reflect a religious attitude; the arrogant demands reflect the magicians' attitude. In essence, possession and "magic" are two distinct paths in the Songhay cosmos. Possession, says Rouch, is open and public. Magic is closed and private (Rouch 1989, 274).

The Magic Spell

The spell or *korte* is the foundation of the sohanci's practice. Rouch traces the putative origin of this word to Manding languages, in which *koroti* means "a bad spell" (Rouch 1989, 298). Rouch was unable to record information about its mythical origin, although Ndebbi, the messenger to the distant God, seems to play a central role in casting spells. When sohanci recite their various incantations, they recite them to Ndebbi, not to God or the spirits.

The magicians, who are usually men, use guides from the spirit world to direct their work. These guides may be genies, various spirits, ancestors, or the Atakurma, the elves of the bush. To maintain their links to their guides, most sohanci possess and nourish ritual objects: stones, altars, consecrated sheep or goats.

But magicians must also be strong; they must fortify themselves so that their "work" succeeds. Through the blood of their fathers and the milk of their mothers, sohanci receive the foundation of their power, but this power must be supplemented. Sohanci eat *kusu*, a millet cake mixed with powdered roots, leaves, and other substances that enhance power. Kusu remains in the stomach, the locus of the magician's power.

Once fortified with kusu, the magician harvests plants and tree barks that are used to make more kusu or are employed in other korte. Each plant or tree must be harvested at a particular time on a particular day. During the "harvest," moreover, magicians must recite the appropriate incantation to demonstrate their respect for the tree or plant. Once they dry the plant in the sun and pulverize it into powder, they are ready to prepare their korte. They mix the powders and recite magic incantations, several of which Rouch quotes in French.

Although there are several groups of occasional magicians, it is the sohanci that interest Rouch the most. The sohanci, he writes, "live by and for magic" (Rouch 1989, 298). They are patrilineal descendants of Sonni Ali Ber, king of Songhay between 1463 and 1491. Sonni Ali Ber or Si was an "unbelievable and enigmatic war chief . . . a magic king who was always the victor and never the vanquished" (Rouch 1989, 299). The sohanci in Wanzerbe told Rouch that it was Ndebbi who initiated Sonni Ali Ber. If one is a descendant of Si from both father's line and mother's line, one's power is triple: blood from one's father, milk from one's mother, and knowledge from one's initiation.

Sohanci use the spirits as allies to do their "work." They also have vultures as familiars. The vulture is the sohanci's spiritual guide and not their totem, which is the lion. The vulture is the only bird that flies through the seven heavens to reach God's house (*Iri Koy do*). Rouch says that the genuine sohanci look for and eat vultures' nests. I have also seen sohanci who buy dead vultures, bake them in the sun, and pulverize them. They then add the "black powder" to their kusu.

The most powerful and knowledgeable sohanci are in continuing contact with the "other" world, which renders them formidable adversaries. They are feared. They protect villages from witches and from the excesses of chiefs. They work alone in huts, usually segregated from their less powerful neighbors. On rare occasions sohanci gather and dance to purify a village or to mourn the death of one of their own. One such dance takes up a scene in Rouch's *Les magiciens de Wanzerbe* (see chap. 6). When the tam-tam music entrances one of the magicians in Rouch's film, the man vomits a small metal chain, the *sisiri,* the physical manifestation of his power. This rare event brings tears to the eyes of grown men in the audience—in a society where men almost never weep in public.

The sohanci's feats are sometimes inexplicable. Just before the most powerful sohanci die, they vomit their chains and tell their successors to swallow them. This act transfers to the successor all of the master's powers: "But a dead magician has not completely left the world of men. He must continue to direct, must continue to watch over the villages just as if he were alive. Yet this presence of the dead among the living demands the disruption of the laws of the world. God created an earth for men and another world for the dead. It is this inexorable law that the magicians stand up against, and with all their fragile powers of men of flesh, they try to triumph over death" (Rouch 1989, 311). The strange power of these men who attempt to defy God is embedded in the images of *Les magiciens de Wanzerbe*. From the very first sequence of frames, one is entranced by the dreamy mystery of Wanzerbe.

PEOPLE OF FORCE, SPIRITS OF POWER

Like the plodding but persistent traveler from Ayoru to Wanzerbe, readers of *Religion* must trudge through page after page of densely written descriptions of Songhay incantations, spells, and ritual objects.

The trail is long, winding its way through the structure of Songhay religion, the mythic origins of the spirits, of the sorko, of the sohanci, through the origin, structure, and practices of the spirit possession cult. Along the way readers meet scores of knowledgeable Songhay, Rouch's informants, who constitute a representative sample of Songhay thought and wisdom.

Like *Contribution à l'histoire des Songhay*, *Religion* is anything but an evocative text. Like a conscientious newspaper reporter, Rouch "lets the facts speak for themselves." He pays attention to the principal journalistic questions: who, what, when, where, why, and how. *Religion* is a vast compilation of data with little or no interpretation. It is a text that reflects Rouch's long-term investment in fieldwork in Songhay. It also exemplifies the mutual respect and trust that evolved from Rouch's "implication" in Songhay.

For the Sahelian specialist, *Religion* is invaluable. Rouch not only recorded the wisdom of men and women whose knowledge can never again be matched, he also observed many rites that are no longer performed. For the film scholar, *Religion* becomes an ethnographic encyclopedia. Its pages contain contextualizing points of reference for Rouch's films on Songhay possession. For careful and dedicated readers, however, there is a more general reward; if one follows the path Rouch has traced in *Religion,* one ultimately confronts the Songhay magicians, the sohanci, people who defy the laws of logic, who deny the ultimate existential absurdity of life: that one is born to die.

No theory could adequately explain the "mechanics" of the Songhay world that Rouch first confronted in the 1940s. In the end he rejects the use of psychoanalytic explanations or ethnological comparisons:

> And to conclude I will simply say that whatever influences or analogies one can discover between Songhay approaches to religion and similar approaches, whatever elementary structures and successive syntheses are revealed, this religion is above all an original religion, complex but coherent, in the image all the same of the men who subscribe to its beliefs, practice its rites, and participate in its cults: . . . the hunter tracking a lion with his reed arrows in the Garuol forests; the fisherman playing in rapids; the young "Gold Coast" looking for adventure in the teeming streets of Kumasi or Accra; the sohanci magician defying God and the devil in his Wanzerbe straw hut. (Rouch 1989, 321)

These evocative phrases close *Religion*. They offer readers a glimpse of Rouch's cinematic vision and demonstrate how participatory ethnographic fieldwork is central to Rouch's cinematic evocation, the drama of life as it is lived in Songhay. While Rouch was gathering data for

Religion, he was also making films. He collected the data on the so-hanci of Wanzerbe while he filmed *Les magiciens de Wanzerbe.* In this way the making of the film stimulated historical and sociological inquiry, and the results of that inquiry further informed the film. Long before his work became well known, there was no artificial boundary separating film from ethnographic writing or film practice from ethnographic practice. As Rouch would say, why not (*pourquoi pas*) use filmmaking to elicit historical and sociological data?

PART

II

Cinema Rouch

Cimi si bundu koogo tayaandi.
The truth will not give its life to
dead wood.
—Songhay proverb

INTRODUCTION

Two Spiritual Fathers and a Critical Son

Haawi ga di buyan bande.
Shame survives death.
—Songhay proverb

We have already seen the influence of Marcel Griaule on the written ethnographies of Jean Rouch. These works are laden with carefully collected data, which provide the basis for Rouch's attempt to interpret the Songhay world as Songhay perceive it. They are neither evocative nor provocative; they are primarily reservoirs of information, painstakingly gathered while Rouch was making ethnographic films.

Griaule urged his students to film ceremonies. For him film was one methodological key that unlocked certain ethnographic doors—the means to the end of more profound written ethnographies. For Rouch film is obviously more than a tool. Although Rouch is most definitely the "son of Griaule" in his written work, the character and quality of his films are inspired by the work of his cinematic spiritual fathers, Robert Flaherty and Dziga Vertov, men to whom Rouch's work pays homage. From the beginning Rouch sensed that the bewildering truths of life in Songhay would not give their vitality—their life—to the dead space of the printed page. Rouch, then, made films to bring life to Songhay truths.

FETING FLAHERTY

Georges Sadoul, the dean of French film critics, has called Robert Flaherty the Jean-Jacques Rousseau of the cinema (Sadoul 1990). Hailed by many film historians as the creator of the documentary, Flaherty was one of the cinema's great geniuses. By the time Rouch met the American explorer-geologist-filmmaker at the Musée de l'Homme in 1938, Flaherty had already made three of his most important films: *Nanook of the North* (1922), *Moana* (1926), and *Man of Aran* (1934). He would make his other significant film, *Louisiana Story,* in 1948.

Flaherty's greatest achievement was *Nanook of the North.* A classic documentary, *Nanook* is still occasionally used to teach anthropology. Like Griaule, who cautioned his students to take their time, Flaherty was an exceedingly patient filmmaker. He once remarked, "Film is the longest distance from one point to another" (quoted in Sadoul 1990).

Nanook was not made overnight. Flaherty was searching for mineral deposits for a mining company when he began to explore the Canadian arctic in 1910. It was only on his third expedition in 1913 that Flaherty began to film the Inuit (see Flaherty 1960; Rotha 1980). However, Flaherty accidentally burned this footage—more than 70,000 feet of it—in Toronto. Film critics agree that the 1913 footage was crude and that Flaherty was displeased with his first efforts (Rotha 1980). He undertook a fourth Canadian mining expedition in 1915 that did not result in a film. In 1921 he lived with Nanook for a year, during which he made *Nanook of the North.*

During 1921–22 Flaherty found the harsh conditions along the shores of Hudson Bay daunting but not insurmountable. In the extreme cold of the northland he built a darkroom and a projection room. In his makeshift screening room, Flaherty showed "rushes" to Nanook and his people and solicited commentary.

Flaherty and Rouch share many traits. Both started their careers as scientist-explorers. Flaherty's most important lesson to Rouch, however, is that of participation. "For Rouch *Nanook of the North* is a celebration of a relationship; it combines the familiarity that accrues from observation with the sense of contact and spontaneity that comes from rapport and participation" (Feld 1989, 232). But Flaherty's participation went beyond living with the people and understanding their ways. He not only asked Nanook for feedback, but also taught him about making films—about the necessity of staging some events. With Flaherty filming becomes a joint enterprise, narrowing the gulf between filmmakers and the people they film. In Rouch's view *Nanook of the North* "is never a detached set of images about anonymous actors but a deliberate selection based on both observations of everyday Inuit routines and Nanook's ability to help stage representative versions" (Feld 1989, 232). This is what Rouch calls the "staging" of reality.

Did Rouch have Robert Flaherty in mind in Ayoru in 1954 when he

An old Dogon man speaks in a ritual language (Siguiso), *Les clameurs d'Amani*. J. Rouch, Comité du Film Ethnographique.

attached a white sheet to a mud-brick wall and projected *Bataille sur le grand fleuve?* Like the Inuit, the Songhay of Ayoru quickly understood the language of the cinema, and from one film other films were born. This experience of "shared cinema" in Ayoru was for Rouch a major event in his initiation as a filmmaker, making Flaherty, along with Griaule, one of Rouch's spiritual fathers.

VERITABLY VERTOV

Whereas Flaherty's creative influence on Rouch is fundamentally methodological, Dziga Vertov's cinematic contributions lead to the heart of Rouch's cinematic art. Vertov's notions of the cine-eye and the radio-ear figure prominently in Rouch's practice of *cinéma-vérité*, in which one edits film as one shoots it—in which the camera becomes an extension of the filmmaker's body. In this sense Vertov's conception of the cinema is the artistic extension of Flaherty's participatory cinema.

Born in Poland in 1896, Vertov, a contemporary of Sergei Eisenstein, became a key player in the experimental Soviet cinema that emerged after the 1917 revolution. Sadoul calls Vertov "the prophet of the cine-eye" (see Sadoul 1990; Vertov 1985). Vertov expressed his most important and revolutionary ideas in *Kino-Pravda* (film-truth), a filmed magazine he founded in 1922, and in *The Man with the Movie Camera* (1929; see Vertov 1985). In *Kino-Pravda* Vertov rejects the theatricality of films and declares the superfluity of film directors, actors, and studios. Vertov's aim was to plunge the cinema into the stimulating depths of real life, a construction of the real prompted by the camera.[1]

Film historians today consider Vertov a visionary whose ideas surpassed the technological possibilities of his day. He called for the marriage of what he termed the cine-eye and the radio-ear—the fusion of image and sound. Indeed, in Vertov's first long work, *En avant Soviet,* the subtitled text is as significant as the screen images. But Vertov's dream of a synchronous sound camera was not realized until the early 1960s.

As Steven Feld points out, Vertov's approach to the cinema attacked the theory of realism head-on. Vertov distinguished the theory of realism from "reality." Opposed to studio fabrications of the real, in *Kino-Pravda* and *The Man with the Movie Camera* Vertov demonstrated methods for capturing a cine-reality of life as it is lived: "For Vertov,

1. Faye Ginsburg pointed this out to me.

film realism was thematic and structural, built up from tiny units of observation of real people doing real things. These units were always organized by the filmmaker to express his version or statement of content" (Feld, 1989, 233). *Kino-Pravda*'s frontal assault on "received realism" required new ways of thinking about and using the camera. Feld cites Rouch, who cites Vertov's famous passage:

> I am the kino-eye, I am the mechanical eye, I am the machine that shows you the world as only a machine can see it. From now on I will be liberated from immobility. I am in perpetual movement. I draw near to things, I move myself away from them, I enter into them, I travel toward the snout of a racing horse. I move through crowds at top speed, I precede soldiers on attack, I take off with airplanes, I flip over on my back, I fall down and stand back up as bodies fall down and stand back up. (Feld 1989, 233)

For Vertov, body and camera are one; the machine-body acquires consciousness as it cine-records. But the camera does not record objective reality; it creates a cine-reality. In this way the camera, an extension of the filmmaker's body-mind, participates consciously in filming life.

Whereas Flaherty is Rouch's model for the method of participatory, shared cinema, Vertov leads Rouch to making *cinéma-vérité* films, the technique Rouch has used extensively. Vertov provides Rouch a theoretical model that reinforces politically and epistemologically his filmic practices.

A CRITICAL SON

Many of Jean Rouch's films have been critically acclaimed. Some are masterworks of cinematic innovation; some evoke the unthinkable, the unimaginable; most are provocative to both European and African audiences. Rouch's films are testaments to a "participatory cinema" pioneered by Flaherty and also pay homage to the Vertovian legacy of what Rouch calls *ciné-vérité*, the filmic truth. Rouch's filmic practice demonstrates a respect for his spiritual fathers: as the griots say, "Shame survives death," but only if sons and daughters fail to respect the traditions of their ancestors.

Enter the critical son. Previously published assessments of Rouch's work are excellent examples of film criticism, but they are ethnographically incomplete.[2] In this part of the book the critical son considers ethnographically five of Rouch's Songhay films as well as his series of

2. There are many excellent studies of Rouch's cinematic practices. Among the best are Eaton (1979); Feld (1974, 1989); *Studies in the Anthropology of Visual Communi-*

films on the Dogon. Two of the films, *Les magiciens de Wanzerbe* (chap. 6) and *The Lion Hunters* (chap. 7), are about Songhay magic. One of the films, *Jaguar* (chap. 8), the only ethnofiction film considered, is about migration and social change. Two other films, *Les maîtres fous* and *Les tambours d'avant: Turu et bitti,* are about Songhay possession (chaps. 9 and 10). The films (chap. 11) on the Sigui ceremonies of the Dogon are about the ritualized transmission of complex cosmogonic knowledge from generation to generation. In Rouchian fashion, the films analyzed here evoke nonethnographic subjects—some philosophical, some methodological, some political—that transcend their West African setting. My purpose is not to replicate the excellent commentary on the historical and technical merits of Rouch's films, but to bring into focus the ethnographic and philosophical themes central to Cinema Rouch. Such is the charge of the cinematic griot's griot. Such is the charge of the critical son who takes seriously the Songhay proverb, "Shame survives death."

---

cation (first four issues); and the papers in Ruby (1989) (special edition of *Visual Anthropology,* "The Cinema of Jean Rouch").

CHAPTER SIX
Les Magiciens de Wanzerbe

Fundi si fun nangu follon.
Life doesn't pass by without battles.
—Songhay proverb

Anyone who has been to Wanzerbe has felt its powerful presence. When I first went there in 1977 I felt but could not understand this presence. Years later Kassey, the head priestess of Wanzerbe, recited to me a myth that shed light on the presence of the past in this village of sorcerers. Listen to Kassey's words:

> The rulers of Gao were once ruled by the Sonnis, the last of whom was Sonni Ali Ber or Si, who was our ancestor. But Si was one day murdered by Mamar [Askia Mohammed Touré]. Si had three sons, Baru, Daouda, and Daouda Albana. After Si's death, Si Baru and Si Daouda escaped to the South. Si Daouda Albana didn't escape. Mamar's men trapped Daouda Albana on the shore of the Niger near Gao. Following the orders of Mamar, they wanted to take Daouda Albana's head back to their king as a trophy. As soon as they severed his head, however, it did not fall to the ground, it rose to the heavens. Frightened, Mamar's men threw Daouda Albana's body into the Niger. The current carried the corpse southward. As the corpse floated south, the head followed its progress from above. When the body reached the place where the Garuol flows into the Niger, it flowed into the Garuol, moving against the current. The head followed its body to the west. Body and head continued. Body and head continued until the body reached a spot that was to become Wanzerbe. There Si Daouda Albana's head came back to the earth and attached itself to Si Daouda Albana's body. Daouda Albana stood up in the shallows. "Here I shall found a village." And so he did. He married local Gurmantche women and fathered many sons and daughters. Some of the sons married Gurmantche women; others mar-

ried their cousins. And so began Wanzerbe. And so it has continued until this very day. (Kassey Sohanci, Wanzerbe)[1]

When Kassey told me the myth of Wanzerbe's origin, I comprehended for the first time the historical depth of its reputation for sorcery. Through skill in sorcery, as Jean Rouch wrote in *La religion et la magie Songhay,* the sohanci battles death itself. After Askia Mohammed's coup d'état Si Daouda Albana became a fugitive, but Askia's men soon captured him. He had already lost his political power; he had lost his freedom and was about to lose his head. But the blood of Sonni Ali Ber ran in his veins. The magical knowledge of his father sparked his consciousness. The milk of Kassey, Sonni Ali Ber's sister, coated his belly. In this way Si Daouda Albana defied death. His severed head rose to the heavens to follow his decapitated body down the Niger and up the Garuol until it reached the site of Wanzerbe. There he became whole again. There he founded Wanzerbe. He was the first sohanci; his story set the standard for his descendants who, like their ancestor, demonstrate that "life doesn't pass by without battles."

In Wanzerbe, mythic past and oppressive present interchange; the everyday and the unimaginable fuse. Si Daouda Albana's pride, bearing, and wariness—his controlled fury—continue to burn in the eyes of Wanzerbe. What stranger could be at ease in such a place?

IMAGES OF WANZERBE

Magiciens begins with the thumping *gbunk* of the double-headed tam-tam drum. As the music continues we see our first image: it is a vulture's head, symbol of the sohanci of Wanzerbe. The vulture flies high, we learn, and listens to God's secrets. The sohanci too know the secrets of the earth, the sky, the trees, and the bush.

Rouch and his entourage travel to Wanzerbe from Yatakala. We see images of the local Tuareg chief and of Sourgya, the Songhay paramount chief. It is market day. Women sit in the shade of the giant *kokorbey* that dominates the market plaza, which separates the neighborhood of Sohanci from Karia.

Rouch begins to speak, telling us that the people of Wanzerbe do not like strangers; they are certainly suspicious of Europeans, but they also mistrust all outsiders. Rouch's guide, Nacio Maiga, is snubbed at the market. Even though he is a Songhay noble, a patrilineal descendant of Askia Mohammed Touré, the people in Wanzerbe refuse to shake his hand and do not speak to him.

1. Interview with Kassey of Wanzerbe, 5 July 1984.

A sohanci in front of his hut.

From the beginning of the film, then, the viewer learns that Wanzerbe is a cold place—at least to outsiders. But despite this hostility Wanzerbe, like any village, has its everyday routines. Young boys, like boys in other villages and other countries, play games to amuse themselves. In Wanzerbe the game is to hop around on one foot. But Rouch does not dwell on amusing children's play, for Wanzerbe is the village of what he calls magicians.

Rouch introduces us to the magicians of Wanzerbe: Barake, Djaje, and Bakari. The dean of the Wanzerbe magicians is an old blind man who wears heavy brass beads and carries a *lolo*, an iron staff to which are attached blood-caked rings. We also see another sohanci's power object: Bakari's silver ring in the form of a horse with a vulture's head, mounted by a horseman who also has a vulture's head. This ring represents Sonni Ali Ber, the first sohanci.

Another of the Wanzerbe magicians is Mossi Bana, who lives in Karia. Although Mossi was not born in Wanzerbe, he is both a sohanci and a zima, the possession priest of Wanzerbe. Rouch's camera follows Mossi into his compound; in the center are four sacred trees and an altar, where Mossi does his magical "work." Among other things, the four trees represent the four cardinal directions. The trees are fed regularly, with sacrificial blood and perfume.

The image of Mossi in his house enables Rouch to talk more generally about the sohanci of Wanzerbe. Many of them are diviners. The best among them, like Mossi, know the technique of *laabu kar,* or geomancy; others know *nor'izo kar,* divining with cowrie shells. People come from great distances to have their "paths" read by such diviners. If a child of Wanzerbe wishes to travel to the Guinea coast, he too will consult a sohanci like Mossi Bana.

The magicians of Wanzerbe are masters of the past, the present, and the future. They are also masters of words, of hundreds of incantations with which they instruct their guides—spirits, genies, ancestors, or Atakurma (elves of the bush)—to perform for them. The sohanci's principal incantation, however, is the *genji how,* which Rouch translates as *attacher la brousse* (tying up the bush). Recited by the sohanci, the genji how brings into balance the mercurial and malevolent forces of the bush. Without such balance sohanci place themselves in great danger; their "work" will not succeed, and they may suffer the consequences of a momentary lapse: weakness, sickness, or death.

Sohanci are also masters of plants used for medical as well as magic "work." Rouch's camera follows Mossi Bana into the bush to record him as he harvests plants. Rouch explains that plants, all housing immaterial forces, must be gathered carefully. Mossi prepares to harvest some tree bark. He recites his genji how and then addresses himself respectfully to the tree, asking its forgiveness. Once these incantations are complete, Mossi cuts portions of bark from the east, north, south, and west sides of the tree.

The portrait of Mossi Bana is impressive. Here is mature man who has completely mastered his world. His knowledge of words, of plants, and of divination enables him to seize power from the universe, to protect his village from malevolent forces. He is a man whose pride and knowledge make him the master of himself.

This portrait of sohanci self-mastery is underscored by Rouch's depiction of a *sohanci hori,* or magician's dance. In the 1940s and 1950s the sohanci's dance was not uncommon. They were staged then to commemorate various Muslim holidays, to purify the *gosi,* or rite of female initiation, to mark the death of a sohanci, or to purify a village. Lately the influences and pressures of Islam have made sohanci dances rare events.

In *Magiciens* the viewer is not told why the sohanci hori is being staged. Has a sohanci died? Does Wanzerbe need to be purified? Nor do we know where in Wanzerbe the dance was performed, though it seems to be the neighborhood of Sohanci. From reading *Religion* we learn that Rouch filmed this purification ceremony on 13 December 1948. Internal dissension had rendered Wanzerbe magic inefficacious. From reading *Religion,* we also learn that the principal dancer was an old sohanci called Yedjo (Rouch 1989, 310–11).

We watch a crowd form on the dusty hilltop that is the village's plaza. There are three tam-tam drummers and an audience, many themselves sohanci. Yedjo is dressed in a black boubou and carries a saber in his left hand, its copper handle in the form of a vulture's head. In his right hand is a baton, his *lolo,* which repels witches. We hear the rhythmic thumping of the tam-tam orchestra.

Yedjo Sohanci prepares to dance. With sand he creates a magic circle on the dance ground, a way of "tying up the bush." He buries a nail in the sand and covers it with a rock. This "work" renders Yedjo invisible to witches but enables him to see them even in distant villages.

He is now ready to dance. Holding in one hand his saber and in the other his lolo, he glides along the sand to his right, to his left, to chase away evil. Griots chant the praise poetry of Sonni Ali Ber.

> Si flies in the night
> Si flies with the first crowing of the rooster
> Si Baru [Sonni Ali's son]
> Si Almine [Si Baru's son]
> Si can kill a man between the hair and the head
> Si can kill a man between the shoe and the foot
> Si can kill a man between the shirt and the neck.
> (Rouch 1989, 100)

After hours of dancing, Yedjo tires and asks for some millet porridge. Meanwhile former Songhay slaves take to the dance space. One of these women pushes a gourd under her dress; another hides a stick under her skirt. Perhaps a bit of sexual diversion?

Soon Yedjo begins to dance again, slowly, majestically, his billowing black cape swirling as he slides across the dance ground. Yedjo's son joins him. Their eyes bulge. Yedjo's son is soon in a trance; he dances wildly. Then Yedjo shudders as if he had been shocked with electricity. Eyes popping, he vomits a small metal chain; it dangles from the end of his tongue for several seconds.

> Now he sees even better than usual. He sees evil in four directions, he pricks surprised *tyarkaw* [witches]. During these several seconds, he is the dangerous master of all the bush and all the villages. Then, bending back with hiccups, he painfully swallows the small, brilliant chain. He makes no speech, he makes no sign; but when members of the audience see the chain, an intense emotion overtakes them. They tremble, raise their arms to the sky, walk about wildly, and weep. (Rouch 1989, 311)

One would think this incredible scene of intense emotion would mark the end of the film, but it does not. Rouch began *Magiciens* with scenes of village life—the market, children's games—that give us a sense of place. He ends the film with a yearly ritual: a sacrifice to the genie of Sargumey.

Men, young and old alike, walk up to the summit of Sargumey to slaughter a cow for the protective genie of the mountain. If the genie accepts the offering, the people of Wanzerbe will expect a year of health and fecundity. If the genie does not accept the sacrifice or if none is offered, the people will suffer. The sohanci of Wanzerbe officiate, and their chief magician carefully cuts the cow's throat. The sohanci watch how the blood flows and determine that the genie of Sargumey has accepted the sacrifice. The men butcher the cow. The sohanci build a fire, then roast the meat and give it to a large crowd of boys. The remaining bits of meat are buried in the soil, ensuring another year of health and happiness for Wanzerbe.

THE IMPACT OF *LES MAGICIENS DE WANZERBE*

Usually listed among Jean Rouch's earlier films, *Magiciens* is one of his less frequently seen works. Yet the image of old Yedjo vomiting his magic chain makes it one of Rouch's most important. One could say that *Magiciens* is simply an ethnographic documentary. There are, after all, panoramic sweeps of an isolated African town, Wanzerbe. There are filmed sequences of rituals: the sacrifice on Sargumey, the harvest of magic plants, the recitation of incantations. There is a portrait of a Wanzerbe magician, Mossi Bana.

Magiciens therefore meets many of the expectations of ethnographic documentary. But in Rouch's hands the film goes one step further, for it confronts the European viewer with a sequence that is frankly beyond belief. How can a man carry a small metal chain—Rouch guessed it was copper—in his stomach? Wouldn't such a chain poison a human being? And how can the presence of such a chain be transformed into what Songhay consider the source of the magician's power?

In *La religion et la magie Songhay* Rouch admits that the sohanci of Wanzerbe challenge the very rules that form the foundation of a scientific worldview. They stand up to and master God. They defy death itself. And they are capable of feats not yet known to us in the West.

Rouch's description of the sohanci dance of Wanzerbe in *Religion* is dispassionate, but his depiction of it in *Magiciens* is unsettling—especially the sequence where the old dancer Yedjo vomits his metal chain and then, with great difficulty, swallows it again. From the Songhay-sohanci perspective, the chain is the peak of personal power. It is so powerful, in fact, that only a few male sohanci—those who have calm and judicious dispositions—are selected to carry one in their bellies.

A sohanci receives the chain in one of two ways. One way that both Rouch and I have documented is for a father to pass it on to his *koycia*, his successor (see Stoller and Olkes 1987). At the moment of death the dying sohanci will vomit his chain—some sohanci have more than one—onto his chest and ask his successor to swallow it. Thus is power passed from generation to generation. Many sohanci die these days without passing their chains on to a successor—there is a dearth of suitable candidates. When a father does pass his power to his son or another successor, the chain is called not *sisiri,* but rather the sohanci's *goy jine,* or "work things."

A second way to receive a chain is by eating a special kusu, or magic cake. The powdered form of a particular tree bark, which remains unknown to me, is mixed with the blood of a goat, added to millet flour and water, and cooked into a paste that is eaten. The kusu makes the stomach expand with gas, and when the person's stomach has returned to its normal state, his kusu is said to have "gone to lie down [*a ga kani*] to sleep." The kusu is said to remain asleep in the sohanci's stomach until it is "awakened" (*tun*) in response to the rhythmic thumping of the tam-tam and the graceful sweep of the sohanci's dance. When the kusu is awakened it transforms itself into a small metal chain, which the sohanci vomits. According to my teachers, when the chain is in a person's stomach it remains in an organic state. In the sohanci's trance the kusu transforms itself into organic matter (Stoller and Olkes 1987; Stoller 1989b).

Viewers of *Magiciens* were intrigued, and several men determined to experience for themselves the village of magicians. One was the French administrator of Tera, the district where Wanzerbe is situated. He went to Wanzerbe to learn from the sohanci. Soon thereafter, French doctors evacuated him to the hospital in Niamey: he had apparently gone mad. Rouch saw this man in the hospital "in a state of disorientation." [2] Unable to treat the administrator's condition, the physicians in Niamey decided to send him to back France, and by the time he landed on French soil, he was again lucid. He did not return to Niger.

A second French administrator in Tera invited Rouch to participate in a Wanzerbe experiment. He did not believe it was possible for a man to live with a metal chain in his stomach. One way to test the veracity of such a claim, he reasoned, was to take an X ray of a magician, preferably old Yedjo, who claimed to have one of these chains in his stomach. Rouch took this man to Wanzerbe. Armed with a portable generator and an X-ray machine, they approached the famous village. Soon after they set up camp in Zongo, dusk settled over the village. They relaxed in director's chairs and sipped whiskey. In the distance Djaje, the chief sohanci of Wanzerbe, strolled by. Just thereafter the scientifically curious administrator fainted. Unconscious, he was rushed to Tera. He did not return; the experiment was never conducted.[3]

A third administrator in Tera, a judge, also attempted to learn about *Wanzerbe-la-magique*. Soon after meddling in the internal politics of Wanzerbe, he became paralyzed from the waist down. As with his predecessors, this serious illness forced the judge's evacuation to Niamey. There physicians treated him, but his condition did not improve. Finally colonial officials decided to return him to France. By the time he reached France, he could walk. He did not return to Niger.[4]

When *Magiciens* was shown in Niger, the sohanci hori sequence disturbed many people. Nigerien intellectuals did not debate the scientific possibilities of the sisiri; rather, they complained about Rouch's exoticism. They did not like the "primitive light" such a film cast upon Nigerien populations. In fact, people in Wanzerbe complained about films "that make us look like simple animals. How can you people understand?" [5] However, *Magiciens* fascinated the students of the University of Niamey when Rouch screened it for them in 1988 (Rouch 1989, 315).

2. Interview with Jean Rouch, 7 March 1990 (Paris).
3. Ibid.
4. Ibid.
5. Interview with Kassey of Wanzerbe, 5 July 1984.

The point of *Magiciens* is neither to provide scientific proof that Songhay magicians carry little metal chains in their stomachs nor to paint an exotically primitive picture of the sohanci of Wanzerbe. As a whole the film depicts the life of the village respectfully. In his writing and in his film, Rouch seems awed by these men who defy death, who vomit and then swallow chains of power.

Rouch's role in this film, as in the other films we shall discuss, is that of a cinematic griot. He tells the story of Wanzerbe, the story of people proudly linked to their history, their ancestors. But the story forces us to confront some fundamental existential questions. How can these men of Wanzerbe defy the laws of physiology? If these men can vomit metal chains and defy the social order, what can they teach us about ourselves? What is possible in the world? The scenes in *Magiciens* force many Western viewers to rethink taken-for-granted categories. By the same token, some scenes may force Western-educated African viewers to confront worlds they had happily forgotten.

THE WORLD OF SONGHAY SORCERY

But a griot—even a cinematic one—rarely tells people how to think or how to react; rather, he demonstrates possibilities and guides people down metaphoric passageways. In *Magiciens* Rouch documents for all time a world of magic in Wanzerbe. In his writing on Songhay religion, he devotes only one short chapter to magic. And yet *Les magiciens de Wanzerbe* asks, What is magic? What is sorcery in the Songhay world? What is it that the sohanci practice alone in their isolated Wanzerbe huts? Viewers receive only partial answers.

In a word, sohanci practice *korte,* the making of "charms." Rouch says that korte is the knowledge that makes sohanci magicians, that distinguishes them from sorcerers. This distinction is unfortunate, since it extends to non-European populations the European division of good and evil. Magic is good unless it is labeled "black" magic, which makes it evil. Sorcery is completely evil, since we have no category of "white sorcery." In Songhay the boundaries between "good" magic and "bad" sorcery are not at all clear; in fact I would say they do not exist (Stoller and Olkes 1987; Stoller 1989b). The world of sorcery, the term I use to encompass what others call magic plus sorcery, is completely amoral. There are no good magicians or bad sorcerers; there are only degrees of power in a world marked by incessant rivalry. The practice of sorcery enables the most powerful of these men to defy the social order, to defy the spirits, and at last to defy the finality of death itself.

Three examples, two from Rouch and one from my own experiences among sohanci, underscore this point. First, according to Rouch, when a sohanci vomits his chain at a sohanci's dance—as in the film—it is a moment of great danger for the dancer. If the dancer is indeed the most powerful sohanci in the crowd, he reveals his chain and swallows it again without incident. If he has overestimated his own power, one of his rivals, perhaps a kinsman, using what is called *dire*, can prevent him from swallowing his chain again, causing his death (Rouch 1989, 304).

Barake of Wanzerbe gave Rouch a second example of amoral rivalry among sohanci: "Two sohanci are eating from the same plate. One is as powerful as the other. Because of his vanity, one of them serves himself before the other, looking at him in a way signifying: 'I am the stronger.' Saying nothing, the other looks at him, and the first one can no longer eat anything. He is forced to recognize the superiority of his comrade: if not he will die" (Rouch 1989, 314). The sohanci must always be vigilant, must always know the relative strength of his power. For him there can be no right or wrong. For him the only morality is power—over life and over death.

The third incident occurred in Sohanci, a village of sorcerers some four kilometers west of Simiri, which is seventy kilometers northeast of Niamey. In 1989 I went to Sohanci to meet the brothers and sisters of Sohanci Adamu Jenitongo, my own teacher, who died in Tillaberi in March 1988. Sohanci is a small village inhabited by members of the Jenitongo lineage, which traces its origin to Wanzerbe. Two patriarchs, Yaya Jenitongo and Koda ("last born") Jenitongo, govern Sohanci. Although they live next door to one another, they have not spoken for years. Rivalry long ago supplanted their fraternal love. Since I had met Koda Jenitongo previously, I elected to lodge with him. My first day there, I took my noon meal at his house and was delighted with the cuisine. As we sat down to a large dinner bowl of millet paste and black sauce, Yaya Jenitongo's wife delivered a large bowl of her own. It too was stuffed with millet paste and smothered with a savory black sauce. I thanked Yaya Jenitongo's wife for her work. She left, and I scooped up with my right hand a little ball of Yaya's millet. As I put it to my mouth Moussa, Adamu Jenitongo's older son, clamped my arm, preventing me from eating it. "That's not for you," Moussa said to me. Koda Jenitongo looked on impassively. Hamidou, Jenitongo's eldest grandson, arrived a bit later carrying yet another bowl of millet and sauce. He sat down in front of me and began to eat. "Aren't you hungry?" he asked me. I looked at Moussa and Koda Jenitongo. They nodded, and I began to eat from Hamidou's bowl. One of Koda's

Preparation of a sohanci's korte.

sons threw the contents of the bowl brought by Yaya Jenitongo's wife into the privy—it was deemed unfit for human or animal consumption.
The life of a sohanci is not a game.

CATEGORIES OF SONGHAY SORCERY

Rouch's *Les magiciens de Wanzerbe* is powerfully evocative, but the
film leaves an incomplete picture of sorcery as it is practiced by the
sohanci in Songhay society. As the film indicates, sohanci are masters
of words, of charms, and of divination. They receive clients and do

work for them. Some sohanci will dance at festivals; some will vomit their chains, becoming the masters of their environs. And yet the life of sohanci is one of interminable vigilance; they live in a world of endless rivalry. Sohanci are both hunters and hunted; they have no peace of mind. Their quest for prestige drives them to "master" their enemies, their friends, even their cousins and their brothers. This underside of sohanci life is central to the experience of the magicians of Wanzerbe but is not part of Rouch's film. Rouch does not treat the more dangerous categories of Songhay sorcery.

There are three general kinds of sorcery. The first is called *dengbeli.* Dengbeli involves the use of topical poisons, placed in powdered form on a bed or some other object the victim is likely to touch. The poison enters the bloodstream through the skin and kills its victim in three days or less. In one case a sorko publicly insulted a powerful sohanci. The sorko died three days later, having defecated his intestines onto the sand (Stoller 1989a). Some of the poisons cause veins and arteries to burst; in this case the victim bleeds to death (Stoller 1989a, b). In dengbeli sorcerers do not recite incantations; it is sorcery limited to the most powerful sohanci.

The second kind of sorcery practiced in Songhay is called *sambeli,* or sending the "magic arrow." Here sorcerers speak to their magic arrow—a ritual object—and then with a magic bow—also a ritual object—shoot the arrow in their compound. If the arrow hits its metaphoric target, which depends on the power of the sorcerer, the victim becomes lethargic and nauseated and may experience violent diarrhea and suffer from shooting pains in the legs. If the victim has protection (wears a special ring or has eaten special foods like kusu), the impact of the sorcery—the arrow, which is invisible to nonsorcerers—is strong but short-lived. If the arrow is not located and removed, an unprotected victim will wither away and die a slow, horrible death. Like dengbeli, sambeli is practiced seldom and only by the most powerful sohanci.

Tengbeli, the third kind of sorcery in Songhay, is more widely practiced. In tengbeli, sickness is brought on by reciting incantations in addition to making offerings to certain spirits. Sorcerers may be hired by an injured party to punish a victim. More likely sorcerers will use tengbeli to vanquish their rivals. By reciting the appropriate incantation, making the appropriate sacrifice to the right spirit, and naming the victim, sorcerers send sickness—and sometimes death. If sorcerers are powerful, the result is immediate. The victim becomes nauseated, delirious, anxious, and partially paralyzed and may shake with palsy.

The practice of tengbeli is as potentially dangerous for the sohanci as for the intended victim. The sorcerer often chooses as victim a rival who is blocking the path to more power, more recognition, more success in the world. But if tengbeli is repelled, its force attacks the person who sent it.

As the griots say, the life of the sohanci is a hard one, full of countless prolonged battles. It is a life in which fear is paramount and respect is often a matter of life and death. In the terse words of *Religion* and in the riveting images of *Les magiciens de Wanzerbe,* Jean Rouch cuts to the truth of sorcery among the Songhay—its unimaginable power, which demands respect. As a cinematic griot, he knew that the life of the magicians of Wanzerbe is a continuous battle in which the sohanci attempts to make others fear and respect him, for shame does indeed survive death. There is no shame—only respect—in Rouch's portrait, *Les magiciens de Wanzerbe.*

CHAPTER SEVEN

The Lion Hunters

Hini kulu nda nga ce dira.
Every power has its incantation.
—Songhay proverb

Like the "old words" of the griot, the surreal images of the cine-matic griot in *Les magiciens de Wanzerbe* make us wonder about the physical and, indeed, psychic capacities of human beings. What can these brave people of Niger teach us about life in the social universe? Despite its ethnographic incompleteness, *Magiciens* forces us to ask these questions. True to the heritage of the "old words," it forces us to respect the isolated people in Wanzerbe who attempt to defy death. In this chapter, which analyzes one of Rouch's better-known films, *The Lion Hunters*, I consider another assumption that Rouch openly questions: that words are neutral instruments of meaning, that words are powerless, that words alone cannot magically alter behavior. For the Songhay, "every power has its incantation."

Songhay hunters master certain powers to pursue their quest. Hunters track lions in the Songhay bush, a vast and dangerous place. From the Songhay perspective, space that appears uninhabited is densely populated by creatures of the night. In the bush, the wise hunter knows that at any moment he may become the hunted. If the hunter kills a hyena, the familiar of Songhay witches, a witch might kill his son or daughter. If the hunter kills a young lion, the soul of the lion might make him so delirious that he would not know, as the Songhay say, "his front side from his backside." The bush is merciless; it kills its enemies. The bush kills the hunter who knows not the words of the hunt.

LION HUNTING IN YATAKALA

Rouch's *The Lion Hunters* is about the conflict between hunter and bush, a war of will and power, of seen and unseen. This conflict, which is the central element of the Songhay story, appears on the screen as a simple narrative. Rouch is the cinematic griot. Viewers are transported to Yatakala, Niger, to sit on a palm-frond mat in a dimly lit mud-brick house. We see angel-faced "little Ali" and hear the cries of the mono-chord violin. We are ready to listen to Jean Rouch's story about men so brave that they face lions armed only with bows and arrows.

One of the major themes of *The Lion Hunters* is the quest. The first

A songhay hunter (*gow*) from Yatakala, Niger. J. Rouch, Comité du Film Ethnographique.

quest in the film takes men from inhabited to uninhabited space, from the secure and safe to the precarious and uncertain. We begin on th Niger River—on an ancient ferryboat that transports Land Rovers Peugeot 404s, camels, and goats across the river. This crossing is some sixty kilometers north of Niamey, Niger, and 140 kilometers south of Ayoru, site of the film's second river crossing. From the crossing, the dirt road leads north to Gotheye and then west to Dargol, Bandio, and Tera, an administrative center. From Tera one follows a well-maintained road some twenty kilometers to Foneko, then turns north onto a track heading toward Bankilare. From Bankilare deep, soft sand and washed-out bridges make the going difficult at times until one reaches Teguey. The road continues to Wanzerbe and then farther north to Yatakala.

For whatever reason, Rouch's camera does not trace this route; rather, we follow a motorized caravan through the desiccated plain, which resembles the route from Dolsul (near Ayoru) to Yatakala. This artistic diversion is unimportant, however, for once the caravan leaves Yatakala and crosses the Erksan dune, we enter the bush that is "farther than far." Here the road is only a track, and soon the track gives away to trackless plains.

We leave the domain of the safe and secure and enter a dangerous place where wild animals roam freely: ostriches, giraffes, wild boars. Human beings once lived in this bush: the *don borey,* or people of the past, that Rouch wrote about in *Contribution à l'histoire Songhay.* They were hunters who left etchings on boulders showing their exploits and their magic. These were men who knew how to harmonize the forces of the bush (*genji haw*), to walk safely along a treacherous path, for they were threatened not only by wild bush animals but also by savage bush spirits.

Now only scattered groups of Fulan and Bella nomads live in this bush that is "farther than far." By living in the isolated and wild bush, the nomadic Fulan who herd cattle, sheep, and goats jealously guard their freedom (see Riesman 1977). The Bella nomads continue to transport salt from the desert to Sahelian markets.

At this point in the film Rouch has established that the bush is a wild and perilous space, unfit for most human populations. The people of the past lived there as hunters, but when the bush is harmonious, as they could make it, all creatures have their own notes and there is balance.

As long as the bush is in harmony, the Fulan and Bella find it a peaceful place. Yet sometimes that harmony is shattered—by lions looking for an easy meal. And so the stage is set for high drama in *The Lion Hunters*, for lions have been attacking Fulan cattle. In these circumstances the Fulan send for the *gow*, the hunters of Yatakala, men who arm themselves only with bows and arrows to battle renegade lions.

From the wild bush Rouch transports us to the cultivated field, field, where a man is harvesting millet. The so-called Gow people, we are told, are sedentary millet farmers who live in villages like Yatakala. In Songhay, however, *gow* designates hunter, and that is all. The gow, like the sohanci or the sorko, are a small subgroup of Songhay who, through long initiation, become hunters. They do not constitute a society.

But the contrast of these sedentary people who live in villages to the animals and spirits of the bush is an important one; it increases the dramatic tension of the film. The gow are dignified men, proud of their heritage and their accomplishments. Rouch introduces us to them: Tahiru Koro, the chief of the hunters; Sidiki, Tahiru's younger brother; Yaya, another of Tahiru's brothers; Issiakia Moussa, a monochord violinist who is the best shot; Issiakia's brother Wangari, who is well versed in the gow oral tradition; Bilabia, the best tracker among the hunters; and Ali, an apprentice who has yet to prove his courage.

What must hunters do to hunt lions? First they must prepare their weapons. Rouch follows the hunters as they select wood for their bows and reeds for arrow shafts. We then go to the village smith, where they purchase arrow points. When the hunters harvest from the forest the wood for their bows, they salute the bush, always a dangerous space for the Songhay. They challenge the bush to combat. To protect themselves, the hunters tie small magic pouches to their bows, filled with powders that ally them to spirits that protect them from the forces of the bush. These spirits constitute much of the hunters' power.

Their real weapon, however, is the poison (*naagji*) they paint on their arrow points. The poison is prepared ritually from a carefully husbanded supply that they replenish every four years, traveling some three hundred kilometers to the south to find the strapotus tree. They open the tree's pods, gather the poisonous seeds, and bring them back to Yatakala. Now ready, this small band of gow leaves the village and enters the bush, where wild and wicked things abound.

Here Rouch uses considerable cinematic skill to portray the drama of a rare Songhay ceremony. Here past becomes present; outside the village on the fringe of the bush, fantasy becomes reality. The hunters create a "magic circle" (*kelle*) like the one depicted on the rock drawing seen earlier. Of all the hunters participating in this rite, only men dressed in *bentia*, the goatskin shorts worn by the men of the past, are allowed inside the circle, where they will brew the poison. As the griot knows, the past infuses its force into Songhay practices of the present.

The rite begins. The officiants, Tahiru and Sidiki, build a fire within a tripod of three rocks, on which they balance a large pot. Into the pot they pour water that has been drawn by a jealous, spiteful woman—to make the water boil with spite. When the water boils, they add the poison seeds. Tahiru Koro, the chief hunter and master brewer, mixes the simmering portion with a long-handled ladle. As he stirs he recites an incantation, which describes in graphic terms how the woman's poison is more wicked than the man's poison, how the poison will make the lion's blood boil and its body burn, how the lion will vomit and die. At the end of his recitation, Tahiru Koro "becomes" the afflicted lion, falls over, and "dies."

When the first batch of poison is ready, the hunters bring broken pottery into which their portion of the poison is ladled. They retire to a tokay tree under which they will brush the poison onto their arrows, covering the point and the contiguous part of the reed shaft. The seeds are conserved to brew a second, less potent batch of poison. The first batch, brushed on arrows, is reserved for lion hunting.

The hunters sit under the tokay tree, coating their arrows with poison and commenting on how strong this particular batch is. Meanwhile Niandu, an old Zerma diviner from Wezebangu, a village about twenty kilometers east of Yatakala, throws his cowrie shells, which see the past and the future. He sees a bad sign.

"Don't go, hunters," he tells the group. "The path is bad. One among you has spoiled the hunt."

This sign troubles the hunters, for the cowrie shells never lie. What will happen to them? Will they be killed by a lion? Will the soul of the lion drive them crazy or kill one of their sons? Issiakia takes up his monochord violin and plays hunter's music. Wangari sings about the past glories of the gow hunters. Although the music encourages the hunters, they nevertheless suspend the hunt.

Five years pass. The lion, which the hunters call Anasara, or the European, has been killing Fulan cows, goats, and sheep. They know it is the same lion because it rarely eats the domesticated animals it kills. Rouch receives a telegram from Tahiru Koro announcing the death of the hunter who years earlier had spoiled the hunt. His death means that the path of the hunt is open. Rouch returns to Yatakala with his film crew of Lam Ibrahim, Damoré Zika, Tallou Mouzourane, and Idrissa Maiga.

The hunters prepare themselves. A possession ceremony is held, and a spirit of the bush, Takum, urges them on. The path is clear, Takum says; the hunt will be good. Protected, the hunters return to the bush that is farther than far.

In short order they learn of more lion devastation. The Fulan chief tells the hunters that the lion kills every day and has wounded his favorite cow. The hunters bury their iron traps several inches deep, covering them with leaves and sand. If the unsuspecting lion steps on one, the trap will snap shut and cut into its leg.

They trap a civet cat and a hyena to test their poison arrows and discover that the poison dispatches them rapidly. The hunters then cut the throats of these animals, transforming bush meat into village meat. Killed but not tainted by the poison, the civet cat and hyena are consumed off camera. Tahiru Koro, the chief of the hunters, recites incantations to neutralize the hyena's soul, because in Songhay it is linked to that of a witch.

There are more lion attacks during the night. The hunters set more traps, leaving bait for the hungry lions. Again they wait for results. The next morning, they find that a young male lion has been trapped. He is agitated but immobilized by the trap. Tahiru Koro speaks to the lion. His words seem to calm the beast. He tells the lion to be brave and to die quickly. Issiakia takes aim and shoots the lion. As Wangari sings praises to the poison, the lion growls, vomits, and dies. To liberate the dead lion's soul, Tahiru taps its head three times. The Fulan praise the skill and bravery of the hunters, but the work is not yet completed, for the hunters realize that Anasara has not yet been captured. They set their traps again and wait through the night.

The next day the Fulan inform the hunters that they have trapped a large lioness, the mate of Anasara. The situation is dangerous, however, for the furious lioness is held only by the toe. The hunters approach. They begin to chant and shoot their arrows. Then, pandemonium. Freeing herself from the trap, the lioness attacks one of the Fulan, but she dies before she can maul the herdsman, who turns out to be the Fulan chief. Here Rouch stops filming, but his tape recorder captures the horrible moment in sound.

The hunt is now spoiled, for a lion has wounded a person. Tahiru Koro taps the lioness's head three times to liberate her soul. He fills her bodily orifices with magic powders to protect human beings from the forces of the bush. One of the hunters retrieves the arrow that killed the lioness—one of Issiakia's. They return to the Fulan camp, where Damoré Zika gives the wounded Fulan chief a series of injections.

Tahiru Koro berates the Fulan for failing to recognize the seriousness of the lion hunt. "It is not a game," he scolds the Fulan chief. He also tells him that he must have done some terrible things if a lion decided first to wound his favorite cow and then to attack him.

The body of the lioness is loaded onto the bed of a truck, and the hunters return to Yatakala singing their own praise songs. They do not return to the village but go to a large tamarind tree under which generations of hunters have celebrated their victories over the bush. There the people of Yatakala gather. Old women sing praises to the hunters, to Tahiru Koro, to Issiakia, to Wangari, to Bilabia, to Bedari, and to Ali, who can now call himself a hunter. With the slitting of the throat the lioness is transformed from taboo bush meat to edible village meat, and the meat is divided among the townspeople. The lion's heart is reserved for Tahiru Koro, who will dry it in the sun and sell it in powdered form. This potent powder will bring high prices in Ghana and the Ivory Coast. Lion heart is a principal ingredient in some of the magic potions prepared by Songhay magicians.

Rouch's camera follows the dispersal of the meat-carrying crowd. A group of men and boys, however, assembles on the dry banks of the Garuol River. There the hunters tell the story of the hunt. They talk about the evasive Anasara and his dead mate, about the hyena and the civet cat, about how Tahiru calmed the young lion, about the undeniable power of the poison.

At the end of the film Rouch takes us back to the beginning. We have returned to the mud-brick room where the story has been told. Issiakia plays his violin, but now angel-faced little Ali is asleep. The little boy has heard about men who hunt lions with bows and arrows. But the winds have swept time away; the world has changed. Little Ali will hear stories of the hunters, but he will never hunt lions himself.

STORYMAKING IN YATAKALA

After seeing the film *Bataille sur le grand fleuve* in Ayoru in 1954, Tahiru Koro invited Rouch and his friends to Yatakala to film his group of lion hunters. One film, as Rouch likes to recount, gave birth to another, but the gestation period was several years. Rouch did not begin filming in Yatakala until May 1957, during the peak of the hot season in Songhay.

From the very beginning this film presented difficulties. Rouch filmed *Les magiciens de Wanzerbe* in one month. *The Lion Hunters* took seven years to complete. It was extraordinarily hot that May, a dusty heat that sapped the energy of both hunters and filmmakers. In the dusty heat, Rouch filmed the poison ceremony. The poison was good, strong, potent, but Niandu, the Zerma diviner from Wezebangu,

Rouch and company during the filming of *The Lion Hunters*.
Comité du Film Ethnographique.

said one of the hunters had spoiled the hunt, so Tahiru Koro suspended it. In Songhay it is said that when one's path is spoiled, one should return home.

Rouch returned to Yatakala and fell ill. He was nauseated, weak, and feverish. On the first day of his illness the children of his Yatakala neighborhood saw Rouch and said: "The white man is pissing." On the second day, they again saw Rouch and said: "The white man is sleeping." On the third day, they saw Rouch once again and said: "The white man is dead."

For Rouch, it was time to leave Yatakala. Damoré Zika drove him to Tera, where the resident French doctor told him to strip and sit under the shower; Rouch had a severe case of heatstroke. Eventually he was taken to the hospital in Niamey, where he spent a month recuperating (Echard and Rouch 1988, interview 8).

During the ensuing years, Rouch filmed bits and pieces of the film. The hunters would send him telegrams. He would gather his crew and truck to Yatakala and the bush that is farther than far. After many such trips, Rouch completed the film in 1964.

The film received widespread critical acclaim. In 1965 *The Lion*

Hunters received the Golden Lion award at the Venice Film Festival. In 1967 Georges Sadoul wrote that *The Lion Hunters* placed Rouch among the greatest French filmmakers (Sadoul 1967, 114). For Sylvie Pierre, *The Lion Hunters* is Rouch's masterpiece: "The effort, the success, the masterpiece of Jean Rouch in *The Lion Hunters* stems from the long patience of a filmmaker who through his fascination took the time to wonder how, through its differences, reality has the right to enchant eye and mind" (Pierre 1967, 66). Pierre also praises the poetic evocation of the lion hunt framed as a child's story. For her the genius of the film lies in its fusion of science and poetry.

These major reviewers, however, miss two essential points. First, they fail to consider the philosophical ramifications of the film. Rouch never pretends that the hunt reproduces what Paul Watzlawick (1977) calls the "really real." We are continually reminded that the film is an instance of "cine-reality." From the beginning, we see that the film is indeed a joint effort. We see Rouch's assistants. We see Land Rovers and trucks. We see telegrams inviting the film crew to Yatakala. During the lion attack, Rouch stops filming but continues to record sounds. We see Damoré Zika ministering to the victim of the lion attack. Here, then, is an implicit critique of documentary realism. Second, the critics do not consider the ethnographic significance of the film; it is much more than an evocative child's story that critiques the theory of cinematic realism.

WORDS AND ACTION

The critics, none of whom are anthropologists, let alone specialists on the Songhay, fail to grasp the ethnographic density and anthropological significance of *The Lion Hunters*. Rouch, too, is silent on this point. For me it is a film in which the fuzzy boundary between fact and fiction is crossed many times. It is also a film with great ethnographic detail. The scene in which the hunters brew poison, for example, is a substantial depiction of sympathetic magic. Tahiru Koro, the chief of the hunters, pretends to die as would a lion wounded by a poison arrow. As the man "dies," the hunters recite the poison incantation. The text is powerfully poetic. Like all Songhay magic incantations, as Rouch demonstrates in *Religion* (see chap. 5), this one begins with a genealogical recitation—a genealogy of power, for power and the secret knowledge that embodies it come from the distant past, from the people of the past. Mention of the ancestors transfers power from past to present.

Later in the film a comparable ritual is enacted each time the hunters shoot an animal. They salute the animal, especially if it is a lion. They shoot it with their poison arrows. They recite their poison incantation as the animal dies. They protect themselves from the animal's soul by tapping its head three times and by filling its orifices with special powders made from tree bark and vines.

This recurrent scene in *The Lion Hunters* illustrates the power of words in the Songhay cosmos, the theme of one chapter in Rouch's *Religion*. For Songhay, words are not neutral elements that *contain* meaning; rather, words carry forces that can alter a substance or change behavior. For Songhay, words have actual might; their power helps control the overwhelming forces of the bush, which, lest we forget, is a very dangerous place. Words exist, then, in and of themselves; they have force (Stoller 1984, 1989b).

Once again Rouch confronts his viewers with a disquieting existential issue: Can words alter behavior? Or to put the matter more bluntly, Can words heal, maim, or kill? (See Stoller 1989b; Favret-Saada 1981.) The Songhay view conforms to that of Western religion, but it contrasts with that of Western science. In the scientific view, words are neutral instruments, tools we use to convey meaning. And yet the notion of the magical word has troubled Western thinkers for a very long time. What is the relation of word and action? Stanley Tambiah (1968) suggests that in *Totem and Taboo* Freud was speculating that the deed preceded the word. Linguistic philosophers, by contrast, suggest that in performative utterances the word *is* deed (Austin 1962; Searle 1968). The writing on word and deed, however, does not answer an essential ethnographic question: Why is it that when a person is asked why a particular ritual or magic rite is effective, the invariable answer is, "The power is in the words"? What then is the relation of words to action? How can words protect the hunters from the bush, a place of great danger?

A partial answer is provided by Walter Ong, who writes that in aural-oral societies, words are regarded as powerful. Words are bound up with action, "for they are always sound." More specifically, in nonliterate societies, "it is thus eminently credible that words can be used to achieve an effect such as weapons or tools can achieve. Saying evil things of another is thought to bring him direct physical harm. This attitude toward words in more or less illiterate societies is an anthropological commonplace, but the connection of the attitude with the nature of sound and the absence of writing has not until recently begun to grow clear" (Ong 1967, 113).

Throughout Africa, and elsewhere in the world, the sounds of words are believed to carry potent powers (Riesman 1977; Lienhardt 1961). Songhay believe that the words of the poison incantation must be recited when an arrow reaches its mark. As with other essentials of hunting lore, the words are passed down from father to son, father to son; the sound of these words enters the wounded lion just as deeply and devastatingly as the arrows, propelling the poison through its body. They bring the lion's blood to a deadly boil and make the animal vomit its death. They protect the hunters from the lion's soul, which seeks retribution for a sudden and violent death.

MAGIC AND THE EVERYDAY

In *The Lion Hunters* Rouch is not content merely to challenge us with profound questions of human existence. His film also forces us to reflect on how we categorize experience, how we re-create our sociocultural universe. From classical philosophy through the Enlightenment to the contemporary era, Western thinkers have dichotomized the world. By expelling the poets and dramatists from his republic, Plato distinguished between art and philosophy, a distinction that would create a boundary between science and the humanities. A cursory glance at the administrative structures of many universities reveals that the classical separation of the sciences and the humanities is still relevant.

During the Enlightenment many classical distinctions were refined. Descartes separated mind from body. British philosophers broadened the chasm between knowledge and sensibility, reason and sentiment. In France Saint-Simon and his student, Auguste Comte, carefully sorted subjective data gathering from objective theory building. Comte's program of theory building in the social sciences is fully realized by his intellectual heir, Emile Durkheim, who in his monumental *The Elementary Forms of the Religious Life* distinguishes between sacred and profane, two distinct sociocultural domains. In the profane realm of everyday life, human beings perform routine tasks that do not inspire them to reflect on the social groups they belong to. In the sacred domain, they engage in rituals during which group emblems or symbols "objectify" society. In the sacred context, Durkheim tells us, individuals sense the social whole to which they belong.

There are a good many closet Durkheimians among sociologists and anthropologists of religion. Jean Rouch is not one of them, for a film like *The Lion Hunters* demonstrates that the sacred and profane are not discrete categories in Songhay. On the contrary, Rouch shows that the Songhay worlds of social life (the profane) and magic (the sacred) are inseparable.

To hunt in the Songhay bush, a profane task, the hunters must engage in a variety of "sacred" activities. To kill lions, they must empower their poison in a ceremony held once every four years. During the ceremony, incantations invoke the ancestors and the spirits of the bush. When poison arrows reach their targets, incantations must also be recited so that the poison will "work." Before leaving on the hunt, hunters seek protection. They consult a diviner and stage a possession ceremony during which Takum, a spirit of the bush, is beckoned. She will tell them if their path is a good one. Forewarning is but one measure of protection the hunters seek; they also attach magic pouches to their bows to guard them from lion attacks.

Critics might suggest that the hunters of Yatakala are exceptions to Durkheim's pattern and that Rouch's film so dramatizes the "magical" aspects of the hunt that it is yet another example of Western exoticism (see Predal 1982). In Songhay, however, most people take metaphysical precautions to protect their quotidian activities (farming, cooking, gathering water, hunting, working in the office). Human beings are metaphorical hunters who are themselves hunted by their rivals, their enemies. This practice is not limited by divisions of social class in contemporary Niger. Not only illiterate peasants in Wanzerbe but educated civil servants in Niamey, Niger's capital city, wear amulets and make offerings to spirits. On occasion university professors as well as lion hunters eat kusu, which protects people from their adversaries in the village as well as the bush (see Stoller 1989b). Although *The Lion Hunters* depicts the fading world of a fraction of the Songhay population, it offers a glimpse of the hidden world of Songhay magic, a world of great contemporary relevance.

In *Les magiciens de Wanzerbe* Rouch confronts viewers with philosophic imponderables: How can people carry metal chains in their stomachs? How can they defy death? These questions challenge taken-for-granted scientific and religious ideas. In *The Lion Hunters* Rouch continues to question our philosophic assumptions. Beyond the story line of a group of men hunting a murderous lion with bows and arrows, the film challenges the applicability of two central themes of Western philosophy. The first of these is the belief in the instrumental neutrality of words; the second is the Durkheimian notion that the social can be divided into distinct categories, sacred and profane.

And so, woven into this "child's story" are themes of great philosophic importance. This artistic elegance is the essence of Rouch's poetry. In the *The Lion Hunters* Rouch becomes a cine-poet who demonstrates the veracity of the Songhay proverb, "Every power has its incantation."

CHAPTER EIGHT
Jaguar

Kureeje danaw si mooru nga guusu.
The blind mongoose is never far from its hole.
—Songhay proverb

The Songhay say that "the blind mongoose is never far from its hole." Like that mongoose, Songhay travelers never stray far from their villages. Even if they go to Kumasi, they are thinking about home—about their villages, their families, and their heroic, gift-laden return to Songhay at the end of their seasonal sojourn.

In the first two films we have considered, Rouch sings the praises of people in an isolated corner of Songhay. The films tell stories of rites that, for the most part, are no longer practiced. In this chapter we turn from Songhay religion and its philosophical consequences to a more sociological theme, the seasonal migrations of Songhay men to the Guinea coast. In chapter 4, we considered why so many young Songhay men traveled so far in search of work; here we shall see how Rouch transforms the empirical findings from *Migrations au Ghana* into a transcendent narrative of "ethnofiction."

Thousands of Songhay men have stories to tell about their youthful trips to the Guinea coast. They are stories of adventure, of change, of fear, of otherness; they are stories of young men journeying into the unknown, not unlike the story of anthropological fieldwork. Although Rouch's writings on migration consider this culturally sanctioned wanderlust as a cultural determinant of Songhay seasonal migration to Ghana and the Ivory Coast, they do not examine in great detail the sociocultural ramifications of economic displacement. What happened to these migratory laborers from Niger and Mali? How did their coastal experiences expand their sociocultural horizons? What happened to them when they returned home? In *Jaguar,* Rouch probes the inner cultural and psychological dimensions of these voyages of dis-

131

Damoré Zika, Lam Ibrahim, and Douma Beso in *Jaguar*. J. Rouch,
Comité du Film Ethnographique.

covery. In this sense *Jaguar* is a film variation of Lévi-Strauss's classic
Tristes tropiques. Like Lévi-Strauss, the protagonists leave home,
travel to a new world (Ghana), and return fundamentally changed;
they are new men in their old world. Western readers expect Lévi-
Strauss to be transformed by his experience among Brazilian others.
Do we expect the same transformation of three "others"—formerly
"objects" of ethnographic observation—who journey to Ghana to discover their own others?

TRISTES TROPIQUES, AFRICAN STYLE

Rouch begins *Jaguar* by introducing the three protagonists. We see Damoré Zika, a Zerma "bandit" tax collector, riding his horse Tarzan.
We see Lam Ibrahim, a Fulan herder, following his cattle. We see Illo
Goudel'ize, a Niger River fisherman, paddling his dugout. The bustling market at Ayoru is an ethnic crossroads that brings together these
young men of varying social experience. Here they notice a number of
men who have just returned from the Gold Coast. Despite their ethnic

differences, the three share a common desire: to leave the confines of their dusty village and seek the unknown, a familiar literary theme. They decide to embark on their own adventure. Lam sells his cow; Damoré appoints someone to give the market people tax receipts in his absence.

In Songhay, any journey away from one's natal village is fraught with peril. One must cross uninhabited territory—the bush—which, as we saw in chapter 7, is a dangerous place. On a journey one also encounters strangers, some friendly, most potentially hostile. For any journey, one must be prepared and protected.

Before beginning their great trip to the Gold Coast, the three protagonists seek assurance about their path. Lam, who is a pious Muslim, goes to a Muslim cleric and asks for the *alfatia*, the prayer of protection. Damoré, the grandson of Kalia, head of the Niamey sorko, attends a possession ceremony. There the spirits tell him to find a vulture's beak and feet to protect him during his travels.

The trio leaves Ayoru for Wanzerbe to consult a diviner, who in this case is none other than Rouch's principal Wanzerbe informant, Mossi Bana. Mossi throws his cowrie shells for the three young men and says their path is bad; he asks them to return that evening. He throws the shells again and foresees accidents and sickness. They can avoid these misfortunes, Mossi tells them, if they separate at the first crossroads after crossing the border.

Although Rouch filmed *Jaguar* between 1957 and 1964, travelers continue to consult diviners before a long trip. In Wanzerbe in 1984, a young man about to travel to Nigeria not only consulted the local diviner but had his uncle, a resident sorcerer, prepare some *daareyan kusu*, a magic paste that, when eaten, protects the traveler from bus accidents. In the summer of 1987 scores of young travelers asked Adamu Jenitongo, the late sohanci of Tillaberi, to "read" their paths and provide protection.

Given their metaphysical bill of health, the three protagonists of *Jaguar* begin their walk southward toward the sea, following old slave and warrior routes. These routes, which are mentioned in Rouch's *Migrations au Ghana*, take them southeastward through what is now Burkina Faso. Gradually the scenery shifts, and so do the people. From Songhay, a dry, rocky desert spotted with thorn trees, we enter the vastness of the savanna. Here the path is lined with elephant grass taller than a man. Here are towering cottonwood trees. Here are small black people, the Gurmantche, who file their teeth to sharp points and whose young women wear only coarse cotton wraparounds. Continuing the march southward, the trio enters Togo: vast rolling grasslands, tall trees, clogged markets, and intoxicating millet beer for sale along with stews made from "bush" meat. The people here recognize our heroes as men from the North, but they do not know how to talk to them. And yet the savanna peoples are hospitable; they give our wayfarers food, drink, and shelter.

Then they arrive in isolated, mountainous Somba country. The water is abundant but is not good. Here our heroes experience for the first time THE OTHER The other is neither European from France nor African from the Sahel. The other is the Somba. Coal black, carrying spears, and adorned only with penis sheaths, the Somba men present themselves in an unembarrassed natural state. For our three modestly dressed travelers, meeting the Somba marks their first experience of the primitive. How can people not wear clothes? How can people eat bush meat? How can people eat dogs? Damoré and Lam marvel, "But they are all completely nude." Are they really men?

At the Somba market they see many, many dogs, and women who smoke pipes. They also witness a ritual dance in which naked men form a circle and move their hips rhythmically back and forth; their sheathed penises flop up and down. With that image in mind, our baffled protagonists leave Somba land. Damoré remarks: "These are gentle people. We shouldn't mock the Somba just because they are nude. God wanted them this way." Like Lévi-Strauss in *Tristes tropiques,* our protagonists finally meet pristine others only to discover they cannot communicate with them.

As they move farther and farther south, the vegetation thickens. The trees are even taller; the earth takes on a copper hue; the moist air weighs heavily on their shoulders. The people here are shorter than the Somba and use a language that sounds more like song than speech.

And then they see it for the first time: the beach and beyond it "the river that does not end." They run out on the beach. Damoré plays in the waves, for sorko like him are "of the water." At first the surf scares Lam, for herders like him are "of the land." They walk along the beach until they come to Lome and the Gold Coast border.

Instead of identity papers for the border crossing, our heroes have amulets. At the border, Damoré brazenly attempts to cross into the Gold Coast. A policeman stops him. Then he sneaks behind the border post and easily enters the Gold Coast. Lam and Illo follow. At the first crossroads in the Gold Coast, the three young men separate. Lam goes off with a Fulan herdsman headed for Kumasi. Illo and Damoré go to Accra.

Rouch's camera follows Damoré to colonial Accra, where he attempts to find his compatriots. We see traffic, the bottle-washing mar-

ket in which Anzuru people work (Anzuru is a region north of Tillaberi in Niger), the market where tin cans are sold, which is dominated
by people from Zermagunda (a region northeast of Niamey in Niger).
With so much traffic, one must be careful crossing streets in Accra.
Finally Damoré comes to a lumberyard run by Songhay from Gotheye.
Yacouba, the head of the lumberyard, hires him as a laborer, but since
Damoré is literate, he quickly promotes him to foreman. Damoré
counts pieces of lumber. He becomes *un petit chef,* "a little chief," and
wears sunglasses, which are very "jaguar," very "with it."

Illo becomes a *kaya-kaya,* a laborer in the port of Accra. He is paid
a paltry two shillings and sixpence for a day of work. Illo complains
that he has to lift five heavy sacks at a time. He is tired and doesn't
make enough money to eat well.

Meanwhile Lam leads a herd of cattle to the Kumasi slaughter-
house. This work is difficult for Lam, who as a Fulan holds cattle in
great reverence: one doesn't walk with cows only to march them to
their deaths. Lam asks his compatriot for his pay. With his ten pounds
he buys a *boubou,* a billowing robe. He puts aside his coarse herder's
tunic until the trip home and joins the world of the Kumasi market.
The market is far larger than in most towns in Niger, and Lam tells us
he must run to see it all. Lam then becomes a *nyama-nyam'ize,* "a son
of disorder," which means he sells a little of everything: perfume,
clothing, combs.

Damoré fares well in Accra. As a foreman, he aids his boss, who has
both a car and a large house in Accra's "Lagostown." Rouch films Damoré as he struts down the streets of Accra. His hair is coiffed, and he
smokes cigarettes and wears sunglasses. As he strolls he watches every-
body around him, especially the young girls. Damoré is very gallant;
he is "cool"; he is "jaguar."

The film now moves between the lives of Lam, Illo, and Damoré.
Lam leaves for Accra to sell blankets. En route he happens upon a gold
mine, where he runs into Duma Beso, a gold miner from Niger. Lam
says that Duma is strong as a bull, that he has a hippo's head and
doesn't care about shoes. We see the brutish Duma walking barefoot,
holding his shoes in his hand. The miners spend eight-hour shifts underground and are paid a pittance. The gold they mine is shaped into
bricks that are stamped and sent off to London. Duma doesn't like working in the mine and decides to follow his countryman Lam to Accra.

Meanwhile in Accra, Illo sleeps in an abandoned dugout. By contrast, Damoré drinks at the "Weekend in California" bar and goes to
horse races. On Sunday, his day off, he wanders along the streets of
Accra. He lingers at the door of a church, waiting for the beautiful

girls to exit. He happens upon a Ga (the majority population of Accra) possession ceremony and an electoral campaign rally for Kwame Nkrumah's Congress People's party. He sees Nkrumah and his associates in front of the Assembly. Dressed in their *kente* robes, they seem regal. Damoré finds these Ghanaian notables *bien nourri*, "well nourished." Damoré and Illo meet on the street, and they repair to Illo's dugout. Damoré talks about his drinking exploits. Ever the pious Muslim, Illo suggests that maybe it is time to leave Accra. They send a telegram to Lam announcing their imminent arrival.

Having returned to Kumasi, Lam continues to sell his *nyama-nyama*, but he takes time off to meet Damoré and Illo at the train depot. Always the promoter, Damoré enters the Kumasi market and reorganizes Lam's boutique. They create a corporation: "Petit à Petit l'Oiseau Fait Son Bonnet" ("Little by Little the Bird Makes Its Bonnet"). In the market, they talk about the ongoing construction of a mosque in Kumasi, the result of the increasing power of the Ghanaian Islamic party.

With the infusion of Damoré's enthusiastic creativity, Petit à Petit expands its inventory. They sell cameras, food, medicines, alarm clocks, and even Michelin maps. They create a "jaguar" boutique. In so doing, Duma, Illo, Damoré, and Lam all become "jaguar."

But it is time to leave the Gold Coast. Rouch's voice cuts into what had been the commentary of Lam and Damoré. He says that these four young men journeyed to the Gold Coast in search of money, but also to find adventure. Like scores of other young Nigeriens, they followed the path of their ancestors, the nineteenth-century Zerma mercenaries Alfa Hano, Gazari, and Babatu, who eventually became the military masters of Gurunsi in the north of the Gold Coast. In the 1950s the heroes were economic warriors like Lam, Damoré, Duma, and Illo. Like the returning heroes of the previous century, they brought back gifts, amazing stories of their experiences, and incredible lies.

Rouch's camera now focuses on the return. Will they have enough money to pay customs taxes and the necessary bribes as well as their taxi fares? In Po, they enter French territory and take French trucks toward Niger. It is the rainy season, and the laterite roads are muddy. Finally they arrive in Ayoru. They say hello to beautiful women and speak a little English. Lam dreams of marrying the beautiful Howa. They give away everything they have brought with them and return to their lives in Ayoru. Duma cultivates his millet field; Illo returns to fishing. Lam finds his herds in good shape; he shields his head from the intense Sahelian sun with his Bergdorf beer umbrella. Damoré concludes the film simply by saying, "The women of Niger are beautiful."

These migrants have returned from far away with rich memories. They remember tall savanna grasses and immense cottonwood trees, meals shared with the pointy-toothed Gurmantche and the beer-drinking people in Sansane-Mango. They clambered up the mountains to Somba land to see truly "primitive" people who danced naked without embarrassment. They go home as men who have played in the ocean surf and worked in the Kumasi market—as "big men" who have stories to tell and European goods to give away. At last back in the dusty peace and tranquillity of their river town, they are forever changed by "the great adventure" of their voyage of discovery. Perhaps they will return the next year and the next year until their wanderlust is sated. Perhaps they will remain home in Niger, filled with the memory of their adventure in the Gold Coast.

IMPROVISATIONAL CINEMA

Damoré Zika conceived the idea of filming *Jaguar* in Ayoru in 1954 when he saw himself on the screen for the first time. He said, "We are going to play." Rouch, Damoré, and Lam knew two things about the film: the beginning and the end. The film, they agreed, would begin and end in Ayoru. As for the rest of the scenario, they knew nothing at all except that upon their return from the Gold Coast they would give away all their treasures: potlatch, African style (Echard and Rouch 1988, interview 7).

How to begin? Like all Nigeriens who travel to the Guinea coast, our trio seeks protection and advice. From Muslim clerics and possession priests they receive protection. From Mossi Bana of Wanzerbe they receive not only advice but a scenario as well. To avoid accidents and sickness, Mossi tells them, they must separate at the first crossroads after the border.

In this way Rouch, Lam, Illo, and Damoré set out for the Gold Coast in Rouch's Land Rover. They follow the old slave routes and film whatever pleases them. In Somba country, Rouch and his camera follow Damoré and Lam, who are the instigators of the action. Farther south in Togo, they drive up to a beautiful red bridge. Damoré and Lam have never seen a red bridge before. Why not shoot a sequence with the red bridge? The red bridge becomes part of *Jaguar* (Echard and Rouch 1988, interview 7).

And so it continues throughout the film. This sense of play, of *pourquoi pas,* accounts for the joy the film conveys. Rouch was replicating the *pourquoi pas* method of his fieldwork in 1947–48. But one problem remained. Rouch shot the film without sound; there were no synchronous sound cameras in 1954–55. How could the commentary be consistent with the playful, joyful ethos of the images? Rouch pondered this problem for some time. In 1957 a colleague from the Film Unit of Ghana invited him to use a sound studio in Accra. Rouch asked Damoré and Lam to watch the *Jaguar* footage and talk. Rouch recorded their image-driven talk. In two days they had a sound commentary that worked marvelously well, for the text was as playful as the film itself.

Rouch's *pourquoi pas* cinema gives *Jaguar* a lyrical quality that, according to the French film critics, captivates audiences. One critic writes what the Songhay had already figured out, that Rouch is a storyteller. "*Jaguar* tells us that what interests [Rouch] is fiction derived from real elements. This introduces myth into reality" (Gauthier 1972, 198–99). Another critic called *Jaguar* an inspiring film, lyrical, filled with feeling and human discovery (Clezio 1972, 15–18). Jean Collet gives voice in his review of *Jaguar* to a Rouchian metacommentary against the dehumanizing tendencies of the human sciences:

> Rouch . . . is a man of science. But when he records the commentary of his films, he has the voice of Jean Cocteau, the voice of a poet. . . .
>
> When he was filming *Jaguar,* he hung a book [from his car's rearview mirror]. It was a very serious book on the migrations to Ghana, full of statistics and numbers. (And today when I compare this book with *Jaguar,* I notice that *Jaguar* provides the best representation because the book lacks a human dimension.) (Collet 1967, 1)

Here I suggest that Rouch, like Lam and Damoré, is playing to an audience of cinephiles; for as I suggested earlier, he *is* a serious scholar of history and anthropology. For him ethnographic data, even of the quantitative sort, are important ingredients in the interactive formula from which he creates the human dimension of his films. For any reader of *Migrations au Ghana,* this fact is evident.

THE SOCIOLOGY OF DISPLACEMENT

Jaguar is first and foremost about social transformation. In the film Rouch poses questions about social change. What happens to young men who travel beyond the boundaries of their cultural experience? What happens to these seasonal migrants as individuals? How are their social roles transformed once they return to the Sahel and Niger?

In this respect *Jaguar* is the filmic extension of Rouch's research on migration conducted in the early 1950s. As we saw in chapter 4, much of his research focused on the economic activities of the migrant groups and how they created their own social institutions in the Gold Coast and the Ivory Coast. Such Rouch films as *Moi, un noir* consider the psychosocial trials and tribulations of young Nigeriens living in Abidjan. *Jaguar* focuses less on the social conditions of the "Coast" and more on the experience of seasonal migration.

In his writings on migration, Rouch is strictly empirical. He presents a vast array of data with little interpretation. His *Migrations au Ghana* is essentially a report, a sociological monograph. In *Jaguar* Rouch plunges into the depths of sentiment, impressions; he exercises artistic license. *Jaguar* is what Rouch calls cine-fiction, a fictitious story based on years of fact-gathering ethnographic research. In his film on seasonal migration Rouch explores the notion of the "voyage" in Songhay experience. He also shows how this veritable rite of passage—seasonal migration—transformed human beings from young men, adolescents, really, into worldly-wise travelers, adults who had seen and experienced the wonders of the Coast. And not to disappoint their compatriots, the travelers usually embellished their adventure stories. And so the story of the voyage is reinforced, becoming the foundation for contemporary myth. These are the stories of Rouch's story of migration, which he tells artfully through the imagery, narrative, and humor of his film.

IN SEARCH OF THE PRIMITIVE

The primary text of Rouch's film, the story of the story of seasonal migration, gives the film a purely sociological texture. This texture is obvious, but there is a philosophical dimension to the film that most the critics have missed. In *Jaguar* Rouch once again defies epistemological expectations by playing with the imagery of the primitive, a discourse of long-standing sociopolitical importance in the Western philosophical tradition. Conrad and Lévi-Strauss are not alone in this search for the pristine primitive; in *Jaguar* they are joined by three young men from Niger, people most Western-educated urbanites would consider "others"—"primitives" searching for their own "primitives."

During the past ten years it has become fashionable to write treatises that criticize our insensitivity toward the "other" and call attention to our epistemological failings. Following the direction of Foucault's *The Order of Things* and the example of Said's *Orientalism,* several recent writers (Clifford's *The Predicament of Culture* [1988], Price's *Primitive Art in Civilized Places* [1990], and Torgovnick's *Gone Primitive* [1990]) have demonstrated how primitivism has shaped our dehumanizing classifications of others in the arts, literature, history, and ethnography. In *Jaguar* Jean Rouch mounted a similar criticism against primitivism, but in the 1950s, when such a stance was most unfashionable.

Let us examine briefly the philosophical edifice Rouch confronts in *Jaguar.* Consider first that Rouch uses a literary motif, the quest, that dates from Greeks and is well represented in French and English literature. What makes Rouch's commentary particularly biting is that he chooses as his heroes men whom Western-educated urbanites would least expect to embark on such a voyage of discovery. Can we expect a petty official, a herdsman, and a fisherman from Ayoru to fill the famous shoes of Richardson's Joseph Andrews? Why is the answer an unequivocal no?

From antiquity to the present, writers from the civilized West have been fascinated by the "otherness of the primitive." This fascination, however, has usually produced textual exoticism. In writings about Africa, our focus here, textual exoticism is largely responsible for our current chauvinistic attitudes about Africans: these people are too limited to educate, too lazy to work, and too lusty to trust with *our* women.

The exoticism about Africa and Africans begins with Herodotus, who described Africans as "dog-eared men that had eyes in their chests." Early Muslim writers on Africa reinforced his imagery. Ibn Battuta (1307–77) maintained the distance between savage (African) and civilized (Muslim) through a discussion of cannibalism. "The pagans hadn't eaten him [a Muslim] solely because of his white color. They say eating a White man is unsafe because he isn't ripe" (Ibn Battuta 1966, 86). In the sixteenth century Mahmoud Kati, a pious Muslim historian (i.e., civilized) wrote that Sonni Ali Ber, king of the Songhay empire (r. 1493–1) was a tyrant out of control. "Sonni Ali Ber was such a tyrannical, hard-hearted king that he would throw an infant into a mortar and force its mother to pound it to death; the flesh was then given to horses" (Kati 1911, 82). According to Kati, Sonni Ali Ber also tortured pious Muslims by putting their heads in the fire until they died. Occasionally he would cut open the swollen stomach of a pregnant woman and pull out the fetus.

Once the "savagery" of African social life was widely known, it became necessary to explain it. Joseph de Gobineau (1967, 205–6) considered race the primary determinant of African savagery:

> The melanin variety is the humblest and lives at the bottom of the scale.
> The animalistic character etched in his loins imposes his destiny from

the minute of conception. His fate holds him within the most limited intellectual scope. However, he is not a pure and simple brute, this Negro with a narrow and sloped forehead, who bears in the middle section of his brain the signs of grossly powerful energies. If these thinking faculties are poor or even nil, he is possessed, by his desire and also by his will, of an often terrible intensity.

The imagery of uncontrolled savagery had its impact on more specific discussion of African (i.e., primitive) religion, which was first known as "idolatry," the absence of belief in a godhead. This absence of belief was thought to imprison the African in a state of unreasoned and uncontrolled madness (see Bousset 1836).

In the eighteenth century idolatry is transformed into fetishism, which Charles de Brosses defined as the worship of any given object, dedicated in ritual, that pleased a person or society. In fetishism, then, anything—trees, rivers, mountains, dolls, crocodiles—could be worshiped in a lavish style. The notion of the fetish, the paragon of unreason, became the frame within which the major nineteenth-century writers on Africa expressed their ideas about primitive African religions (see Bousset 1836).

In nineteenth-century texts heathenism and cannibalism also become important subjects that categorize the African as unreasoning and uncontrolled, a person living in savage circumstances. Describing the bounty of Manyema country, David Livingstone (1872, 529) was puzzled by Manyema cannibalism:

> It was puzzling to see why they should be cannibals. New Zealanders, we are told, were cannibals because they had killed all their gigantic birds, the moa, etc., and they were converted from the man-eating persuasion by the introduction of pigs; but the Manyema have plenty of pigs and other domestic animals, and yet they are cannibals. Into the reason for their cannibalism they do not enter. They say that human flesh is not equal to that of goats or pigs. It is saltish, and makes them dream of the dead.

Livingstone's explanation for this seemingly irrational choice? The Manyema were pagans who had not yet been converted to Christianity.

Livingstone also complained of the heathenism of Africans. Among the Makololo he was fed well and treated well but "had to endure dancing, roaring, and singing, the jesting, ancecdotes, grumbling, quarrelling, and murdering of these children of nature" (Livingstone 1872, 127).

Toward the end of the nineteenth century all these images of Africans and their primitive ways—cannibalism, gluttony, fetishism, and heathenism—are fused into the notion of "darkness," the absence of the light of European values. The ultimate text of darkness is of course Joseph Conrad's remarkable *Heart of Darkness,* first published in 1899. It is a novel in which the European, Kurtz, is stripped of his culture—his senses—and sucked into the void of African darkness, the antithesis of European light. Practitioners of religions lost in time, the savages of *Heart of Darkness* have abandoned distinct human qualities in the shadows of night. Conrad's savages live in a lost world infused with madness that lures the European inexorably into its barren heart. "We were cut off from the comprehensions of our surroundings; we glided past like phantoms, wondering and secretly appalled, as sane men would be before an enthusiastic outbreak in a madhouse. We could not understand because we were too far and could not remember because we were travelling in the night of the first ages, of those ages that are gone, leaving hardly a sign—and no memories" (Conrad 1971, 105).

The nineteenth-century search for the primitive led to an exotic imagery that reinforced European racism and denied "primitives" their humanity. As recent work in cultural studies documents, the discourse of primitivism is very much with us today; it has become a commodity (see Torgovnick 1990; Price 1990; MacCannell 1978).

In the face of this gargantuan beast, Jean Rouch made *Jaguar,* a story of the others' others, a narrative about a voyage of discovery. As such is it a fundamental challenge to the totalizing discourse of the primitive. In the film Rouch restores to the "primitives" their humanity. "Primitive" social life is varied, heterogeneous. Southern Ghanaians think Sahelians are barbarians, but we see northerners running a bustling lumberyard. Northern Sahelians, the descendants of Mande and Songhay princes, consider the southern Ghanaians barbaric slaves, but we see them together on Accra's streets and in Kumasi's market. Like Lévi-Strauss and Conrad, young primitives dream about adventure in the lands of others—others who are just as strange to Rouch's protagonists as they are to the viewer. Like Conrad, our young primitives construct stereotypes about others. Considered this way, *Jaguar* is a powerful critique of the European's long-standing racist and chauvinist search for the primitive and an affirmation of Montaigne's classic statement (1943) that "each man calls barbarous whatever is not his own practice."

ETHNOFICTION

In *Jaguar* some of Jean Rouch's filmic iconoclasm becomes evident. Damoré, Lam, and Rouch dreamed up the idea for *Jaguar*. Damoré, Lam, Illo, and Duma Beso are actors, playing roles. The divination of the sohanci Mossi Bana of Wanzerbe provides Rouch and company their scenario. In this way the company rolls through the West African countryside creating their *pourquoi pas* film, *comme ça*.

Such a film defies categorization. It is not a documentary that attempts to "capture" observed reality. By the same token, it is not a melodrama the filmmakers dreamed up to titillate our emotions. Rouch calls his creation "cine-fiction." Other critics have called films like *Jaguar* and *Moi, un noir* "ethnofiction." These films are stories based on laboriously researched and carefully analyzed ethnography. In this way Rouch uses creative license to "capture" the texture of an event, the ethos of lived experience. Here again Rouch defies expectation, throwing a monkey wrench into the carefully considered distinction between fiction and nonfiction, participation and observation, knowledge and sentiment. In the 1980s scholars in anthropology and cultural studies have deconstructed many of the dualistic distinctions that are fundamental to what they call logocentrism. Through the methods, composition, and realization of *Jaguar*, Rouch had already made many of the same arguments—filmically—in the 1950s.[1]

JAGUAR IN NIAMEY

In spring 1977 Cheryl Olkes and I went to the Centre Franco-Nigerien to see an outdoor screening of Rouch's *Jaguar*. Most of the audience was Nigerien—of several ethnic groups, from the polyglot chatter. The film began, but the babble persisted. Many of the spectators conversed with the images on the screen. Some recognized faces in the Ayoru market scene. Some saw friends who had since died. Some noticed people who had since moved to Niamey or to Lome. Some recognized a market, a village, a road where they had been. For older viewers images of the Kumasi market or the border post at Po triggered memories of their own adventures. For young viewers, *Jaguar* opened an entirely new world.

1. See chapter 12 of this book for more on Rouch's philosophical contributions. Rouch's major ethnofiction films are *Jaguar* (1967), *Moi, un noir* (1957), *La pyramide humaine* (1959), *Petit à petit* (1969), *Babatu, les trois conseils* (1975), and *Cocorico, Monsieur Poulet* (1974). For specific criticism of these films, see the extensive bibliography in Predal (1982), *Jean Rouch, un griot gaulois*," a special issue of *CinemAction* 17.

When images of the Somba appeared on the screen the audience exploded with laughter. Old and young alike pointed at the spear-carrying men dressed only in penis sheaths, at the women who smoked pipes. We heard one older man say in Songhay, "I was there. Those Somba eat dogs. I've never seen so many dogs." A younger man chuckled in Songhay: "They are completely nude; they are the true savages." This crowd of "primitives" in Niamey had found or redis-covered their own primitives.

CHAPTER NINE
Les Maîtres Fous

A ne n'inga bia weyna no nda weyna n'inga bia no.
He says that his shadow is the sun and that the sun is his shadow.
—Passage from a praise song to Dongo, deity of thunder and "father"
of the Hauka

In the Hausa language, *hauka* means "crazy." From the Songhay perspective the behavior of Hauka spirits is crazy, indeed. In the bodies
of their mediums, they handle fire, put their hands in pots of boiling
sauce, eat poisonous plants. Sometimes Hauka spirits vomit black ink;
saliva froths from their mouths. The Hauka also burlesque French colonial society. They often wear pith helmets and mock European behavior—especially French and British military behavior. This Hauka
mockery has led several scholars to consider the emergence of the
Hauka in Niger about 1925 as a form of cultural resistance to French
colonial rule (see Fugelstad 1975, 1983; Stoller 1984, 1989a). For
many Songhay this bravado stems from the Hauka's "kinship" with
the mercurial and ever-powerful Dongo, deity of thunder and adopted
son of Harakoy Dikko, goddess of Niger's waters.

Images of the Hauka captivated Jean Rouch when he first witnessed
them in 1946 during the filming of *Au pay des mages noirs*. His fascination with the Hauka spirits increased as his field studies advanced.
In 1953–54 he traveled to the Gold Coast to follow the trail to Accra,
the Mecca of the Hauka. When several audiences of Hauka mediums
saw the Hauka possession sequences of Rouch's *Bataille sur le grand
fleuve,* they arranged for him to film their yearly ritual in the rural
compound of the Hauka high priest, Mounkaiba. The result of that
invitation is *Les maîtres fous,* Rouch's most controversial film.

A Hauka spirit in the body of his medium, *Les maîtres fous*. J. Rouch, Comité du Film Ethnographique.

MASTERS OF FOLLY

Like *Jaguar, Les maîtres fous* is about the migration of Songhay and Zerma peoples from Niger to the colonial Gold Coast. Whereas *Jaguar* treats the journey as much as the destination, *Les maîtres fous* focuses exclusively on the sociocultural adaptations of the Zabrama (Songhay and Zerma) community in the Gold Coast.

From the initial frames there is music in *Les maîtres fous,* the sound of a brass band playing Ghanaian High Life music. Viewers then read a short contextualizing note about the meeting of North (Songhay, called Zabrama in the colonial Gold Coast) and South (the peoples of the Guinea coast), the confrontation of traditional and modern. From these abrasive confrontations is born a new religion, the Hauka cult.

Rouch shifts directly to the world that gave "birth" to the Hauka cult. In 1954, the year Rouch filmed *Les maîtres fous,* Accra was the capital of the colonial Gold Coast. In the film Accra is a cosmopolitan crossroads: Europeans drive their cars along narrow streets clogged with bicycles, pushcarts, buses, and trucks; Ghanaian brass bands play on the parade grounds; votaries of the Daughters of Jesus proclaim their faith in the streets; Hausa prostitutes parade downtown for higher wages; Yoruba dance to their own music, crossing the thoroughfare. This cacophony of sound, blur of movement, and confluence of peoples constitute the world to which the men from the North, Zerma and Songhay from Gao and Niamey, must adapt. Their adaptation, viewers are led to believe, takes the form of a new religion "not yet known to us." It is based on the Hauka, spirits that possess their mediums violently in demonstrating their otherworldliness: wide, wild eyes slice the darkness like beacons; foaming saliva covers black chins like scraggly white goatees; bellows, grunts, and groans shatter the silence of night. We see the Hauka for a brief, unsettling moment, long enough to fix our attention.

The scene cuts back to Accra. Rouch shows us images of Zabrama at work in the colonial Gold Coast: Stevedores carrying ships' cargo in Accra's port; miners descending into the depths of a gold mine; bottle washers cleaning their bottles; agricultural workers cutting rice; cattle herders steering their charges through Accra's streets; sanitation workers spraying insecticide on stagnant ponds to kill malarial mosquitoes. These examples, of course, give the viewer only a glimpse at the world of work in the Zabrama community. In *Migrations* Rouch says the Zabrama played an important commercial role in both Accra and Kumasi. Indeed, Zabrama merchants were in some cases among the cities' wealthiest residents.

The sociocultural and economic contexts set, Rouch takes his viewers on a short journey from city to countryside, from the known to the unknown. We leave Accra en route to Mounkaiba's compound, the site of a special Hauka ceremony. Mounkaiba is the high priest of the Hauka "religion" in the Gold Coast. We travel in large trucks, first on a paved highway and then on dirt roads, penetrating deeper and deeper into a thickening forest. Finally we can go no farther, and the participants continue on foot until they reach Mounkaiba's fairly substantial compound, with several houses and an impressive array of "union jacks"—sections of cloth each representing a Hauka deity.

The ceremony begins with the nomination of an initiate and with penance. The initiate is suffering from prepossession sickness. For the Hauka medium this means he has nightmares, somnambulates, and unearths corpses of cemeteries. He presents himself to Mounkaiba, who accepts his nomination. The scene shifts to the altar, a rounded mass of bloodstained concrete, over which the "sinners" will beg forgiveness. One penitent asks his Hauka to forgive him because he has had sex with his best friend's girlfriend. As he begs forgiveness, he swings a chicken back and forth in front of and behind his body, a way of symbolizing his past transgression and his future diligence. Other penitents follow suit. Mounkaiba, the officiating priest, cuts the chicken's throat. Blood spurts onto the altar, and the penitents surround it and touch its edge with their forefingers. Should they violate their oaths, their Hauka may make them ill or even kill them.

The music begins with the wail of the monochord violin and the syncopated thumps of gourd drums played like bongos. The Hauka mediums form a circle. They march counterclockwise to the rapid beat—sounds that beckon the spirits. Some of them wear pith helmets. Some crack whips fashioned from automobile fanbelts. A shrill whistle pierces the air. Some of the penitents attempt to join the medium-dancers, but they are expelled from the circle by Mounkaiba's sentries, who carry wooden rifles. Their "sinful" presence among the dancers could ruin the ceremony.

As the music pulses in the background, the first Hauka, Kapral Gardi, arrives. He belly flops to the ground, then jumps to attention. He salutes people in the audience and is given a red sash—his trademark. He collects the wooden rifles, which is his job in this military theater of the absurd.

Other spirits approach their mediums. Rouch gives us a closeup of the onset of possession. A young man sits on the ground, his legs extended in front of him. His left leg shakes as though he is shivering, then his right leg trembles. "It" moves through his body. His arms

The statue of the Governor-General in Moukaiba's compound, *Les maîtres fous*. J. Rouch, Comité du Film Ethnographique.

stiffen; his head jerks back; foam bubbles from his mouth. His breathing is heavy, and his eyes are white and distant.

Soon Mounkaiba's compound is literally jumping with Hauka spirits who flop on the ground and ask for fire to burn themselves. If the spirit is truly in a body, fire will not burn the medium's flesh. One of the spirits, Commandant Mugu, the wicked major, torches his clothing. Even though his shirt is consumed by fire, his flesh is miraculously spared. Rouch introduces us to other Hauka: General Malia, the general of the Red Sea; Madame Lokotoro the doctor's wife; Gomno, the governor-general; Samkaki, the truck driver; Chemoko, the son of the corporal of the guard.

Mounkaiba makes an offering of an egg to his wooden statue of the governor-general, a rotund white figure with a pith helmet and a mustache. He recites an incantation and breaks the egg on the governor-general's pith helmet. This action represents the plume worn by the British governor-general on formal occasions in Accra. In fact the comportment of the Hauka recreates in exaggerated form the theater of British military ritual: salutes; the protocol of military rank; marching with weapons; "round table" conferences among the notables.

The notables call a round table conference to discuss their sacrifice to the spirits. They choose to kill a dog and eat its meat to demonstrate their otherness, for no Songhay would ever eat dog meat. There is discussion about whether to eat the dog raw or cooked, but they decide to cook it. Mounkaiba slits the dog's throat on the Hauka altar. The Hauka gather around the dog's throat and drink the gushing blood. They stand up and lick their lips. Rouch zooms in on the spirit Samkaki: his eyes flash as dog blood reddens the bubbling saliva on his chin.

The dog is skinned, butchered, and cooked in a pot of boiling water. When the dog meat is ready, the Hauka put their hands into the pot to grab pieces. The boiling water does not scald their hands. With their teeth the joyous Hauka rip cooked dog meat from the bone. They chew and smile. They pronounce the ceremony a great success. Mounkaiba saves the uneaten dog meat and broth for those Hauka mediums who had to remain in Accra.

Daylight is dying, and one by one the Hauka slip away from their mediums. The mediums must depart for Accra, but the "truck driver" is still in his medium's body. Samkaki is deleriously happy because the festival has been a wonderful event. He tells Mounkaiba that two such ceremonies must be held the following year. Mounkaiba agrees. The cries of the violin and the thumps of the drums dissipate in the air. The last Hauka departs amid soiled cloth, blood-soaked altars, and the ever-present "union jacks." Night sweeps into Mounkaiba's compound.

The next morning Rouch's camera takes us back to Accra to see how the Hauka mediums are getting along in the everyday world. Rouch uses these reintroductions to juxtapose the profane and the sacred. We discover that Madame Lokotoro, for example, is a highly esteemed clerk. We learn that General Malia is in fact "just a private." Other mediums are pickpockets, bottle washers. Finally Rouch focuses on the general staff of the previous day, all of whom work for the Accra waterworks. They are digging a ditch, it so happens, in front of the Accra mental hospital. These men, Rouch tells us, are among the best workers of their service. He wonders whether these men of Africa have discovered through their "new religion" a cure for the dehumanization of modern society that causes the proliferation of mental disorders.

CRAZY CONTROVERSY

Les maîtres fous loosed a torrent of controversy even before it was released in 1955. When Rouch took his film to France in 1954, he showed it to a small and select audience at the Musée de l'Homme. Since there was no sound track, Rouch provided commentary from the projection booth. As the minutes ticked by, Rouch sensed the mounting tension in the room. Griaule was furious; he suggested the film be destroyed. Several African intellectuals agreed with Griaule. Luc de Heusch saw merit in the film. According to Rouch, Griaule didn't like Africans burlesquing white Europeans so wildly; Griaule was ashamed of the film. The African scholars in the audience found the film's images offensive, especially Rouch's closeups of wild-eyed black men foaming at the mouth, drinking dog blood, and eating dog meat. They feared these images would reinforce racist myths about black Africa (Echard and Rouch 1988, interview 7).

These comments disturbed Rouch profoundly, but he was convinced he had filmed something extraordinary, something that should not be destroyed. In the end he did not destroy *Les maîtres fous,* which in the words of his producer, Pierre Braumberger, became Rouch's "masterpiece." Released in 1955, the film caused quite a storm.

Dan Yakir (1978, 3) writes: "*Les Maîtres Fous* was controversial everywhere. It was criticized by the British and by young African intellectuals. The late Senegalese director Blaise Senghor told me that when he came out of the theatre in Paris, the spectators looked at him saying to each other: 'Here's another one who is going to eat a dog!' " In 1957 *Les maîtres fous* won first prize for short films at the Venice Film Festival, reflecting the widespread European praise for the work. "In the image of his *maîtres-fous*, Rouch is a possessed filmmaker who gives birth to a veritable magic dance whose effect is to capture the movement of the real." [1] For critic Michel Delahaye (1961), *Les maîtres fous* exorcises the hatred Africans and Europeans hold toward one another. The widespread European praise for the film stems in part from Rouch's intercutting of scenes of the Hauka and the military ceremonies of the British colonial government, an instance of Vertovian juxtaposition. [2]

Fearing more racist interpretations of the film, African scholars condemned it. Sensitive to these fears, Rouch made sure the film was not distributed very widely (Echard and Rouch 1988, interview 7). The most vituperative comments about Rouch's ethnographic films, especially *Les maîtres fous,* came in 1965 during a debate between Rouch and the Senegalese novelist and filmmaker Ousmane Sembène. Ousmane Sembène stated his preference for Rouch's films of fiction, like *Moi, un noir,* as opposed to his more ethnographically oriented films, like *Les maître fous.* "I would like to know," Rouch asked, "why you don't like my purely ethnographic films—the ones that depict, for example, traditional life." Ousmane Sembène answered with a classic response. "Because you show it [traditional life] and you dwell on a reality without showing its evolution. What I reproach them for, as I reproach Africanists, is that you observe us like insects" (Predal 1982, 78).

Ousmane Sembène's telling point was motivated by his sense of postcolonial representational politics. Several scholars have complained about the incomprehensibility of Rouch's film, which stems from a lack of ethnographic contextualization.

Although he considers *Les maîtres fous* a remarkable document, Jean-Claude Muller, an anthropologist specializing in West Africa, criticizes the film's ethnographic decontextualization.

> The main trouble—and this is not intended to be a criticism—stems from the fact that it is almost impossible to fully understand and hence appreciate a film that concerns religion and symbolism—and there is a lot of this in the film—without prior knowledge of something about the

1. Grob (1962, 3). Grob does not discuss how Rouch creatively adjusted to the technical limitations he confronted in filming *Les maîtres fous.* Jay Ruby (personal communication) suggests that Rouch shot the film with a spring-motored camera with hundred-foot rolls. No sound was recorded, so the sound track had to be dubbed. The crude technology of the day (1954) therefore had a profound influence on the texture of the film.

2. Faye Ginsburg and Jay Ruby pointed this out to me.

religious setting of the population filmed. The film is still a complement—a very important one—to the written ethnographic account, and
not the other way around. This applies even more so to a film dealing
with religious matters. . . . The great wealth of details portrayed in the
film can be mastered only after the reading of the ethnographic material.
(Muller 1971, 1472)

The ethnographic materials Muller refers to are, of course, *La religion
et la magie Songhay* and *Migrations au Ghana*. Muller goes on to sit-
uate the Hauka movement in the broader perspective of Songhay possession, a contextual fact not evident from the film.

Muller here suggests that *Les maîtres fous* is underdetermined. I
cannot agree that films are the complements of written ethnographies
(see MacDougall 1975; Banks 1990), but his review reinforces a major
theme of this book: that Rouch's films, including *Les maîtres fous*,
cannot be considered apart from his painstaking longitudinal ethnographic research.

THE HAUKA IN SONGHAY POSESSION

Many Europeans have applauded *Les maîtres fous* for its technical
merit, its compelling images, and its penetration of a world rarely if
ever experienced by Europeans. By many accounts, the film influenced
la nouvelle vague in France. African intellectuals, by contrast, have
deplored the content of *Les maîtres fous*, suggesting that it perpetuates
a racist exoticism. In the film Africans can be seen as savages practicing barbaric religions from another age.

The undeniable brutality of the Hauka, however, is but one manifestation of possession among the Songhay. Out of context, images of
men torching themselves, frothing at the mouth, drinking the gushing
blood of a freshly slaughtered dog, and eating boiled dog meat underscore the exoticism that African intellectuals deplore. Here again are
images of brooding primitives engaging in savage acts that disgust European audiences and reinforce racist stereotypes. *Les maîtres fous* is
long on images and short on explanations. The presence of provocative scenes is the film's greatest strength; the absence of an explanatory
context is its greatest weakness.

The Hauka phenomenon in the colonial Gold Coast is a very short
chapter in the story of Songhay possession (see Rouch 1989; Stoller
1989a). The Hauka are among the most recently arrived Songhay spirits, and their place of origin is not the colonial Gold Coast of the early
1950s—as Rouch suggests in his film—but colonial Niger in 1925 (see
Fugelstad 1975; Stoller 1989a; Rouch 1989).

It all began during a dance of girls and boys. During the dance a Soudye woman, Zibo, who was married to a Timbuktu *sherif,* began to be possessed by a spirit. They asked her who it was. It said: "I am Gomno Malia" [governor of the Red Sea]. The people said they did not know this spirit. Then others came and took the bodies of some of the young boys. They too spoke their names, and the people did not know them. The spirits said: "We are the Hauka, the guests of Dongo." This occurred at Chikal, very close to Filingue. A few days later, all the boys and girls of Filingue had been possessed by the Hauka. (Rouch 1989, 80)

In fact, when the Hauka first appeared, the reaction of Songhay possession priests was not unlike the reaction *Les maîtres fous* provoked from audiences of Europeans and African intellectuals: they dissociated themselves from the outrageous behavior of these "unknown" spirits. The grotesque antics of these "outlaw" spirits, however, soon caught the attention of the local Filingue authorities, who notified French colonial officials in Niamey. Soon the colonial government threw the original band of Hauka mediums and priests into jail. Major Croccichia, the commandant of Niamey, imprisoned the sixty participants for three days—punishment for their outlandish behavior. After their release the group staged a dance, where Zibo began to shake from the presence of Gomno Malia.

Enraged by the insolence of these young people, Major Croccichia had them arrested again. He brought Zibo to his headquarters, slapped her, and asked: "Where are the Hauka?" He slapped Zibo until she admitted there were no Hauka. The soldiers brought the other Hauka mediums to Croccichia, and he and his soldiers slapped them until they too admitted there were no Hauka. Humiliated in public, the Hauka mediums were sent back to Filingue.

But they found no peace there. The chief expelled them from town. They trekked to other villages in Filingue and to other districts and founded new Hauka cults. The Hauka movement spread widely. By February 1927 the colonial administration noted that there were Hauka adepts in all the villages of Filingue district. They considered the Hauka rivals "of the established order represented in the chieftaincy, the backbone of the administrative system created by the French" (Fugelstad 1975, 205).

In March 1927 Gado Namalaya, the old chief of Filingue, died. The French supported the candidacy of Chekou Seyni, one of Gado's sons. Chekou, however, was not unopposed. Manifesting themselves as a political force, the Hauka supported a rival candidate. This action was an intolerable affront to French authority. To make matters worse from the French perspective, the Hauka founded their own villages in the bush and created their own society, which was overtly anti-French.

The French found in the Hauka "a clear opposition to the traditional chieftaincy. They discovered the presence of an open dissidence, a society, the members of which openly defied the social, political, and religious order. It is here that we discover that the most original aspect of the Hauka movement: their total refusal of the system put into place by the French" (Fugelstad 1975, 205).

Although the Hauka cult was born in Chikal, it found its first real home in the colonial Gold Coast. According to Rouch, the Hauka came to the Gold Coast about 1929 and first appeared in Asuom. Driven by the zeal of a Zerma called Ousmane Fode, the Hauka movement spread rapidly in the Gold Coast. Ousmane Fode was born in Dosso in Niger and served with the British army in World War I (Rouch 1956, 176). In one year he had become the great ritual priest of the Hauka of the Gold Coast and the subject of contemporary myth.

Sometime about 1935, there was a violent dispute between a Hauka dancer, most likely possessed, and a young Hausa girl. As a result, the local authorities forbade further Hauka dances. After forty days, the Muslim period of mourning, Ousmane called a meeting of all the Hauka mediums of the Gold Coast. In the words of Rouch's informant, Tyiri Gao, the possession priest of Kumasi:

> The celebration began about seven o'clock in the morning, but at noon the police arrested everyone. That evening, a guitar player played in the prison. The Hauka possessed their dancers. They broke down the prison door and escaped. Then, that same night, two fires broke out. In Koforidua the church burned, half the village of Kibi burned, and eight Hauka dancers were killed; the governor of the Gold Coast became alarmed— Is it because we arrested the Hauka that in only one night there have been so many accidents? Who are these Hauka? The governor ordered Ousmane Fode and Amani to explain what the Hauka were. The governor authorized them to have a place in Nsawam, Accra, and Akwatia. In this way the Hauka remained in the Gold Coast. (Rouch 1956, 177)

Rouch doesn't know whether this story corresponds to real events, but he does say that the "golden age of the Hauka" occurred from 1935 to 1943, until the death of Ousmane Fode, a golden age despite the fact that the autochthonous populations found Hauka ceremonies bestial, the same negative reaction of many African and European audiences to *Les maîtres fous*.

By the time of Rouch's filming in 1954, the Hauka movement was well ensconced in the Gold Coast. Mediums emerged from among the Zabrama migrants. Although mediumship was sometimes stigmatized in Niger, in the Gold Coast it became prestigious. Rouch does not say whether this prestige was reserved for the Zabrama community or whether it stretched to other migrants and to the indigenous communities.

One of the problems with *Les maîtres fous* is that it depicts only a limited aspect of colonial history in West Africa. Viewers have little idea of the origins of the Hauka movement and less about how the Hauka deities fit into the Songhay pantheon of spirits. The Hauka were flourishing in 1954 when Rouch filmed them. What happened to the movement in 1957, when Ghana became independent? What happened to the mediums who returned home to Niger? Did they take along their Gold Coast spirits? Did independence in Niger render the Hauka movement superfluous, or does it continue as an expression of Songhay cultural resistance?

These contextualizing issues are missing in *Les maîtres fous*. To some extent they are present in *La religion et la magie Songhay* and in *Migrations au Ghana* Rouch suggests that many of the mediums returned to Niger with their spirits, but his writing about the Hauka does not assess the movement after independence.

My recent experience suggests that the Hauka are alive and well today in Niger, though there is no longer a separate Hauka movement as there was in 1927. Opposition to European rule ceased to be the underlying theme for the Hauka when France granted independence to the republic of Niger in 1960. But just as the conceptual residue of slavery remains among the former slave populations of Songhay, so the psychological yoke of colonialism has remained with many peoples in Niger. Although Europeans are no longer the political administrators of districts in the republic of Niger, they still hold many important positions both in the capital city of Niamey and in rural regions of Songhay country. Europeans are technical advisers to various Nigerien ministries. They play important roles on the staffs of the national and regional hospitals. Europeans are the technicians responsible for a wide variety of internationally funded development projects. They still teach in Niger's university. The "force" of the European continues to be strong in all regions; the need for many Songhay to make sense of this "force" remains equally strong (Stoller 1989a, 161).

Just as the need remains to make sense of the ongoing European force, so the presence of the Hauka persists. There are Hauka mediums living in most Songhay towns. In larger towns like Tillaberi, the Hauka mediums are loosely attached to the major possession groups; they frequently meet informally, stage their own ceremonies, and perform their own sacrifices.

Hauka are not merely comedians who make social commentary. They have specific roles to perform during spirit possession ceremonies. They are protectors—the sentinels, really, of the Tooru, the nobles of the Songhay spirit world. When the Tooru possess the bodies of their mediums, several Hauka soon arrive to protect them. Sometimes they escort people in the possession crowd to an audience with the Tooru spirits. The Hauka are also clairvoyants. They often call individuals into their circle to read the past, present, and future. Above all, Hauka are witch hunters, the first line of defense against Songhay witchcraft. When Hauka brandish fire above their heads—as they do in *Les maîtres fous*—it stands as a warning to witches in the area: beware the "force" of the Hauka, a force derived from their "father" Dongo. In some communities Hauka mediums patrol their villages until the early morning hours to protect them from the noctural ravages of witches (Stoller 1989a, 161).

THE MEDIUM IS THE MESSAGE

Les maîtres fous is not a film that merely documents what Rouch inaccurately calls an emerging African religion. There are documentary elements in *Les maîtres fous*. Rouch gives us glimpses of the busy life of the Zabrama workers in the colonial economy. He shows us the teeming multiethnic streets, the busy port, the productive gold mines. He teaches us a bit about the Zabrama, the men who migrate from the North, whose bodies become the mediums for the Hauka. He takes us to a yearly Hauka ceremony at which possessed mediums put their bare hands into a caldron of boiling stew without injury. Foaming at the mouth like rabid dogs, the Hauka slaughter a dog and eat its cooked flesh.

Clearly, Rouch's intent is not to depict the broad ethnographic context of the Hauka in Songhay possession. *Les maîtres fous* is not an observational film that depicts its subject from objective, eagle-eyed heights; rather, the filmmaker takes the viewer into the heart and soul of Songhay possession.[3] One is unmistakably "there," and Rouch *doc-*

---

3. DeBouzek (1989, 308) comments on Rouch's narration in *Les maîtres fous:* "Although Rouch tried to translate directly the dialogue of the Hauka—a glossolaliac melange of broken French and English—he realized that the task was an impossible one. After working extensively with one of the members of the cult on an interpretation of the events and the recorded speech, he decided to set his notes aside, doing the final voice-over without a written script. According to him, that first narration was part of his own 'possession' by film, part of his personal cine-trance."

uments the scene in such a way that the unmistakably there becomes the unforgettably there.

Is Rouch's intent in *Les maîtres fous* a kind of being there in body as well as mind? Partially. But my own suspicions suggest a much grander intent. Despite its ethnographic decontextualization, *Les maîtres fous* is nothing less than a challenge to our way of thinking. Like *Jaguar,* it is a film that defies the imperious arrogance of the Western "gaze."

Rouch provides no reductionist theory of the incredible events depicted in *Les maîtres fous*. This tack is consistent with his orientation in *Religion*. Instead, Rouch challenges us to reflect on the following questions: How can men put their bare hands into boiling caldrons without scalding themselves? How can "trance" be so violent, so irreverent, so brutal, and so funny—all at the same time? Rouch provides no answers to these unsettling questions; he provides, rather, images that *document* the scientifically unthinkable. Surely there must be some trick, some sleight of hand, as Lévi-Strauss argues in his influential "The Sorcerer and His Magic" (1967). Others have suggested that mediums can handle fire without injury only for fifteen seconds or less (Kane 1982). Still others write about the power of mind to overcome the ravages of physical pain and such physical forces as fire (see Adair 1960). The Songhay have a simple explanation: possessed mediums are no longer human beings; they are spirits. Spirits see the past and the future, have the strength of ten men, and withstand fire and boiling water. They are the presence of the immortal on earth—in the bodies of human beings. And all we need to do is watch the screen to observe—never impassively—incontrovertible evidence of the Hauka's otherworldliness.

Rouch wants to shock viewers into confronting these imponderables, to disturb their cozy epistemological presuppositions. On each of the more than fifty occasions when I have shown *Les maîtres fous,* one of my students has vomited. Several students invariably wonder how people as "primitive" as the Songhay could know something about which we know nothing. Many students desperately seek scientific explanations for trance: they want to demystify the inexplicable. Some are insulted, believing the film is racist.

No one discounts the power of *Les maîtres fous*. For anthropological critics like George DeVos, the power of the film stems from its brutal honesty. Unlike many anthropologists, Rouch does not believe indigenous peoples must always be presented in a positive way: "Let's compare Rouch with *Roots*. *Roots* romances rites. Rouch, on the contrary, is honest in regard to rites as well as in the psychological and sociological attitude he carries with him. It is this that explains the impression of discomfort. The spectator is ill at ease, but at the same time he must take in what he has been given to see" (DeVos 1982, 59). Is it "unethical" to depict "others" only in positive terms?

COLONIALISM FROM BELOW

In 1988 Rouch spoke at a New York University retrospective on his films, during which he proclaimed that his African colleagues, who at first denounced *Les maîtres fous* as racist, now consider it the best depiction of African colonialism on film—a kind of colonialism from below. Rouch's assertion is, of course, arguable. One could suggest that Rouch, as a Frenchman, was incapable of "knowing" the colonial situation from an African perspective. As the late Oumarou Ganda, a Nigerien filmmaker who once worked with Rouch, said: "Rouch is a European who sees with a French eye." Other African filmmakers agree with Ganda (Predal 1982, 71, 63–76).

But do they consider some mitigating factors? Rouch filmed *Les maîtres fous* some thirteen years after he first set foot in Africa. During this time he remained in touch with his informant-friends. Rouch also sought the advice of his collaborators, especially Damoré Zika. This long personal contact is the foundation of films like *Les maîtres fous*. Listen to filmmaker Inoussa Ouseini's words about Rouch: "He is close to the people, he is in permanent contact with the people, and this you see on the screen, because when the people do not accept you this pops through the cinema! Therefore, Rouch created this cinema of contact with the people, and when you practice this genre of cinema, you cannot cheat [to trick or stage], because if the people do not accept you beforehand you cannot film" (Predal 1982, 76).

For Reda Bensmaia, *Les maîtres fous* captures in images the essence of colonialism in the Gold Coast: the British exploitation of Africans. Sensitive to colonial excesses, Rouch finds the correct tone: "Rouch's path is correct not only because he doesn't ignore colonialism, but because leaving constantly his own environs and exhibiting nature through the massive effects she produces elsewhere, it at no time allows the spectator to remain indifferent, but compels him in some way if not to take a position, at least to change" (Predal 1982, 55). According to Bensmaia, Rouch demonstrates in *Les maîtres fous* that to understand the meaning of decolonization, a European must begin with his own decolonization.

The reason *Les maîtres fous* is one of Rouch's masterworks is that it ingeniously brings together the complex themes of colonization, decolonization, and the ontology of trance, in thirty-three minutes of extraordinary cinema. In a direct manner, Rouch thrusts the "horrific comedy" of Songhay possession upon his viewers, challenging them to come to grips with what they are seeing on the screen (see Stoller 1989a). *Les maîtres fous,* like Rouch's Songhay ethnographies and some of his other films (*Les magiciens de Wanzerbe*), *documents* the existence of the incredible, the unthinkable. These unexplicated scenes challenge us to decolonize our thinking, to decolonize ourselves.

In May and June Songhay farmers watch the eastern sky. They see a bank of black clouds building and sense a wind shift from west to east. And then they listen for Dongo's rumble—his "groan," as the griots say. These are the sounds that carry to parched villages lifesaving rain. If the rain comes one hears the groans of Dongo's children, the Hauka, as they run frolicking in the muddy streets toward the zima's compound.

They arrive half-naked, their chests covered with mud. "My zima," they say. "My father came today. He is mean. He wants blood. He is mean. My father came today. Give him his blood, and you will have a safe and productive rainy season. My father came today. He is mean."

Dongo is still the master of Songhay skies. His children, *les maîtres fous,* are still a force in the dusty byways of Songhay villages.

CHAPTER TEN
Les Tambours d'Avant: Turu et Bitti

Boro kan mana gaanu si windi.
The uninitiated cannot join the circle of possession dancers.
—Songhay proverb

Songhay villages are situated in a climatic zone, the Sahel, where famine has a long history. If rainfall deviates even slightly from the prescribed pattern, the life-giving millet crop is threatened. Even if the rain is abundant, rats, locusts, and insects can ravage a healthy crop and bring on a deadly famine. To protect themselves from the scourge, Songhay communities stage possession ceremonies to make offerings to the Black Spirits, the deities in the Songhay pantheon that control soil fertility and pests. They are the spirits that urge the Songhay to seek "the truth of the bush."

Rouch's *Les tambours d'avant: Turu et bitti,* the subject of this chapter, is about one such Black Spirit ceremony that took place in the village of Simiri in March 1971. The film is not only about "the truth of the bush," but also about the truth of the field, a space that, in Rouch's oeuvre, is the product of cooperative plowing, watering, and weeding. And just as the uninitiated person can never join the circle of possession dancers, so the uninitiated anthropologist, Rouch demonstrates, can never plunge into the real—of the field.

BLACK SPIRITS IN SIMIRI

As *Les tambours d'avant* begins, Rouch's camera walks us to a desiccated landscape just outside Simiri, Niger: vast stretches of sand are dotted with scraggly plants and occasional thorn trees. In the background we hear drums. It is 11 March 1971, the last day of a four-day festival for the Black Spirits, the Genji Bi, which control locusts and other pests. The people of Simiri know that if they make offerings to these spirits, the spirits will protect the crops. On the first three days of the ceremony, however, not one deity has entered the body of a medium.

Listen to Rouch's words: "To enter into this film is to plunge into the real." And Rouch can plunge into this real only because his path of initiation has led him to the heart of things Songhay.

Here Rouch becomes the camera, and we see what he sees. We approach Simiri and the compound of Sido Zima. We pass by a kraal in which several sheep are tethered to small wooden posts. Perched on Rouch's shoulder, we approach the dance grounds. We see the *tunda*, or sacred canopy, under which sit Simiri's spirit mediums. Rouch focuses on an old man dressed in a billowing indigo cape—Sambo Albeda. Sambo, a medium to Hausa spirits, is tired. He has been dancing more than four hours in the hot March sun. His spirit is far, far off, and the day is slipping away. Will the festival be a total failure? Will the spirits refuse to descend upon Simiri? Will the locusts devastate the millet in the Simiri fields during the rainy season?

Rouch-the-camera now approaches the musicians, for they are playing the drums of yore, the *turu* and the *bitti*. The turu is fashioned from a large gourd over which is stretched sheepskin. The bitti is a cylindrical drum whose ends are covered by stretched sheepskin. Unlike the gourd drums played at most possession ceremonies, these are struck with the hand, not with bamboo drumsticks. We see the musicians playing these drums of yore. We hear the drum rhythms. Sambo Albeda resumes his dancing.

Suddenly the music stops. The violinist senses that the spirits are close. The old dancer no longer is Sambo Albeda but is now Kure, the hyena. The turu drummers call for meat; Kure wants meat. Kure dances; he is hungry.

Daylight is fading, but Kure's presence compels old Tusinye Wasi to dance. Soon she too is possessed by Hadjo, the Fulan slave who is a Black Spirit.

Rouch-the-camera takes us to a conference between Kure and Daouda Sorko, son of Sido Zima. He is inside the circle of possession dancers. "I want meat," Kure says to Daouda. Daouda nods and says: "We want a good harvest." Soon Hadjo joins Kure, Daouda Sorko, and Rouch-the-camera. The deities want goat blood—a sacrifice. As they wait for the goat, Daouda Sorko douses them with perfume.

The sun is setting. Rouch moves away from the action so that the

Drummers playing the turu and bitti in Simiri, Niger, *Les tambours d'avant.*
J. Rouch, Comité du Film Ethnographique.

camera sees what the children of Simiri are seeing. The sun sets on
Simiri and Rouch's film.[1]

POSSESSION CHEZ ROUCH

Songhay possession possessed Jean Rouch in 1942. Since then he has
devoted most of his anthropological attention to this cultural phenom-

1. *Les tambours d'avant: Turu et bitti* is an experimental single-shot film. Feld
(1989, 229) writes that the single-shot sequence films are "filmed while Rouch is walking
among the participants. Rouch calls these 'shot-sequence' films 'ethnography in the first
person' because he plays the roles of participant and catalyst as he films. The purpose of
these films is not to break down and explicate events but to show how the familiar
observer perceives and interacts with them and authors a subjectively experiential account of them the moment he films. This style of shooting long sequences with a single
focal length lens (frequently 10 mm) and extensive walking is also considered by Rouch
to be an answer to the problem of editing; namely, to edit everything in the camera as it's
being shot, and then string the shot sequences together." The last shot of *Les tambours
d'avant,* in which Rouch captures the setting sun, is according to Jay Ruby (personal
communication), Rouch's ironic reference to a Hollywood cliché, which is part of notion
of single-shot experimentation.

enon. Possession occupies center stage in his anthropological writings; it is the subject of most of his ethnographic films.

But what is it about Songhay possession that so possessed Rouch? He has already stated that the possession ceremony he saw in 1942 compelled him to think of Paul Eluard's surreal poems. Is possession, for Rouch, the source material for automatic writing or automatic film? To Rouch, possession is the enactment of life and death; it is playing—in its deepest sense—with existence (see Geertz 1973; Bentham 1931). In Songhay, possession ceremonies set the stage for contract negotiations between human beings and the gods who control the forces of the universe. Human beings engage in these negotiations with their total being—their hearts, the Songhay griots would say. If this contract between human beings and the gods is "signed"—in blood—there will be health, happiness, fecundity, rain. If for some reason the negotiations fail, there will be sickness, sorrow, barrenness, drought, famine (see Stoller 1989a).

As Rouch points out graphically in his books and films, climate is a major player in the Songhay story. As one sees at the beginning of *Les tambours d'avant*, Songhay is a flat, sandy, barren desert, its vast stretches broken by periodic mesas (see Sidikou 1974; Stoller and Olkes 1987). A good year will bring perhaps twenty inches of rain. Rainfall, however, usually averages between ten and fifteen inches a year. Soil quality is generally poor. Many cultivators sow their millet crops in rolling fields of sand. Songhay is also the home of locusts, rats, birds, and other pests that attack millet at various stages of its development.

Even with sufficient rain and no pests, a bountiful harvest is not guaranteed. The rain must fall at the right times in the growth cycle of the millet plant. At the beginning of the rainy season, it should rain no more than once a week. Too much rain will flood the young millet shoots and kill them. Too little rain early on means the Sahelian sun will scorch the young shoots. This sporadic rain pattern should continue until August, when it should rain heavily seven to ten times. In August the growing millet stalks need much moisture. In September the rain should drop off gradually; too much rain in September will rot the stalks. In October, the time of harvest, a bright, hot sun is required to ripen the mature seeds. Rain in October will also ruin the crop. Any variation from the ideal climatic pattern substantially reduces crop yields. Too little food means less resistance to the common illnesses and tropical diseases that ravage Songhay children and adults (Stoller 1989a, 127–31).

Faced with uncertainties of climate, Songhay consider themselves powerless against the mercurial forces of nature. Too "hard" to beg, Songhay use the framework of possession to negotiate with the deities that control natural forces, which in turn control human destiny. This idea of negotiation is apparent in *Les tambours d'avant*, especially when Kure, the spirit, speaks to Daouda Sorko, the man. Kure wants meat. Kure and his spirit sister Hadjo want blood. Daouda Sorko, who represents the social world of Simiri, wants a good harvest. In exchange for blood and meat, Kure and Hadjo vow to protect Simiri from pests.

Possession ceremonies also set the stage for other negotiations: men seeking wives; women seeking husbands; people seeking "protection" for a long journey, as in *Jaguar;* people seeking cures for illness; communities seeking a defense from epidemics; communities seeking to avoid pests; communities asking for rain—in the prescribed pattern.

This last request is made during the most important possession ceremony of the year—the *yenaandi,* or rain dance. In the 1989 edition of *Religion* Rouch describes the yenaandi as a "pact" between human beings and the gods. Rouch's notion of a pact or contract is an apt one. But a yenaandi is more than a pact between human beings and the spirit world; it also entails a pact among the people of a community.

It is expensive to stage a yenaandi. Organizers must buy sacrificial animals (at least one black goat and four chickens) and find kola and tobacco for participating musicians, mediums, and priests. Further, organizers must pay musicians, mediums, and priests. Where does the money come from? Often local government officials and chiefs will collect money for the festivals. Just as often, a Muslim official or local chief will refuse to sponsor a "pagan" ceremony, which means that the troupe will have to cancel the rite or perform it incorrectly by skimping on the preparations. When rites are canceled or incompletely performed, priests fear the ultimate punishment: a deadly drought.

In other words, there must be local harmony, local support for the spirits. This harmony sets the stage—the yenaandi dance ground—for a dramatic ceremony during which the masters of the sky, Dongo (thunder), Cirey (lightning), Moussa Gurma (wind and clouds), and Manda Hausakoy (iron), visit the social world. Seated on their thrones, actually overturned mortars, they judge the community. They assess the quality of the sacrificial animals as well as the quality of social relations in the possession troupe and the community. If they are satisfied, the spirits accept what the priests offer them and promise rain. If there is dissension, the spirits will withhold their support.

Possession ceremonies therefore mark the drama of life and death

A medium dances to the rhythms of the turu and bitti, *Les tambours d'avant.*
J. Rouch, Comité du Film Ethnographique.

in Songhay. Possession priests know the life and death consequences of
ceremonies like the yenaandi. The musicians know their sweet music
may save a life. Mediums know their bodies will house spirits that may
bring rain. Sorkos know their "old words" will bring spirits. Possession, then, is a dramatic stage of real life in which performers play
their roles with great seriousness.

In 1984, during a serious drought, a gourd drummer told me a story
that stresses the seriousness of his possession tasks. During one possession ceremony he left his drums to eat lunch. When he returned, he

> struck his drum once. But something was strange. Had he heard a noise
> under the calabash? Had something moved under it? With a long stick
> [he] lifted his calabash, and then sprang from his spot behind the drum.
> In his absence, someone had put a viper under the drum. He killed the
> snake. . . .
>
> "There are mean people everywhere. There are people who wish me
> harm, and I do not even know why. That day, I wanted to leave that
> damn place, but I could not. As a drummer I have a responsibility to
> myself and to the spirits." (Stoller 1989a, 121)

This resilience, this strength of character, is common among possession players. Rouch no doubt found this strength of character and

depth of will in old Kalia of Niamey, in Wadi Godje, in Sido Zima, in Daouda Sorko of Simiri, and in Mossi Bana of Wanzerbe. In the summer of 1942 old Kalia introduced Rouch to Songhay possession. The drama and power of the ceremony immediately captivated him. "Old Kalia's purification ceremony of ten men who had been killed by lightning was so moving. . . . that I was incapable of writing about it or even taking photographs of it" (Rouch 1978c, 7). The romance has lasted more than fifty years, during which the major focus of Rouch's ethnographic writing and films has been Songhay possession. For him possession is a dramatic dreamscape where characters' actions have life and death consequences.

THE PHENOMENOLOGY OF SELF IN SONGHAY

By the time he filmed *Les tambours d'avant: Turu et bitti* in 1971, Jean Rouch had spent almost thirty years among Songhay possession players; he had long since joined the circle of dancers. Rouch first visited Simiri in the late 1940s; he filmed a yenaandi there in 1951, twenty years before *Les tambours d'avant*. The people of Simiri did not consider Rouch an "observer" or a strange foreigner; rather, they called him "the one who follows the spirits," someone who had been initiated. Viewers get a sense of this nickname in *Les tambours d'avant,* in which Rouch, camera strapped to his shoulder, walks effortlessly among spirits, priests, musicians, and praise singers.

This experience and the film that resulted prompted Rouch to write an article on the notion of the self in Songhay. A version of the article, originally published in 1971 in France, is part of the postface of the 1989 edition of *La religion et la magie Songhay:* "As a result of this experience [*Les tambours d'avant*], I attempted to write about the Songhay interpretation of the notion of the 'self' of the possession medium, the magician (*sohantye*), the victim of the witch (*tyarkaw* 'soul eater'), as well as the self of the observer-filmmaker" (Rouch 1989, 337–38).

Rouch begins his essay by considering the "self" of the possession medium. Possession priests explain that possession occurs when the spirit, a mass of invisible energy, displaces the "double" of its medium. The double or *bia* of all human beings manifests itself in several ways, according to Rouch. It is our shadow; it is our reflection in a mirror or on the surface of water. It is also our soul. It leaves the body during sleep, which accounts for our dreams, and escapes from the body at death in quest of its own adventures.

If one is a medium, one's double can be displaced during a possession ceremony. According to Rouch, this is what happens to the medium about to be possessed:

> Following numerous indirect accounts [it is already indicated that the dancer must not remember the possession] the dancer *sees* the spirit [eventually the old initiates see it too] penetrate the dance circle and direct itself toward him or her; the spirit holds in its hands the skin of a freshly slaughtered animal and presents the bloody side of it to the dancer three times:
> —the first time, tears flow from the dancer's eyes;
> —the second time, mucus flows from the dancer's nose;
> —the third time, the dancer cries out. (Rouch 1989, 339)

On its fourth pass, the spirit places the bloody skin over the dancer's head. In this way the spirit captures the double and enters the dancer's body. During possession, the dancer's double is protected under the bloody skin. When the spirit leaves the body, it lifts off the bloody animal skin, liberating the dancer's double. The medium opens his or her eyes. Sometimes mediums are unconscious for several minutes. They always cough as if they had just left an airless vault (Rouch 1989, 340).

Songhay possession priests have presented other theories. Adamu Jenitongo of Tillaberi said the dancer's double resides in the sacred *lolo,* an iron staff owned by sohanci who, like him, are also possession priests. Other zima have said that the possessed dancer's double resides in one of the poles of the sacred canopy under which the possession musicians play (Rouch 1989, 340).

Whatever the mechanism, the paramount fact of possession, according to Rouch, is that the medium's double is displaced. Among the sohanci, the notion of the self is quite different. The sohanci, Rouch says, is the master of his double, which is not displaced by a spirit. Here Rouch contrasts possession with shamanism. The self of the possession medium is displaced, but that of the shaman travels great distances. In *Les magiciens de Wanzerbe* we have already encountered the magician's chain, the sign that the "self" of the magician has taken the form of a "vulture" that flies great distances and masters his enemies (Rouch 1989, 340–42).

In the Songhay world, the magician and the witch (*cerkaw*) are linked through combat—the combat of doubles. Witches operate at night. When they travel in the darkness their trail is marked by flashes of light, which are in effect the trace of their doubles. Meanwhile the body of the witch remains in the village in a dream state. The magician combats the witch in Songhay villages. As the magician sleeps, the

double goes on witch patrol, carrying the lolo to prick and thus inca-
pacitate the witch. Here it is worth quoting Rouch at length: "The
stories of these imaginary fights are fabulous: armed with the lance
[lolo, or double], the magician tries to prick the witch, which defends
itself by throwing millet stalks at the magician. But when the doubles
return to their respective bodies at dawn, they mark on the bodies [of
the real witch or magician] the wounds they received: raised scars that
they display proudly" (Rouch 198, 344). If the double of the witch
escapes detection, it will hunt the doubles of other people. Occasionally the witch's double steals the victim's double. In this vulnerable
doubleless state, the victim sickens and sometimes dies. Songhay frequently claim that witches have killed their children. In villages people
ask a sohanci or sorko to make them an amulet to defend them against
a witch's attack (Stoller and Olkes 1987).

But what is the "self" of the observer or, in Rouch's case, the ethnographic filmmaker? Here Rouch compares his own "self" with that
of the possessed medium. In filming *Les tambours d'avant* Rouch literally attached himself to the ritual and entered a "cine-trance of one
filming the trance of another" (Rouch 1989, 348). Cine-trance, however, is entered only by filmmakers who practice *cinéma-vérité*, who
hunt for images in the real world. Cine-trance is, in effect, a kind of
profound dialogue between ethnographer and other, leading to a phenomenologically informed and shared anthropology.

But cine-trance is more than a film version of dialogical anthropology. As DeBouzek describes it (1989, 305), cine-trance occurs when
the filmmaker is possessed by film itself:

> The process of filmmaking is an act of belief, the belief that his [Rouch's]
> films are as much a product of his unconscious "filmmaker's" mind as
> they are the careful documentaries of an "ethnographer." For example,
> in the short, but revolutionary film *Tourou et Bitti* [1971], Rouch uses
> narration to explain the circumstances of the film—it was shot in one
> continuous take of a ten-minute magazine—and to wonder aloud if it
> was his own act of filming—his cine-trance—that he believes precipi-
> tated the possession trance of the dancers.

CONFRONTING POSSESSION

Faced with the power of possession in person or on film, many of us
are skeptical about its "reality." Possession is drug induced, we might
say; the mediums are fine actors. In many cases these explanations are
valid. In some possession cults drugs are ingested; in some rites mediums fake possession. In Songhay, however, possession is rarely in-

duced through drugs. And if a possession priest detects charlatanism, he publicly humiliates the offending medium (Stoller 1989a). The point is that possession is not automatic. When troupes stage ceremonies, as *Les tambours d'avant* documents, the outcome is unpredictable. If there is dissension in the troupe or the community, as we have seen already, the spirits often refuse to take the bodies of their mediums.

Les tambours d'avant also documents the possibility of cine-trance. From a reading of *Religion,* it is evident that the spirits know Europeans. They aided Rouch in his attempt to work with the sohanci of Wanzerbe. They greeted him in the audiences of possession ceremonies. Just as Rouch treated the Songhay spirits with reverence, so they have "worked" for him with kindness and consideration.

Most anthropological writers and filmmakers have a realistic view of the gulf separating self and other. It is difficult enough to communicate with acquaintances who share our culture and language; communicating with ethnographic others is much more difficult. In the field we attempt to learn "their" ways and their languages, hoping to make sense of their worlds. But the chance for misinterpretation is great, and we cannot completely immerse ourselves in their worlds, no matter how genuinely they invite us to join them.

Jean Rouch's fifty years of experience in Songhay does not undermine this realistic appraisal of the differences between self and ethnographic other. But his work, especially *Religion,* suggests that we can enter the other's world more profoundly that we may have imagined. *Les tambours d'avant* reflects Rouch's profound immersion in things Songhay. It is a film that *documents* the possibility of obviating, however temporarily, the barrier between European and African. This barrier is surmounted through the combination of Rouch's personal history among the Songhay and the presence of his camera, through which he entered a cine-trance. Had someone else been filming the sequence that day in Simiri, I am certain the mediums would not have been possessed. Such is the power of Rouch's persona in Songhay.

THE PHENOMENOLOGY OF FIELDWORK

In ten minutes of footage, *Les tambours d'avant* indexes a radical method, that of a shared, participatory anthropology. In a sense the subtext of "shared anthropology" runs through most if not all of Rouch's films. "Shared anthropology" is the story behind the story of Rouch's films. It is a story in which Rouch has used the medium of film

An offering to the spirits during a yenaandi, *Yenaandi, ou Les hommes qui font la pluie*. J. Rouch, Comité du Film Ethnographique.

to share with the "other" the results of his work. Sharing results builds a solid foundation of respect between ethnographer and other.

It would have been impossible for Rouch to film *Les magiciens de Wanzerbe* had the spirits not given their consent. In Wanzerbe Rouch "shared" his enterprise with such men as Mossi Bana and Barake Sohanci. In *The Lion Hunters* Rouch's collaborators are present in the film. Damoré Zika conceived the idea for *Jaguar* after seeing images of himself projected onto a white sheet in Ayoru, Niger. Mossi Bana's divinatory directions became *Jaguar*'s scenario. Rouch shot *Les maîtres fous* at the invitation of Mounkaiba, the high priest of the Gold Coast Hauka in 1954. In Simiri, Rouch was *en famille* as he walked among the possession players at a Black Spirit festival. Rouch was not a visiting filmmaker on location but a person who had willingly entangled himself in Songhay social life. This entanglement in the maze of Songhay relations gave him personal access to the marvels of the Songhay world. It also built a foundation of mutual respect that, in my view, is evident in his films. Rouch writes:

> The field changes the simple observer. When he works, he is no longer one who greeted the oldtimers at the edge of the village; to take up again Vertovian terminology, he "ethno-looks," he "ethno-observes," he "ethno-thinks," and once they are sure of this strange regular visitor, those who come in contact with him go through a parallel change, they "ethno-show," they "ethno-speak," and ultimately, they "ethno-think."
>
> It is this permanent "ethno-dialogue" that is one of the most interesting slants of today's ethnographic approach: knowledge is no longer a stolen secret, which is later devoured in western temples of knowledge. . . . [Knowledge] . . . is the result of an endless quest in which ethnographers and others walk a path which some of us call "shared anthropology." (Rouch and Fulchignoni 1989, 298–99)

Years before Rouch spoke these words, he had put this method into practice. He opened his being fully to the Songhay world during fieldwork in 1947–48. Influenced by Flaherty and Vertov, Rouch's ethnographic filmmaking became a shared enterprise—part of his life in Songhay. But we can never forget the substantial influence of Rouch's Songhay friends, whose ideas shaped his thoughts on field methods and filmmaking. For Rouch the contributions of Damoré Zika, Lam Ibrahim, Boubou Hama, Talou Mouzourane, Mossi Bana, Wadi Godji, Sido Zima, and Daouda Sorko—to name only the core of Rouch's Nigerien cast—have been of prime importance. They not only have shaped Rouch's life in the field but have given life to his films.

But what is this Rouchian notion of shared, participatory ethnography? Here Rouch's ethnographic practice sets an example. Participatory anthropology means spending many years in the field; it means mastering the language or languages of the field; it means conceding *our* ignorance and *their* wisdom; it means admitting our mistakes (in public and in print); it means fashioning works (in prose and film) that attempt to capture the seamlessness of thought, action, and feeling in the world, resulting in ethnographies that are fully rather than partially sensual; finally, it means expanding our audiences and our accountability. Such a radically empirical tack will not lower our scientific standards, as some critics argue, but will raise them (Jackson 1989).

The prescience of Rouch's ethnographic practice has yet to be acknowledged. During the 1980s North American anthropologists began to focus on the politics of ethnographic representation.[2] Some of these writers called attention to the death of ethnographic authority; others called for dialogic ethnographies. Still others, proclaiming the end of logocentric representation, advocated more poetic evocation in a postmodern anthropology in which kinesis had replaced privileged mimesis (Tyler 1987). All these theoretical positions and counterpositions are familiar notes in the symphony of discourse on ethnographic representation in recent anthropological prose.

Rouch's films of the 1950s and 1960s embodied themes of ethnographic postmodernity articulated in the well-known works of recent years. His ideas on participatory anthropology are, like poetic truths, embodied in his ethnographic practice, within and between the frames of his films, in his notion of cine-trance. For this reason Rouch's philosophic contributions have heretofore been underappreciated or ignored. (See chap. 12 for more on Rouch's philosophical contributions.)

The griot's charge is to speak the "old words," words that sometimes criticize people in the past. But is not the griot's task also to sing praises of the past so that, in the words of the elders, honor can replace shame, which the ancestors tell us is so powerful it survives death itself?

That too, as it is said, is the griot's task.

2. See Tedlock (1983); Clifford (1988); Marcus and Fischer (1986); and Clifford and Marcus (1986) for general arguments about dialogic and "critical" anthropology.

CHAPTER ELEVEN
The Dogon Passion

Don borey fonda, cimi fonda no.
The path of the ancestors is the true path.
—Adamu Jenitongo, late sohanci and zima of Tillaberi,
Niger

Each of the previous chapters in this part of the story has treated the ethnographic and philosophical issues of a single Jean Rouch film. Besides depicting aspects of Songhay social life and culture, these films have either documented the unthinkable or criticized the primitivism of Western academics. The previous chapters have also probed the rewards of adopting a more phenomenologically grounded stance toward ethnographic fieldwork. In this chapter my words take us to the west of Songhay to consider Rouch's series of Dogon films that follows the sixty-year cycle of Sigui ceremonies—the Dogon Passion. They demonstrate that these films are more than complements to the ethnographic texts of Marcel Griaule and Germaine Dieterlen; rather, the films are keys to the mysteries of the Sigui.

In West Africa the indeterminacies of the "old words" sometimes create puzzles. The path of the ancestors may well be the true path, but it is often difficult to follow, with many obstacles and detours along the way. In the case of the Sigui it was ultimately Rouch's camera—not Griaule's notebook—that cleared a path toward a profound ethnographic understanding of the Dogon Passion.

MARCEL GRIAULE'S DOGON

The Dogon are cultivators who live along the Bandiagara cliffs in Mali, not far from Mopti. Some Dogon villages, like Yougou and Bongo, nestle into the cliffs; others, like Amani, are on plains or plateaus. The climate is hot and rainfall is spotty; soil quality is poor.

Such a harsh environment has until recently kept the Dogon isolated from outside influences (Muslim and European). Despite the difficult conditions, Dogon men have raised millet and sorghum for centuries. More recently, Dogon women have cultivated onions as a cash crop. The Dogon are best known in the West for their art, through which they express the deep themes of their religion. The complexities of Dogon religious life—the multifaceted worship of the ancestors—have been described in the various works of Marcel Griaule and his intellectual descendants.

In the thirteenth or fourteenth century, the Dogon left Mande country and began their hundred-year migration to the Bandiagara cliffs. Although the Dogon were Keita, descendants of Sundiata Keita, founder of the Mali empire, they left their mountainous homeland of Kangaba because they refused to convert to Islam. They followed the Niger River, spending years in Segou and Djenne. During their migrations, the Dogon developed a close relationship with the Bozo, who became their joking partners. They also lived among Mossi and Kurumba during their long travels (Palau-Marti 1957; Dieterlen 1982).

The Dogon wanderings may well be indexed in their language. Even

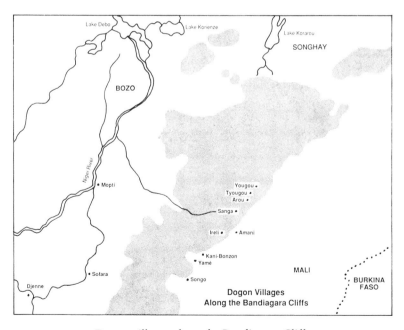

Dogon villages along the Bandiagara Cliffs.

though the Dogon are a Mande people, their tongue, according to Dieterlen, is a Voltaic language that has more in common with Mossi,
Gurmantche, and Kurumba than with Malinke or Bambara. Despite
its Voltaic syntax and morphology, the Dogon language features many
lexical items borrowed from Mande languages (Dieterlen 1982).

When the Dogon left Mande, they carried with them the soil of their
homeland, soil in which had been buried one of their mythic ancestors,
Lébé, the first person to "die"—though in appearance only. When the
ancestors opened Lébé's tomb, they discovered a living serpent surrounded by *duge* stones that had been transformed from the ancestor's
skeleton. Followed by the serpent, the Dogon traversed underground
tunnels to the Bandiagara cliffs. In Kani Bonzon, near Kani Kamboli,
they founded the first shrine to Lébé, the oldest living man of the
eighth family of Dogon ancestors.

In the thirteenth or fourteenth century the Dogon consisted of four
families. The Dyon, the Ono, and the Dommo were the offspring of
Lébé's first son, and the Arou were the descendants of Lébé's second
son, Dionou, who was the first person to truly die. At Kani Bonzon the
Dogon families divided the sacred ancestral soil among themselves and
settled the countryside. The Dyon settled the plateau; the Ono and
Dommo spread out onto the plain. The Arou remained among the
Bandiagara cliffs and became the guardians of Lébé's original shrine.
For this reason the *hogon* (priest) of Arou not only is the priest of
Lébé's shrine but is the supreme priest of all the Dogon (Paulme 1988;
Dieterlen 1982): "The various Dogon families that are descended from
these families keep alive the feeling of their original identity, even if,
following secondary migrations, they find themselves mixed together
in a single territory (especially when it comes to the Arou and Dyon)"
(Palau-Marti 1957, 12).

In the fourteenth century the Dogon seem to have occupied much
more territory than they do at present. Before the Mossi invasion, Dogon apparently lived with Kurumba populations in the region of Yatenga, north of Ouahigouya in Burkina Faso. The Mossi invasion
forced the Dogon into their current territory, north of Yatenga in contemporary Mali. Isolated by the imposing cliffs, windswept plateaus,
and parched plains, the Dogon flourished despite a succession of
peoples who claimed authority over them. These included the Songhay
(ca. 1475), the Bambara of Segou and Kaarta (ca. 1700), the Fulan of
Macina (ca. 1830), and the Toucouleur of El Hadj Omar (after 1860).
In 1893 the Frenchman Archinard took control of the Bandiagara
cliffs and followed with the conquest of Sanga after three days of
battle. Between 1893 and 1902 the French administered Dogon

through Aguibou, whom the French recognized as the king of Macina, sovereign of the Fulan. In 1902 Dogon came under direct French supervision, but it was not completely pacified until 1921 (Palau-Marti 1957, 12–13).

Marcel Griaule's Dakar-Djibouti mission arrived in Bandiagara on 28 September 1931. He and his colleagues (Michel Leiris and André Schaeffner) remained among the Dogon until 26 November of the same year. During their two months among the Dogon, Griaule and company spent most of their time in Sanga, but they also visited Yougou, the place where the Sigui begins, Tyougou, Bongo, and Songo, where the Sigui ends after its seven-year odyssey. Upon arriving in Yougou, Leiris wrote: "Arriving on foot at Yougou, in a countryside that is indeed the end of the world (a knot of houses, sacred huts, enormous crumbling caves), we made the difficult ascent, pilgrims of the Sigui, joking and thinking of Wagner. Then we camped on the highest *togu na*, or shelter for men, built well above the village in the midst of burial caves and on a rock so sheer and narrow that our beds were literally at the edge of a precipice." They slept next to the cave where the first Dogon masks had been placed. Leiris called Yougou the "lunar Rome" (Leiris 1981, 124).

During this first sojourn in Dogon, Griaule found principal informants such as Ambara Dolo, witnessed several mortuary rituals and the five-year festival of masks (*dama*), attended several sacrifices, and photographed the mysterious cave etchings at Songo.

Griaule returned to Dogon year in and year out. As a result of his long-term Dogon studies, he developed his well-known multidisciplinary method, which, as we have seen, emphasized elaborate documentation. Griaule's methods produced stunning results. He and his talented colleagues published monographs that became anthropological classics: *Masques dogons* and *Conversations with Ogotemmêli* (Griaule); *Les âmes des Dogons* and *Le titre d'honneur des Arou* (Dieterlen), *L'organisation sociale des Dogon* (Paulme); *Ethnologie et langage: La parole chez les Dogon* (Calame-Griaule); and *La langue secrète des Dogon de Sanga* (Leiris). Except for Denise Paulme's work, most Griaulian Dogon studies, whether linguistic, religious, or historical, focused on Dogon cosmogony and cosmology. For Griaule and his followers the Dogon were and continue to be the philosophers of the Sahel, a people whose ancient cosmology remained untainted by outside influences.

Several British anthropologists have wondered whether Griaule's Dogon are an invention, an expression of his own predisposition toward philosophy, a reflection of his attitudes toward the lost worlds of "the primitives." In a revelatory article Mary Douglas asks: What if the Dogon had been studied by Meyer Fortes? What if the Tallensi had been studied by Marcel Griaule? Had Griaule camped among the Tallensi, she suggests, he would no doubt have written about their complex cosmology. Had Fortes slept under the highest *togu na* at Yougou, she argues, he would no doubt have written about Dogon kinship and clanship. How much of what we "see" is conditioned by formal training, by our own epistemological predispositions, by our personal experience in the world? (See Douglas 1967; van Beek 1991, 139–67.)

Despite Douglas's playful speculation, one can neither deny the complexity of Dogon cosmogony and cosmology nor overlook the way Griaule's depiction of Dogon thought has captured our imagination. Above all, Marcel Griaule's portrait of the Dogon demonstrates powerfully that so-called primitive people do possess systems of thought whose complexity rivals that of our own. This theme runs throughout the books and films of Jean Rouch.

DOGON MYTH AND THE FIRST SIGUI

As for the myth of the Dogon, listen and learn from the wondrous tale.

In the mythic past, the god Amma threw a lump of clay into the air. As the clay flew through the air, it spread to the north, the south, the east, and the west. Amma was male; the earth was female. The anthill was the earth's vagina; the termite hill was her clitoris. Amma desired sexual relations with the anthill, but when he approached it, the termite hill erected itself and blocked his passage. No intercourse could take place until Amma cut down the termite hill. Amma had sex with the "excised" earth, but the harmony of the world was upset by Amma's act, which resulted in the birth of the pale fox, creature of disorder. Amma continued his relations with the excised earth, producing twin spirits called Nummo.

> Water, which is the divine seed, was thus able to enter the womb of the earth and the normal reproductive cycle resulted in the birth of twins. Two beings were thus formed. God created them like water. They were green in color, half human beings and half serpents. From the head to the loins they were humans: below they were serpents. Their red eyes were wide open like human eyes, and their tongues were forked like the tongues of reptiles. Their arms were flexible and without joints. Their bodies were green and sleek all over, shining like the surface of water, and covered with short green hairs, a presage of vegetation and germination. (Griaule 1965, 18)

From heaven the Nummo pair looked down upon their mother, the earth. She was without clothes and without speech, a result of her illicit relations with Amma. To remedy the shameful plight of their mother, the Nummo pair descended to her. They brought with them fibers they had grown in heavenly gardens and fashioned them into two strips that would cover their mother's front and back. The fibers were filled with the moisture of Nummo, which contained the vapors of the first language: "Thus clothed, the earth had a language, the first language of this world and the most primitive of all time. Its syntax was elementary, its verbs few, and its vocabulary without elegance. The words were breathed sounds scarcely differentiated from one another, but nevertheless vehicles. Such as it was, this ill-defined speech sufficed for the great works of the beginning of all things" (Griaule 1965, 20).

The role of speech was to organize the world, but from its mythical origins speech precipitated disorder, for the pale fox, the first son of Amma, coveted the speech of his mother, the earth. The pale fox attempted to steal his mother's skirt, whose vapors embodied speech. The earth buried herself in an anthill—in her own womb—only to be followed by the pale fox. As a result of this incest, the pale fox became imbued with language. Thereafter diviners sought him out to learn the desires of God.

Meanwhile, the blood of menstruation flowed from the earth for the first time. God abandoned his violated wife; he decided to create living beings himself. God threw the ingredients of human life—two lumps of clay—to earth, and the Nummo pair descended to earth to perfect human life. As the lumps changed into human beings, the Nummo pair drew the shadows of a man and a woman on the ground. The first man pulled both of these shadows into his being. The first woman followed suit. In this way the first man and woman were hermaphrodites. The soul of the woman was in the man's prepuce; the soul of the man was in the woman's clitoris. As long as the first man and woman were hermaphrodites, there could be no procreation. Just as the termite hill, the male aspect of mother earth, blocked God's penetration into her passage, so the presence of prepuce and clitoris would prevent harmonious procreation. The Nummo pair circumcised the man. "The man then had intercourse with the woman, who later bore the first two children of a series of eight, who were to become the ancestors of the Dogon people. In the moment of birth the pain of parturition was concentrated in the woman's clitoris, which was excised by an invisible hand, detached itself and left her, and was changed into the form of a scorpion" (Griaule 1965, 22–23).

The first four children of the primordial couple were male; the last four were female. These eight children were able to produce offspring without external intervention.

One day, the oldest of these eight children of the first man and woman entered the anthill in which the Nummo resided. The Nummo took the child into the depths of earth, in whose moisture he received language. The other ancestors followed their oldest brother's lead. But the seventh ancestor was a special case, for she received a perfect knowledge of the Word.

> What the seventh ancestor had received, therefore, was perfect knowl-edge of a Word—the second Word to be heard on earth, clearer than the first and not, like the first, reserved for particular recipients, but destined for all mankind. In particular, it enabled mankind to take precedence over God's wicked son, the pale fox. The latter, it is true, still possessed knowledge of the first Word, and could still therefore reveal to diviners certain heavenly purposes; but in the future order of things he was to be merely a laggard in the process of revelation. (Griaule 1965, 27)

Before the oldest ancestor's descent into the anthill, human beings lived like animals in holes dug in the earth. Thereafter they took notice of the anthill's shape and fashioned dwellings in its image. In this way they sheltered themselves from the elements.

The strictly human phase of the first eight ancestors was short-lived. The original Nummo pair whisked them up to heaven and trans-formed them into Nummo who were, of course, subordinate to the original Nummo pair. They became the Nummo ancestors.

But there was great disorder in the world of human beings, and the eight Nummo ancestors decided to descend to earth to help organize the world. The first ancestor, the smith, went into the world of human beings and lived among them as a man. He taught them technology. But the smith could not reorganize the world by himself. The other ancestors followed their oldest brother to earth in the order of their birth. The eighth ancestor was impatient; she came to earth before the seventh Nummo ancestor, the ancestor of speech. The seventh Nummo was so angry at her younger sibling that when she came to earth, she turned into a great serpent, which moved toward the smithy, where human beings killed it. The smith butchered the great serpent. He divided the carcass among humans and kept the head, which he buried under his anvil in the primordial field.

The seventh Nummo ancestor was the master of speech, but the eighth "is the foundation of the speech which all the other ancestors used and which the seventh taught" (Griaule 1965, 48; see also Echard and Rouch 1988, interview 10). The problem was that human beings needed to learn the third Word, which would have been taught by the seventh Nummo ancestor had she not been killed at the instigation of the smith. Someone had to die to pass into the other world, and so the oldest living man of the eighth family, which most perfectly embodied the Word, died. He was known as Lébé.

Actually Lébé did not really die, for death was unknown at that time. He only appeared to die. Human beings buried Lébé in the primordial field, which now contained the body of the oldest man of the eighth family and the head of the seventh ancestor under the smith's anvil.

The smith struck his anvil, and the sound carried underground, awakening the spirit of the seventh ancestor. He took his Nummo form of half-human, half-serpent and made his way to the grave of Lébé. He ate the first man, head first, and then vomited eight *duge* stones in the form of a person's soul. These are the stones that the *hogon* (priests) of the Dogon wear around their necks. The stones embody the eight original ancestors as well as the bones of Lébé.

Much later, human beings, led by Dyon, wanted to leave the primordial field, but not without the soil of Lébé's grave, which would protect them on their journey. And so they opened the grave and found the *duge* stones and the seventh Nummo ancestor in the form of a living serpent. In this way human beings learned that the essence of Lébé, the oldest man of the eighth ancestor family, was embodied in the *duge* stones. Lébé was the essence of the third Word, which would organize the world of human beings: "The seventh ancestor, dead only in appearance, ate Lébé, also dead only in appearance. In eating the man he took what was good in him but, for his own part, he gave his life-force to the human flesh of man, that is to say to all mankind. Thus because the seventh ancestor consumed Lébé, descendant of his brother the eighth ancestor, their respective life-forces were mingled" (Griaule 1965, 59). Lébé and Nummo became one, a fact the Dogon celebrate every year during the great Lébé sacrifice, officiated by the hogon, the oldest man of a Dogon region, who is the guardian of Lébé's shrine.

The first Lébé shrine was founded by Dyon at Kani Bonzon. The Dogon had come to the Bandiagara cliffs from the primordial field in Mande. The seventh Nummo ancestor, whom the Dogon found in Lébé's grave, followed them. The hogon is the living manifestation of Lébé and the Nummo.

In the distant past the Dogon ancestors were immortal. Lébé died only in appearance. When the seventh Nummo and Lébé died, their resurrection restored harmony to the world, though it was short-lived.

The fibers that the original Nummo pair had given to their mother the earth had been soiled by menstrual blood because of the indiscretions of the pale fox. The fibers, now red with blood, were placed on the primordial anthill to dry.

In time the fibers were stolen by a woman who terrorized human beings, for no one had ever seen such brilliant fibers. She made herself a queen. Eventually men took the fibers away from the queen and dressed themselves in the regal clothing. Women were no longer permitted to wear them.

The men who had stolen the fibers did not tell the oldest man of their theft. This omission was a serious affront to the old man, who expected respect from younger men. Like his forebears the old man, now at the end of his life, had been transformed into a Nummo. Like them he had not yet ascended to heaven; rather, he slithered along as a great serpent.

> One day when the young men had dressed themselves in their fibers, which hey kept hidden in caves, and were on their way to the village, the serpent met them and barred the way. Angry at having been flouted, he violently reproached them, speaking in the Dogon language so that they could understand; and this was the cause of his death. For, since he no longer possessed human form, the language of which was the third revealed Word, he ought to have used the language proper to spirits, into whose world he had come, that is to say, the first Word. By speaking to men in language that was familiar to them, he was transgressing a prohibition and cutting himself off from the superhuman world, in which he was now an impure element, and so could no longer live there. It was equally impossible for him to return to the world of men. Accordingly, he died then and there. (Griaule 1965, 170)

The serpent lay lifeless across the road. The frightened young men fled back to the village. They returned to the scene of death with the village elders, who decided to take the dead serpent to a cave and wrap it in the very fibers that had precipitated its demise. The soul and the force (*nyama*) of the man-serpent rose from the carcass and entered the body of a pregnant woman who was wearing a red fiber dress. This woman gave birth to a child who came out red and spotted like a serpent. He did not become normal until the village elders organized a ceremony to celebrate the death of the ancestor.

The elders put the child in seclusion while they staged the ceremony. Three years after the death of the serpent, they fashioned a great mask carved and painted in the form of a serpent (*imina na*) and made a sacrifice over it to attract the *nyama* of the dead ancestor from the temporary and insufficient home in the body of the child (Griaule 1938). The elders made the child part of the cult the village created in honor of the dead ancestor, the first person to die.

With the first death, the Dogon created the cult of the dead, whose ceremonies placed a heavy burden on the living. The most important rite of this cult is the Sigui, which is performed by all the Dogon every sixty years, the life span of the first human. The key element of the Sigui is the great mask, which is used once every sixty years.

Griaule devoted an entire section of *Masques dogons* to the description and analysis of the Sigui. He wrote:

> The goal of the Sigui rites is to renew the great mask, provide for the soul of the mythic ancestor in his serpent form, and place new initiates under his care as new recipients of the ancestral spirit.
>
> The first Sigui honored the ancestor whose death was caused by his breaking a taboo, which itself was caused by the young generation's transgression of social rules. They danced the Sigui to atone; it was also to expiate ancient sins committed by men that resulted in the introduction of death. (Griaule 1938, 166)

Through the Sigui, then, all Dogon people are imbued with the spirit of the first dead ancestor.

Griaule and his team were fascinated by the Sigui, which had last been celebrated in 1913, eighteen years before his first trip to the Bandiagara cliffs. Griaule nonetheless found many informants who were *olubaaru*, Sigui initiates who had drunk the millet beer brewed for the ceremony. With the aid of these wise men, Griaule gathered information and reconstructed the ceremonies of 1907–13, during which the great masks were brought out of caves in ceremonies that occur once every sixty years. Griaule described the Sigui costumes, the manner of dancing, aspects of Siguiso (the Sigui's ritual language), and the Sigui liturgy. Had Griaule lived another eleven years he might have witnessed the 1967 Sigui—in Yougou—himself.

THE SIGUI FILMS (1966–74)

Marcel Griaule died prematurely in 1956, leaving to Germaine Dieterlen, his dedicated associate, and is daughter Geneviève Calame-Griaule, among others, the task of continuing his longitudinal work on the Dogon. In 1965 Geneviève Calame-Griaule published her exhaustive *Ethnologie et langage: La parole chez les Dogons*. Germaine

Olubaaru dignitaries, *Les clameurs d'Amani.* J. Rouch,
Comité du Film Ethnographique.

Dieterlen, who first went to the Bandiagara cliffs in the 1930s,
dreamed of witnessing the Sigui ceremonies. During these ceremonies,
as we have seen, the Dogon celebrate the origin of death and of speech,
expressing these mythic themes through dance, costumes, and the presentation of the great serpent mask as well as through Siguiso, the lan-

guage of the Sigui. To realize the dream of recording the celebration of a Sigui, Dieterlen asked Jean Rouch to film the ceremonies that would begin in 1967.

In 1966 Rouch returned to the craggy outcroppings of the Bandiagara cliffs, to the land of the Minotaur, a land that evoked for him the paintings of Yves Tanguy, Giorgio De Chirico, and the early Salvador Dali. He and Dieterlen trekked to Arou to visit the head hogon of all the Dogon, the priest of Lébé and the descendant of the first person to die. The hogon informed them that the Sigui would begin the following year in Yougou. The hogon could not witness the ceremonies, since custom dictates that he never leave his dwelling in Arou. Rouch and Dieterlen journeyed to Yougou and found a village depleted of young men. "They'll return next year," the Yougou elders told them.

Why does the Sigui start in Yougou? In 1965 Dieterlen and Rouch may have discovered one of the keys to this mystery. At the beginning of time, God threw a celestial anvil to earth so the ancestor of smiths could shape materials with his hammer:

> The celestial anvil that had fallen into Lake Bosumtwi (a sacred lake in Ashanti) had rebounded to Yougou Dogorou in Dogon country. It was an enormous sandstone turret . . . that dominated the village and that during its second falling had crushed the first of God's creatures, the little Andouboulou elves, who preceded the first humans. And it is from there, from this anvil of Yougou, that each sixty years the Sigui begins its tortuous itinerary, following the cliffs for seven years. (Rouch 1978c, 16)

In 1967 Rouch, Dieterlen, Gilbert Rouget, and a sound technician, Guindo Ibrahim, returned to Yougou. They now found the village filled with young men more than ready to dance the Sigui. Shaded by a giant baobab tree the Sigui initiates, most naked to the waist, danced in a serpentine procession.

> I will always remember this sequenced plan (one of my first experiences with synchronous sound shooting without interruption) of several minutes, where I discovered the Tai square overrun little by little by a serpentine line of men, classed strictly by age ranks, all dressed in indigo cotton trousers, bare-chested, wearing on their necks and ears and arms their wives' or sisters' adornments, their heads covered by white embroidered bonnets . . . carrying in their right hand a fly whisk, and in their left hand the *donno,* the T-shaped chair, and singing to the rhythm of the drums, "The Sigui takes off on the wings of the wind." (Rouch 1978c, 17–18)

As Rouch filmed statues of the Andouboulou (the elves of the bush) on the third day of the Sigui ceremonies, two uniformed Malian gendarmes appeared and informed him that the permit to film that year had been revoked. By orders of the government in Bamako, Rouch had to turn his footage over to the Malian authorities.

> We then advanced a fine-grained argument: because our films are sensitive to heat, we had installed two butane refrigerators on Yougou mountain, and if one took the films to Bamako without refrigeration, they would be lost. The gendarmes went back up to Yougou mountain, saw that we had refrigerators, and at dawn we left in a Land Rover (with a refrigerator) for Bamako, a thousand kilometers away, accompanied by a police commissar. (Rouch 1978c, 18)

Somehow Dieterlen obtained a new permit to film the next day in Bamako. Rouch and Dieterlen returned to Yougou at once, sans police, and continued to film.

Rouch returned to France and showed the film, *L'enclume de Yougou* (The anvil of Yougou) to Denise Paulme and Michel Leiris. These Dogon veterans saw their first Sigui and understood nothing (Echard and Rouch 1988, interview 10). But this ceremony was very different from those described in Griaule's writings: no great serpent mask had been displayed at the Yougou Sigui. Why?

In 1968 Rouch and company went to Tyougou, a village of the plains rather than the cliffs. As in the first ceremony at Yougou, dancing proved to be the central element of this second of seven Siguis. In contrast to the dancers at Yougou, the men in Tyougou wore bright sashes and cowrie shells. There were other new elements at Tyougou:

> Another new element was the presence of a little girl, the *Yasiguine* "the sister of Sigui," carried on her father's shoulder to represent the community of women in the midst of the community of men. Something had stunned me in what Griaule had said. He said that in the Sigui, they carved and painted a great mask, the mother of all masks, which is never worn and which represents the first dead ancestor who was reborn in the form of a serpent. In Tyougou it was in front of the cave of masks, recently carved, in the form of a serpent with a tail like a bird's head, but totally unpainted. In the neighboring cave there were three large masks. Those from the Sigui of 1908, of 1848, and of 1788. (Rouch and Fulchignoni 1989, 287)

When Rouch asked when they would paint the new mask, they answered, "Next year" (Rouch and Fulchignoni 1989, 287). The film Rouch shot in 1968, *Les danseurs de Tyougou,* raised another fascinating question. Why didn't the elders paint the mother of masks?

In 1969 Rouch and Dieterlen returned to the cliffs to film *La cav-*

L'enclume de Yougou. J. Rouch, Comité du Film Ethnographique.

erne de Bongo, which I described in the introduction to part 1. To
recapitulate briefly, the ceremonies at Bongo celebrate the death of the
first ancestor, represented by an earth mound that symbolizes Lébé,
who died and was reincarnated as a serpent. At this ceremony four
great masks are displayed, depicting the dead ancestor and his resto-
ration to life. To dance the Sigui, the men don black trousers and wear
beads and cowrie shells.

A problem presented itself the following year for the Sigui at
Amani. The elders told Rouch that no one had ever seen more than
three Sigui ceremonies. Would it be dangerous for Rouch and Dieterlen to attend the ceremonies at Amani? The Dogon elders consulted
the pale fox, God's wicked first son who reveals heavenly secrets. The
diviner drew figures in the sand, and during the night the tracks of the
passing pale fox provided answers to the diviner's questions. The pale
fox indicated that Rouch could film the ceremony at Amani, but there
would be many problems.

Although Rouch and company did experience many problems with
the Malian government and with an Algerian television crew, they
were able to film *Les clameurs d'Amani.* In this ceremony the mythic
theme of the Sigui shifted from death to life—the invention of language and the creation of the world. An old master of Siguiso recounted the entire creation myth in the ritual language. The dancers
wore double sashes and no cowrie shells.

The next year, 1971, the team proceeded to Idyeli, a beautiful village squeezed against the base of a cliff and cooled by the waters of a
permanent spring. They arrived for the Sigui in the evening only to
learn that all the men were going to leave the village to begin the Sigui
on the adjacent dune. In the morning the elders permitted Rouch to go
to the dune if he promised not to eat or drink. He encountered an
incredible scene—all the men were popping out from under the sand,
having buried themselves in the dune. Rouch describes the scene he
filmed:

> In fact, the dune was dug full of burrows in which the men hid. They
> stuck out their heads like rabbits. In the shade of a tree, curled up in a
> fetal position next to their bull-roarers, slept the dignitaries, the *olu-
> baaru.* They were waiting for the awakening, for birth. Around three in
> the afternoon an old man came from the village and the *olubaaru* turned
> to the bull-roarers. The old man cried out in Siguiso and all of a sudden
> the entire dune was covered with people. New men came out of their
> placentas in the sand. Accompanied by the bull-roarers they went back
> to the village in procession. (Rouch and Fulchignoni 1989, 288)

When they reached the village, an old man cried out: "Masks, stop." The men had become masks. Like the mother of masks, they had become the first ancestor. They washed and dressed and danced, a celebration of birth, all captured in *La dune d'Idyeli*.

Back in Paris, Rouch and Dieterlen realized that no two Sigui were the same. Each ceremony constituted one chapter in the complex of the Dogon myth. The Sigui at Yougou symbolized the death of the ancestor near the smith's anvil. At Tyougou the Sigui represented the funeral of the ancestor and the beginning of her transformation into a serpent. Because the process was not complete, the great mask of Tyougou had not yet been painted. The ceremony at Bongo referenced the *dama* of the ancestor, the end of mourning. Now the metamorphosis of the serpent was complete. It was clear to Dieterlen and Rouch that death was the theme of the first three Sigui ceremonies. The Sigui at Amani, however, recounted the story of procreation and the birth of language. Here the elders teach the new initiates Siguiso and the serpent dies once again, as in the myth. The Sigui at Idyeli represented the birth of a new form of ancestor (Rouch 1978c, 20–21).

In 1972 they traveled to Yamé, a village in an Islamized zone and the site of the sixth Sigui, recorded in *Les pagnes de Yamé*. The initiates presented themselves for the Sigui, but many Islamic Dogon left Yamé; they did not want to witness a pagan rite. In Yamé the men dressed like women, wearing jewelry and women's clothing. Here the mythic theme was motherhood. "The most dramatic moment of the ceremony was when the men lined up facing one old man who said, in Siguiso, 'The Sigui has come from the east, he has come on the wings of the wind.' The men turned toward the east, then toward the west and they waited a moment, then they turned back toward the east" (Rouch and Fulchignoni 189, 289).

Circumcision, the only element missing from the mythic cycle, was no doubt the theme of the seventh Sigui at Songo in 1973. But drought sapped the Malian countryside in 1973. With millet in such short supply, people could not spare enough grain to brew the necessary amount of millet beer, which had to be drunk in large quantities. Rouch and Dieterlen did not attend the ceremonies in Songo in 1973.

In 1974 they went to Songo to reconstruct the seventh and final Sigui in *L'auvent de la circoncision*. They sacrificed a goat and took its skin and some leftover millet beer to Yougou, the site of the first of the seven Siguis. When the leftover beer and the goatskin, symbol of the circumcised foreskin, reached Yougou, the Sigui was officially over . . . until 2027, when the anvil falls from the sky, announcing the death of

Les pagnes de Yamé. J. Rouch, Comité du Film Ethnographique.

the first ancestor and the arrival of the Sigui. In the seventh and final Sigui, "the ancestor becomes a young child who returns to the hole of the anvil where he is always alive, the immortal reincarnation of Diounou Serou" (Rouch 1978c, 21).

For its finale, the Sigui returns to the hole of the smith's anvil, where in primordial times the ancestor smith kept the head of the serpent (the seventh Nummo ancestor), which humans had killed—in appearance only.

The Dogon are truly the great philosophers of the Sahel. They dramatize their most profound thoughts every sixty years during the seven-year Sigui cycle. The first three years of the cycle represent death; the final four symbolize life. The sixty years between ceremonial cycles represent the sixty-year life of the first human being. That Rouch was able to film the Sigui cycle of 1967–74 is itself a remarkable ethnographic achievement. Through the process of filming the Sigui, moreover, Dieterlen and Rouch grasped the full significance of this rarely performed rite. Here is a case in which film played the central— not a peripheral—role in an ethnographic investigation. Such had been Jean Rouch's ethnographic practice for twenty years.

FILM AND ETHNOGRAPHY

Rouch's example of shared cinema demonstrates that film is not merely a complement to the ethnographic text. From the beginning of his field research Rouch used the camera as a epistemological tool. Filming *Les magiciens de Wanzerbe* provoked questions that led him to collect magic incantations, to photograph the power objects of the sohanci, and to record historical texts. This body of field data inspired Rouch to make other films.

None of Rouch's ethnographic films can be isolated from his ethnographic research interests. In *The Lion Hunters,* Rouch made a film that tells an ethnographic tale within the frame of a child's story. But the film also raised questions about "the men of the past" and the meaning of the ancient etchings on rocks—the magic of "the men of the past." These are questions Rouch continues to reflect on, continuing to offer hypotheses—and films. *Jaguar* and *Les maîtres fous* are films about the experience of Songhay migration to the Gold Coast in the 1950s. Making these films prompted Rouch to think about the problems of social adaptation, symbolic syncretism, academic imperialism, French colonialism, and racism. Many of Rouch's political views on these themes are expressed in his admirable *Petit à petit* (1969), especially when Damoré Zika uses calipers to take the body measurements of his Parisian "informants." Rouch's experience with *Les tambours d'avant* prompted him to ponder the phenomenology of fieldwork, which for him is never dissociated from the camera. The Sigui films enabled Rouch and Dieterlen to understand more completely the complex symbolism of the Sigui rituals. In this way they

added the brushstrokes necessary to complete Marcel Griaule's ethnographic portrait of the Dogon.

During the period of the Sigui films (1967–74), Rouch teamed with
ethnomusicologist Gilbert Rouget to investigate the relationship
among music, dance, ethnography, and film. The collaboration produced two films on spirit possession: *Porto Novo* and *Horendi*.

Rouch and Rouget traveled to Porto Novo, in what was then called
Dahomey (now Benin). Rouch filmed a series of possession dances.
The footage presented a serious problem, however. Listening to the
possession music, Rouget found the patterns of variation incompre-
hensible. Rouch suggested they put some sequences in slow motion to
find an answer to this ethnographic question. They found that varia-
tions in rhythm occurred because the dancers had taken charge of the
orchestra, becoming conductors. Through *Porto Novo* they discovered
a cardinal principle of African ethnomusicology; in Africa, music follows movement.

To test this hypothesis, Rouch and Rouget traveled to Niger to film
the initiation of a Songhay possession medium. Using the same techniques, they made the following discoveries. In Songhay a possession
orchestra consists of a monochord violinist and usually four gourd
drummers. Studying the film in slow motion, Rouch and Rouget found
that three of the four drummers played the rhythm of the dance. The
fourth drummer followed the dancer, just a measure behind the other
drummers; he struck his drum to "push" the dancer. Taking their cue
from the dancer's movement, the three principal drummers adjusted
their tempo and rhythm. In this way the dancer "leads" the orchestra.

This work prompts the more general question of the role of film in
ethnography: "Is ethnographic film filmic ethnography?" (Ruby 1975;
Banks 1990). For most anthropologists ethnographic film is a frill. Until the 1970s ethnographic films resulted from nonanthropological
projects: travelers' records, politically inspired documentaries, and anthropological projects using film to complement a written ethnography. As Homiak (n.d., 4) has recently written:

> Why, given the sustained critique in recent years of "visualism" within
> anthropological epistemology, has this aspect of anthropological praxis
> [representation] not raised the same kinds of unsettling questions about
> the use of the camera as a Western technology of control used to "cap-
> ture" and represent the Other? The simplest answer here is that photog-
> raphy (and film), although almost always present in field practice, has
> never been taken seriously by anthropologists. It is seen merely as a mar-
> ginal practice used to supplement the "real" work of ethnographers—
> producing texts.

Many anthropologists have attempted to use films to reproduce objectively social reality. These "observational films" try to reproduce faithfully the texture of life in the field. "They are observational in their manner of filming, placing the viewer in the role of an observer. . . . They are essentially revelatory rather than illustrative, for they explore substance before theory" (MacDougall 1975, 110). In observational films the camera is seen as the means of documenting objectively the last flickering lights of dying cultures. Observational filmmakers therefore refrain from interacting with the people they film for fear of tainting reality. They also spend long periods in the field so that the subject people will lose interest in the camera—as if the camera were not there. As MacDougall notes (1975, 110), "Invisibility and omniscience. From this desire it is not a great leap to begin viewing the camera as a secret weapon in the pursuit of knowledge. The self-effacement of the filmmaker begins to efface the limitations of his own physicality. He and his camera are imperceptibly endowed with the power to witness the TOTALITY of an event. Indeed, they are expected to. Omniscience and omnipotence." In short, observational cinema corresponds not so much to the epistemology of *cinéma vérité* à la Vertov or Rouch as it does to a theory of realism, which creates a kind of numbness. MacDougall writes that in observational films, "the relationship between the observer, observed and the viewer has a kind of numbness."

MacDougall (1975) cited Rouch's notion of "shared cinema" as a solution to the epistemological, political, and artistic problems of observational cinema. In "shared cinema" filmmakers refuse to hide their presence. In Rouch's case, the presence of the filmmaker or his team is openly acknowledged in *Jaguar, The Lion Hunters, Les maîtres fous, Les tambours d'avant, La pyramide humaine,* and *Chronique d'un été.* In all these films, moreover, the context of filmmaking plays a central representational role. For Rouch the camera does not capture reality, it creates reality—or cine-reality—a set of images that evokes ideas and stimulates dialogue among observer, observed, and viewer.

For Rouch film is not a device for collecting data but an "arena" of inquiry. *Les magiciens de Wanzerbe* not only presents Songhay magic incantations but recounts the story of Wanzerbe, of feats of magic that are so unsettling that we are driven to question some of the assumptions of our worldview. *The Lion Hunters* not only depicts the technology of how to hunt lions but is a child's story that explains how words imbue objects with force, how magic words and objects fill hunters with the courage to face killer lions with only bows and arrows. *Jaguar* not only portrays the migration of three Nigeriens to the colonial Gold Coast but is the tale of the quest of three young dreamers, "primitives" who encounter their own "primitives" on their journey. *Les maîtres fous* not only represents the Hauka movement in the Gold Coast of 1954 but is the story of another world, the world of spirits "not yet known to us," whose grotesque strength amazes and repels us. *Les tambours d'avant* not only portrays a Songhay possession ceremony but is the story of a filmmaker who crosses an ethnographic boundary in Simiri, Niger, and enters the netherworld of the Minotaur, the world of cine-trance. The Sigui works are the filmic record of a complex ceremony; they are also the story of how films become dreams, of how the origin of the Dogon is re-created every sixty years. These achievements in film set the anthropological standard for ethnographic film.

Two recent articles on the state of ethnographic film urge future ethnographic filmmakers to follow Rouch's path of shared cinema. Akos Östör bemoans the way visual anthropologists are still discussing "tired old questions, such as: Can there be a scientific anthropology on film? Can film serve the purposes of anthropology in research and teaching (but not, apparently, in interpretation or analysis)? The concern is still mainly with first principles, abstractions, and initial conditions. Where are the *anthropological* accounts of films? Any films?" (Östör 1990, 715). Östör suggests that anthropologists concern themselves with the anthropological analysis of film. He cites the work of Jean Rouch as a case in point: "Whether filming a funeral or creating ethnographic fiction, Rouch is aiming at the best film can offer anthropology. . . . He seems to regard himself as a technician of the anthropological film and, for all his imperfections, his body of work gives us the measure of what we have to strive for. Rouch's oeuvre is unequaled in its scale and range, whether in written or filmed ethnography, a fact which alone should entitle him to serious attention. An anthropological analysis of his work has yet to be written" (Östör 1990, 722). This book is an attempt to write just such an anthropological analysis of Rouch's work.

The importance of Rouch's ethnographic practices has also received recent attention from Jay Ruby, who ruminates on the politics of cinematic representation. He suggests, among other things, that we forget the notion that film will enable us to see ethnographic worlds through the eyes of the other. What to do in the future? Ruby provides one possibility:

> Between the extreme alternatives of the subjugation of the subject by filmmakers and the domination of image production by the subject lies a third path—one found expressed by filmmaker/anthropologist Bar-

bara Myerhoff shortly before her death in 1986. Myerhoff proposed that the researcher/filmmaker seek to locate a *third voice*—an amalgam of the maker's voice and the voice of the subject, blended in such a manner as to make it impossible to discern which voice dominates the work. In other words, make films where outsider and insider visions coalesce into a new perspective. Rouch's *Jaguar* appears to be the sole documentary experiment in third voice. (Ruby, n.d., 22)

How can anthropologists represent others so that no one voice dominates the text or the film? I suggest the answer lies in Jean Rouch's notion of "shared anthropology," in which mutual trust and familiarity are built up over a long period in the field. In this way anthropologists become implicated participants in the lives of the people they represent.

At Cinema Rouch, films go "beyond observational cinema," which means they are more than empirical; they are radically empirical. At Cinema Rouch the limits of ethnography are the limits of the imagination. Ethnographers participate fully in the lives of their others. Dreams become films; films become dreams. Audiences are moved. Feeling is fused with thought and action, and viewers are awakened from their sleep.

At Cinema Rouch, as the Songhay elders like to say, one follows the path of the ancestors into a world where we not only encounter others but also encounter ourselves.

PART
III

*When Films
Become Dreams*

The poet of the future will surmount
the depressing notion of the irreparable
divorce of action and dream.
—André Breton

INTRODUCTION
Postpositions

Albeeri saani i siiro no, amaa nga no ga haw ga kay.
An old man's talk may appear to be twisted, but in the end it
   straightens itself out.
—Songhay proverb

Pundits have recently proclaimed the end of description
   and even the end of anthropology. There are also a growing number of anthropologists who believe that "scientific
anthropology" as it is currently constituted is a philosophic
impossibility. In the postmodern world, we are told, the modernist notion of representation is irrelevant. What can we
hope to describe when the Enlightenment truths we took for
granted have been undermined, when the others, no longer a
foil for our cogitative exercises, refuse to let us define them?

Scott Malcomsen (1989, 11) reports that the primitive has
disappeared. In the early days there came to the "savannahs,
pampas, atolls and yam gardens . . . pale emissaries in usually
large wooden boats. . . . The primitives of yesteryear would
be anything that was not Europe, which was their allure and
their crime." Malcomsen suggests that anthropology will end
not with a bang but a burp. "Modern white civilization—
which is but a burp, really, in the meal of history—is losing its
Others, and they are the air it has needed to breathe. The
primitives are gone and with them, one hopes, the white
people of yesteryear will depart."

Stephen Tyler (1987, 99) takes a decidedly more philosophical perspective in considering the end of description and the
end of (modernist) anthropology:

> Thus, the ethnographer's text reveals a vision of a way of life
> only inasmuch as it takes away the living dialogue, for the let-

199

ter of ethnography killeth. The ethnographer is the symbol of doom. His appearance among the natives is the surest sign of their disappearance, a disappearance that is effected as much by the textualization that purports to record and save their way of life, not for them, but for the good of science or the implicit moral lesson it has for the West, as it is brought about by political and economic domination that enables the ethnographer's presence and which his presence symbolizes.

For Tyler, "postmodernism is the name for the end of a kind of writing that begins by reading"; it is a rejection of the "plain style" of scientific discourse. In the postmodern era, according to Tyler, anthropologists are busy constructing postmodern ethnographies, texts that evoke rather than represent, texts that seek "not the thought that 'underlies' speech, but the thought that is speech" (1987, 4). More specifically,

> A postmodern ethnography is a cooperative evolved text consisting of fragments of discourse intended to evoke in the minds of both reader and writer an emergent fantasy of a possible world of commonsense reality, and thus to provoke an aesthetic integration that will have a therapeutic effect. It is in a word, poetry—not in its textual form, but in its return to the original context and function of poetry which, by means of its performative break with everyday speech, evoked memories of the *ethos* of the community and thereby provoked hearers to act ethically. (1987, 202)

Was Tyler thinking about images in *Jaguar, The Lion Hunters,* or *Les maîtres fous* when he wrote those lines? For embedded in those Rouch films are the very themes Tyler writes about. Indeed, one can say that the works of Jean Rouch meet many of the criteria Tyler sets for a postmodern anthropology, and they do so with humor and artistry.

The epistemological depth and artistic verve of Rouch's ethnography take us beyond the artificial boundary that marks the end of anthropology. Consider Tyler's notion of evocation. Rouch is indisputably the master of evocative ethnographic film. As we have already seen, his films of the Songhay do not analyze the social phenomena they seek to portray. Instead, they move viewers through powerful imagery and transcendent stories. Some are repelled by the brutality of the film *Les maîtres fous,* in which Hauka spirits chomp the boiled meat of a freshly slaughtered dog. Others are awed by the power of spirits who let mediums put their hands in pots of boiling stew with no ill effects. The images of this film transport most viewers to the Gold Coast of 1954, compelling them to consider the rigors of life in the physicosocial milieu of colonial Africa.

Rouch's films and writings repudiate intellectualism, the foundation of what Tyler calls modernism. The power of Rouch's ethnography stems from the sensuality of his cinematography and the poignancy of his narratives. He is a storyteller who fuses thought, action, and feeling to make an incontrovertible point: Songhay and Dogon, despite their lack of technological sophistication, accept and try to placate unseen, inexplicable forces that are beyond the experience of most of us in the West.

Rouch's ethnography is like the talk of a Songhay elder: it carries us off in many directions simultaneously, but in the end it straightens itself out into a wholesale critique of classical humanism, academic imperialism, and intellectualism—all of which fragment rather than reintegrate the experience of social life. Rouch's theoretical positions are embedded in his characters, in his cinematic techniques (Vertovian juxtaposition and wide-angle camera work), and in his narratives. That is the path of an artist, a twisted path that straightens itself out. The expositions of Tyler and Malcomsen, by contrast, are postpositions that do not fully consider the relevance of film to the postmodern or to the future course of ethnographic expression.

In chapter 12 I consider Rouch's contributions to anthropology. Why is it that Rouch—and ethnographic film—is marginal to premodernist, modernist, and postmodernist anthropological discourse? That discussion leads to the analysis of embodied poetic truths, narrative force, and the truth, to use Chinua Achebe's words, of fiction. At the end of this winding path, as the griots say, we return to Rouch's ethnographic practice, which has compelled him to follow a course toward a radically empirical destination. Along the way, I argue, radically empirical Rouch has blazed a trail toward future ethnographic practice—after the end of anthropology.

Chapter 12, then, considers Rouch's creative and scholarly contributions to Euro-American intellectual life in the postmodern era. In the Postface, I return to where it all began—Kalia's Niamey compound in 1942. I return to Songhay notions of word and image to consider the cultural contributions Rouch has made to Songhay intellectual life à la fin de siècle.

CHAPTER TWELVE
Rouch, Theory, and Ethnographic Film

The image is a pure creation of the mind.
It cannot be born from a comparison but from a juxtaposition of
   two more or less distant realities.
The more the relationship between two juxtaposed realities is
   distant and true, the stronger the image will be—the greater its
   emotional power and poetic reality.
—Pierre Reverdy

In chapter 11 we saw that Rouch's shared filmmaking is, in David MacDougall's words, "beyond observational cinema." In this chapter I extend the notion of shared cinema to general ethnography, for in Rouch's notion of participatory anthropology one moves beyond observational ethnography into a world of radical juxtapositions, of poetic evocations, of children's stories that frame epistemological critiques. Some critics have called Rouch's methods phenomenological. I find William James's idea of radical empiricism a more apt description of Rouch's method of ethnographic research and his theory of ethnographic representation. In this final chapter, then, I shall describe Rouch as a radical empiricist for whom lived experience is a primary component of fieldwork. The result of Rouch's radical empiricism, I suggest, is a corpus of ethnography that provides a model for a more empathic, more faithful, and more artistic kind of anthropological expression. In the end Rouch's ethnography is suited to a world in which the mirror of reality has been not merely cracked, but shattered and scattered to twinkle like so many rhinestones in the fading light.

WORD AND IMAGE

There is little mention of film, photography, or Rouch in recent anthropological discourse, postmodern or otherwise. The reason is put forward by Jean-Claude Muller (1971) in his review of Rouch's *Les maîtres fous*. Among other things, Muller says that films are complements to ethnographic texts; they are, in the words of John Homiak (n.d.), "images on the edge of the text." The straight lines of the text shape anthropological discourse, molding a variety of right-angled structures. These precise constructions create fine-tuned order out of the chaotic disorder of social life.

Nietzsche would have called such an epistemological tack the flight from truth's terror (Heller 1988; Nietzsche 1871). Whatever one calls it, the need to create textual order out of experiential chaos has a long history in the Western philosophical tradition; it dates to the post-Socratic creation of mimesis.

In scholarly representation, the creation of order out of chaos is embodied in the Baconian notion of plain style. Plain style reduces the ambiguous, contradictory nature of experience-in-the world, replacing it with a transparent, unencumbered, clear language sapped of life, a style "of language so perfectly fitted to the world that no difference could insinuate itself between words and things. . . . The great goal was to create an order of discourse that mirrored the mind that mirrored the world that mirrored the discourse" (Tyler 1987, 7). In plain style rhetorical flair is frowned on, and metaphors are out of bounds. In plain style narratives are suspect, for they reflect the contingent rather than reinforcing the certain.

Plain style fills the pages of anthropological journals, monographs, and abstracts, which are supposed to be written in disinterested third person. Plain style also fills the frames of observational films. Plain style reduces the complexity of the world to simple structures, principles, laws, axioms, all expressed in simple, bloodless sentences or numb, indifferent images. Such bloodless texts or films about Africa prompted Ousmane Sembène to remark that Africanists "observe us like insects." The theoretical assumption of plain style ethnography is that the observing eye captures the "really" real—realism.

Plain style usually stands for scientific discourse. In plain style theoretical arguments are evaluated not by the aptness of their metaphors, but by the consistency of their internal logic. Theories should be spelled out point by point. Logical relations are sequenced in space; they are linear. Logical arguments, by consequence, call for literal readings and literalist evaluations. In the arena of plain style there is little space for metaphor, for poetic images, for evocative prose. These either are complements to the argument (the text) or are beside the point. Because most anthropologists are engaged in plain style discourse—the writing and reading of plain style—most of them have

Damoré Zika and Lam Ibrahim in *Petit à petit*.

difficulty evaluating the significance of the implicit messages of photography and film. It is for this reason that Jean Rouch is well known
for his technical innovations in film but not for the contributions his
films make to theories of ethnographic representation.

DREAMLANDS

There have been many artists, novelists, and filmmakers who, like the
plain stylists of the human sciences, have dreamed of re-presenting reality. In painting there is, of course, the work of Courbet and Delacroix. In literature one thinks of Zola, Dickens, and the much-
ballyhooed contemporary "social" realism of Tom Wolfe. The vast
majority of ethnographic films are "observational"; they attempt to
record life as it is "really" lived.

And yet during the twentieth century any number of avant-garde
movements have attempted to break the realist hold on the arts and
philosophy. Movements like Dadaism and Surrealism bred experiments in painting, poetry, fiction, and film.

Led by André Breton, the Surrealists coveted the human imagination, crating a kind of *pourquoi pas* stance toward life. Listen to Breton in his *First Surrealist Manifesto:*

Threat is piled upon threat, one yields, abandons a portion of the terrain to be conquered. This imagination which knows no bounds is hencefor-ward allowed to be exercised only in strict accordance with the laws of an arbitrary utility.

Breton's enemy, of course, is logic:

> We are still living under the reign of logic: this, of course, is what I have been driving at. . . . The absolute rationalism that is still in vogue allows us to consider only facts relating directly to our experience. . . . Under the pretence of civilization and progress, we have managed to banish from the mind everything that may rightly or wrongly be termed super-stition, or fancy; forbidden is any kind of search for truth which is not in conformance with accepted practices. . . . The imagination is perhaps on the point of reasserting itself, of reclaiming its rights. (Breton 1924, translated in Lippard 1970, 10, 12)

Breton's insights compelled his friends to create artistic images that defied the established intellectual order, that *embodied* in tableaux, sculpture, poetry, and film the oneiric qualities of the human imagina-tion. The Surrealists carried their art beyond observational represen-tation into a kind of dreamland of irreducible images that defied cate-gorization.[1]

The vast potential of film attracted the attention of the Surrealists. During the Surrealist era Philippe Soupault wrote cinematographic poems; Robert Desnos, Antonin Artaud, Salvador Dali, and Luis Buñuel wrote film scenarios. Since the primary interest of these writers was to experiment with such cinematic techniques as montage, few of their scenarios were made into films, the most notable exception being Dali and Buñuel's *Un chien andalou*.

Writing of Surrealist films in general, Kuenzli (1987, 10) says: "In order to rupture the symbolic order, the Surrealist films rely on char-acters, on narrative, on optically realistic effects which hook the viewer into the world portrayed by the film. Only through the viewer's identification with the familiar world invoked by the film can the film's sequential disruptions of that invoked familiar world have the poten-tial to disrupt the viewer's symbolic order and open up surpressed un-conscious drives and obsessions." While Kuenzli may have been think-

---

1. There are too many texts on Surrealism to cite here. Among the most useful are Balakian (1986) and Lippard (1970); the latter contains comments from the Surrealists themselves. Some of the best comments from Surrealist painters can be found in Char-bonnier's collection of interviews (1980). Anthropologists should compare Clifford's comments on Surrealism (1988) with those of the Surrealists themselves, such as Breton (1924, 1929). For commentary on Rouch and Surrealism, see DeBouzek (1989).

ing of *Un chien andalou*, his prose aptly describes the filmic techniques of Jean Rouch used in the *Les maîtres fous* and the *Les magiciens de Wanzerbe*, both of which disrupt viewers' symbolic order, their taken-for-granted assumptions about the world.

From a realist perspective, Surrealist poems and films are illogical; they were—and are—largely dismissed from the theoretical discourse in philosophy and the human sciences. Such has been the case for most artistic experiments. Art may move people to think new thoughts and feel new feelings, but it does not articulate theories that enable us to "know" the truth. Getting back to the canon of plain style, theories should be presented in linear and logically cohesive arguments. In the arts, as Yeats first noted, human beings cannot "know" truth, they can only "embody" it (Graff 1979, 6). Jean Rouch's films make no claim to representational truth, but the images in his works embody the truths of the worlds and peoples they portray. This is why Rouch is known more for his artistic innovations than for his philosophical sophistication.

The split between no-nonsense plain style and metaphorically nuanced narrative style is unfortunate. Anthropologists have much to learn from artists and novelists, whose images and narratives evoke themes that we stumble upon years after their artistic creation. Self-referentiality, for example, is one of the key themes of the postmodern debate that raged ten years ago in literature and rages today in anthropology. The notion of self-referentiality in a fragmented world where classical boundaries have disappeared is a central theme in the plays of Luigi Pirandello, who wrote his most important works between 1917 and 1930, and Bertolt Brecht, who was most active in the 1930s and 1940s. These plays evoked postmodern themes years before philosophers and literary critics articulated them in plain style (Gaggi 1989).

What is true for the plays of Pirandello and Brecht is also true for the novels of Franz Kafka and Milan Kundera. In "fictional" works these Central European novelists evoke powerful, incontrovertible truths. Kundera says:

> Novelists draw up *the map of existence* by discovering this or that human possibility. But again, to exist means: "being-in-the world." Thus *both* the character *and* his world must be understood as *possibilities*. In Kafka, all that is clear: the Kafkan world does not resemble any known reality, it is an *extreme and unrealized possibility* of the human world. It's true that this possibility shows faintly behind our own real world and seems to prefigure our future. That's why people speak of Kafka's prophetic dimension. But even if his novels had nothing prophetic about them, they would not lose their value, because they grasp one possibility

of existence (a possibility for man and for his world) and thereby make us see what we are, what we are capable of. (1988, 43)

Have the novelist's images, characters, and narratives cut a clear path through the obfuscating vines and creepers of philosophical discourse? Have they seized elements of human being that are beyond the reach of social thought? Kundera thinks so. These are his concluding comments about Kafka:

> If I hold so ardently to the legacy of Kafka, if I defend it as my personal heritage, it is not because I think it worthwhile to imitate the inimitable (and rediscover the Kafkan) but because it is such a tremendous example of the *radical autonomy* of the novel (of the poetry that is the novel). This autonomy allowed Franz Kafka to say things about our human condition (as it reveals itself in our century) that no social or political thought could ever tell us. (1988, 117)

Kundera's novelistic practice is a case in point. His books about love, laughter, life, and death in totalitarian Czechoslovakia evoke the insanity of that world better than any polemic political tract or dispassionate academic analysis.

What is it about some fiction that cuts to the heart of the human predicament? Discussing the *The Palm-Wine Drinkard,* the principal work of Nigerian novelist Amos Tutuola, Chinua Achebe (1989, 144) writes about what he calls the truth of fiction":

> Tutuola performs the miracle of transforming us into active participants in a powerful drama of the imagination in which excess in all its guises takes on flesh and blood. Afterwards we can no longer act as hearers only of the word; we are initiates; we have made our visit; we have encountered ourselves in the Drinkard in much the same way as the Drinkard had encountered himself in the course of a corrective quest— albeit unknowingly—in that preposterous clump of unpleasantness that is his own son, the half-bodied baby. The encounter like much else in the novel is made unforgettable for us because of Tutuola's inventiveness not only in revealing the variety of human faces that excess may wear, but also in his deft exploration of the moral and philosophical consequences of breaching, through greed, the law of reciprocity which informs like a gravitational force the seemingly aberrant motions of his bizarre, fictive universe.

In ethnographic and ethnofiction film, Rouch carries his viewers onto an almost Tutuolian dreamscape. *Jaguar* takes us there, as do *Les magiciens de Wanzerbe, Les maîtres fous, The Lion Hunters,* and *Les tambours d'avant.* On this dreamscape, Rouch provokes us to consider aspects of the human condition in ways, to paraphrase Kundera, that no theoretically sophisticated cultural analysis can do.

Does this mean that former models of ethnography and ethnographic film are riddled with useless illusions, that their shelf lives have long since expired? Not at all. It does mean that techniques associated with the fiction side of the spurious opposition fact/fiction must be incorporated in future ethnographic practice and representation. To cope with the dizzying vicissitudes of contemporary life in the era of late consumer capitalism, we need to adopt ethnographic forms that defy classical genre classifications, that express the notion of simultaneity through such cinematic techniques as montage (see Marcus 1990; Stoller 1989a; Morrissette 1985; Deleuze 1989).

There are two models worth following here: that of Herman Broch in prose and that of Jean Rouch in film. Dan Rose (1990, 56) argues that Broch's *The Sleepwalkers* captures the major theme of our fragmented era: the loss of cultural values. In the novel the "theme is manifest at two levels: (1) in the lives of the characters who live between its covers, and (2) in the multiple genres used by Broch to convey narrative, poetically induced feeling and idea."

Rose's comments on Broch are applicable to most of Jean Rouch's films, which crisscross the boundaries between documentary and fiction, observer and participant. In film Rouch makes us confront a world in the throes of change, a world rocked by racist expectations that his characters continually defy. Are Nigerien peasants supposed to take philosophical journeys? Are hapless stevedores supposed to express their existential angst with poetic feeling? Are illiterate peasants in Wanzerbe supposed to know secrets beyond our comprehension? Are anthropologists supposed to become socially entangled and fall in love with the people they portray?

Rose argues (1990, 56–57) that a future ethnography—in prose—will have to be "a polyphonic, heteroglossic, and multigenre construction" that will include:

(1) the author's voice and own emotional reactions.
(2) critical theoretical humanist mini-essays that take up and advance the particular literature and subliterature of the human sciences and particular disciplines (perhaps an ethnography will develop one or two ideas that provide coherence to the entire book).
(3) the conversations, voices, attitudes, visual genres, gestures, reactions and concerns of daily life of the people with whom the author participates, observes and lives will take form as a narrative and discourse in the text—*there will be a storyline.*

(4) poetics will also join the prose.
(5) pictures, photos, and drawings will take up a new more interior relation to the text—not to illustrate it, but to document in their own way what words do in their own way.
(6) the junctures between analytic, fictive, poetic, narrative and critical genres will . . . cohabit the same volume.

Rose's comments about prose ethnographies can apply to ethnographic films, which, to capture the oneiric quality of life in a thoroughly wired world, will also have to defy genre restrictions, a practice Jean Rouch introduced more than forty years ago.

Rose is suggesting, in the end, that social life today is far too complex to be reduced to either plain style or narrative style. Indeed, Broch's fiction and Rouch's films are more than surreal dreamscapes; they are radically empirical attempts at representation—attempts to depict the tangible and evoke the intangible. For me, radical empiricism is the model for future ethnographic practice and representation, a model inspired by Jean Rouch's example. In the remaining sections of this chapter, I describe the roots of radical empiricism and then consider Rouch's oeuvre in radically empirical terms.

RADICALLY EMPIRICAL ROOTS

Radical empiricism springs from two sources: the Continental phenomenology of Edmund Husserl and the American pragmatism of William James and John Dewey. Both of these philosophies constituted minority currents in the stream of Western metaphysics. They were critiques of the received wisdom of classical humanism and the experiential distancing of intellectualism, in which the pure thought of the mind is considered an objective domain beyond the subjective excesses of the sensual body (Hiley 1988).

European phenomenology emerges from Husserl. In his transcendental phenomenology Husserl, like so many before him, attempted to resolve the European crisis in philosophy, which emanated from the chasm that divided self and other, subjective and objective, idealist and realist. Husserl's solution was the *Epoche*, a methodological device that would mystically fuse self and other, sensible and cogitative.

> The strategy for beginning, in Husserl's case, was one which called for the elaboration of a step-by-step procedure through which one viewed things differently. His model was one of analogy to various sciences, often analytic in style; thus he built a methodology of steps: *epoche*, the psychological reduction, the phenomenological reduction, the eidetic

reduction and the transcendental reduction. At the end of this labyrinth of technique what was called for was a phenomenological attitude, a perspective from which things are to be viewed. (Ihde 1976, 19)

In the end, the *Epoche* was an effort "to return to things themselves, to let things speak, to let them show themselves" (Husserl 1960, 12). In the view of Don Ihde, Husserl's transcendental phenomenology constituted a philosophy of experience, a kind of radical empiricism.

Richard Zaner underscores Ihde's conception of phenomenology as a form of radical empiricism. The empiricism of Locke and Hume considered philosophical knowledge either as individual things in space or as commonsense perceptions. Zaner writes (1970, 38):

> What that form of empiricism obscured, and led one to believe was non-existent or to ignore officially, is that our experience is far richer than empiricism would admit. Not only are there different ways of experiencing the same things—sense perceptually (in different modes), remembering, imagining, depicting, expecting and still others—but some things are not at all accessible or reducible to sensory perception. . . . Thus while phenomenological philosophy, as critical philosophy, shares empiricism's insistence that philosophy be attentive to things themselves as experienced, it differs from empiricism in its contention that experience is seen to be, when critically viewed, much wider, more articulated, and far more complicated than empiricism traditionally acknowledged it to be.

In his various writings, Alfred Schutz extended phenomenology from the philosophical plane to the social arena. Like Husserl, Schutz concerned himself with human intentionality in everyday life. How do we make decisions in a given social setting? Schutz suggested that our social decisions derive from our biographically determined situations (Schutz 1962, 1967). Again, like Husserl, Schutz focused on what he called "the natural attitude," which is tantamount to everyday life. He also wrote about a variety of other attitudes that constitute the experiential matrix: dreams, fantasy, and the scientific approach. In his writing on "multiple realities" Schutz demonstrated how these various "attitudes" interpenetrate as experience in the flux of social life. Schutz's phenomenology is therefore profoundly cultural, for the play of attitudes guides our social behavior in the world and helps us interpret that of others. In addition, his minute focus on the relation of self to other, which inspired the work of Harold Garfinkel and Erving Goffman, cuts to the heart of the anthropological field encounter; it pinpoints the complexity of simple interaction in our own culture, let alone interaction in an alien culture.

Much of the phenomenological literature, especially the writings of Husserl, is obscure and inaccessible. Some of its themes nonetheless share common ground with aspects of William James's philosophical doctrine, especially his notion of radical empiricism. As James Edie, among others, has pointed out (1965, 116), William James failed to articulate his philosophical ideas in a rigorous manner, resulting in much confusion about ideas like radical empiricism. It is clear, however, that James and Husserl worked toward many of the same goals. Like Husserl, James took an antimetaphysical, anti-intellectual stance. Like Husserl, James wanted to erase artificial metaphysical boundaries by giving philosophical priority to the flux of experience. Like Husserl, James considered the question of meaning at the center of philosophical reflection, which meant that human being-in-the-world became the cornerstone of a philosophical anthropology.

James's radically empirical philosophical anthropology focuses on experience, reality, reason and belief, the self, and action. Although these topics are woven seamlessly through James's thought, it is in his writings about experience and reality that we get the most concrete statement on radical empiricism, a return to the apprehension of "pure experience" as it is perceived in "the immediate flux of life": "To be radical, an empiricism must neither admit into its constructions any element that is not directly experienced, nor exclude from them any element that is directly experienced. For such a philosophy, *the relations that connect experiences must themselves be experienced relations, and any kind of relation experienced must be accounted as 'real' as anything else in the system*" (James 1943, 42). For James the stream of consciousness "is not composed of 'substantive parts' only but also of 'transitive parts'—not only of experiences designated by nouns, but of those designated by conjunctions, prepositions, adverbs, syntactic forms and inflections of voice as well" (Edie 1965, 116).

The radical empiricist is therefore confronted with a world of immense complexity, full of phenomenological contradictions, that defies the rarefaction of system building and the reductionism of intellectualist theory building.

What are the epistemological consequences of a radical empiricism? First, radical empiricism expands the scope of the philosophical gaze:

> More generally, radical empiricism confers equality of status on all the intellectual and spiritual activities of man. It shows up the superstition that science alone is in touch with the real and can say anything useful about it. It disposes of the thought-cliché that "the sciences of nature have progressed but the sciences of man are in their infancy." It settles

the question of art—is it illusion or a path to reality? Does beauty, emotion, meaning, sublimity reside in the object or the beholder? The empiricist critic or connoisseur understands that qualities are relational but genuine. As for the artist, if he sees his work as done within and upon experience—the endlessly malleable medium—he is freed from the tyranny of previous "rules" and of contemporary dogmas; he can create a taste by which he is to be judged and live to see nature imitating his art. The moralist also, or the mystic, or the simple believer is entitled to treat his experience as a reality when he comes upon it, instead of being bound to discount it at once as illusory. (Barzun 1983, 120)

In short, James's notion of radical empiricism questions the certainty of science, the certainty that through proper scientific methods the investigator—of social life, in our case—ultimately discovers the truth.

In large measure John Dewey's philosophy, especially the ideas spelled out in *Art as Experience* and *The Quest for Certainty,* continues—in a more rigorous manner—James's battle against intellectualism. In *Art as Experience* Dewey focuses some of his attention on what Keats called "negative capability." Dewey notes that for Keats, Shakespeare was a man of enormous negative capability, the capacity for "being in uncertainties, mysteries, doubts, without any irritable reaching after fact or reason" (Dewey 1980a, 22). To have negative capability is to embrace, even relish, the ambiguities, uncertainties, and imponderables of lived experience.

Experience, of course, is what Keats's "negative capability" is all about. As Dewey strongly suggests, experience is a radically empirical domain in which thoughts, feelings, and actions are inseparable. Experience is continuous for every human being; it is not only ethereal, but fundamentally aesthetic. For Dewey the aesthetic, an intrinsic component of experience, " is not an intruder in experience from without, whether by way of idle luxury or transcendent ideality, but . . . is the clarified and intensified development of traits that belong to every normally complete experience" (Dewey 1980a, 46). For Dewey, then, there is no intellectualist separation of ideal expression—Art—and prosaic expression—art or folk art. There can be no idealization of experience, aesthetic or otherwise. In the tradition of the skeptics from Sextus Empiricus to Nietzsche, Dewey writes that truth "never signifies correctness of intellectual statements about things or truth as its meaning is influenced by science" (Dewey 1980a, 3). It denotes the wisdom human beings live by. Jean Rouch's ethnographic films bring to life the very issues Dewey writes about; they bring into respectful relief the wisdom the Songhay and Dogon of West Africa life by.

RADICALLY EMPIRICAL ANTHROPOLOGY

A radically empirical anthropology is one that places a premium on field experience; it is field anthropology that does not privilege theory over description, thought over feeling, and sight over the "lower" senses (touch, smell, taste). It is an anthropology in which investigators practice Paul Riesman's notion of "disciplined introspection," in which they are more than passive observers in quest of ever elusive objectivity, more than methodical treasure hunters in search of buried truth. It is an anthropology that recognizes blatant incongruities, confounding ambiguities, and seemingly intolerable contradictions—the texture of life as it is experienced in the field. It is the implicated anthropology of phenomenological explorers who have the temerity to peek at what lies behind the mirror of reality (Bergé, n.d.). It is the sensual anthropology of scholars intent on describing social life from the perceptual orientation of the other. It is an anthropology of commitment in which scholars return to the field year after year to glean new insights from changing sociopolitical or socioeconomic conditions, insights that enable them to "know the place for the first time" (Eliot 1942).

Experience in the Field

In *Paths toward a Clearing* Michael Jackson (1989, 3–4) demonstrates the relevance of radical empiricism to the anthropological field encounter:

> The importance of this view for anthropology is that it stresses the ethnographer's *interactions* with those he or she lives with and studies, while urging us to clarify ways in which our knowledge is grounding in our practical, personal and participatory experience in the field as much as our detached observations. Unlike traditional empiricism, which draws a definite boundary between observer and observed, between method and object, radical empiricism denies the validity of such cuts and makes the *interplay* between these domains the focus of its interest.

Jackson goes on to compare a radically empirical anthropology to quantum mechanics, arguing for the centrality of the *interaction* of observer and observed. The difference between physical science and anthropology, of course, is that the latter comprises two-way relations with living, creative beings.

> The orderly systems and determinate structures we describe are not mirror images of social reality so much as defenses we build against the

unsystematic, unstructured nature of our *experiences* within that reality. Theoretical schemes and the neutral, impersonal idioms we use in talking about them give us respite from the unmanageable flux of lived experience, helping us create illusory word-worlds which we can more easily manage because they are cut off from the stream of life. In this sense, objectivity becomes a synonym for estrangement and neutrality a euphemism for indifference.

Jackson's critique of anthropological neutrality and indifference is consistent with Tyler's censure of the epistemology of plain style and MacDougall's characterization of the "numbness" of observational cinema. In a radically empirical anthropology, according to a phenomenologically and pragmatically informed Jackson, our experiences are central to the field enterprise and to the construction of anthropological knowledge. In this mode, our experiences become primary data. As in Jean Rouch's "shared anthropology," experience "becomes a mode of experimentation, of testing and exploring ways in which our experiences conjoin or connect us with others, rather than the ways they set us apart" (Jackson 1989, 4).[2]

Participation

Radically empirical anthropologists participate fully in the lives of those they seek to describe. How could it be otherwise if one is committed to a sensorially aware, experience-driven kind of fieldwork? In this sense, however, participation does not mean "participant observation," anthropology's most famous oxymoron; rather, it means that anthropologists open themselves to other worlds as they acknowledge their implication—their entanglement—in networks of social relations.

Immersion or fuller participation in other worlds can yield striking results. Take Jean Rouch's years of association with the Songhay of Niger. In his case the spirits—in the bodies of mediums—told the great magicians of Wanzerbe to teach him about Songhay sorcery and possession. In my case, thirty years later, the spirits also paved the way for my entry into the world of Songhay sorcery. We both became apprentices—full participants in Songhay life. As apprentices our first lesson was that one is ignorant; one knows nothing. From that time on we built our knowledge, and we continue to build it. Apprenticeship demands respect. If there is one underlying theme in Rouch's films and

2. See also titles on the anthropology of the senses, which are part and parcel of a radically empirical anthropology: Howes (1988a,b, 1990); Seeger (1981); Corbin (1986); and Feld (1982).

my books, it is that a deep respect for other worlds and other ideas, ideas often preposterous to our own way of thinking, is central to a future ethnographic practice.

RADICALLY EMPIRICAL ROUCH

Although Jean Rouch would heartily consider himself an ethnographer, an anthropologist, a filmmaker, an artist, and a poet, he probably would not classify himself as a radical empiricist. As I have already mentioned, Rouch, like William James, prefers to spin revelatory tales in films or interviews rather than to rigorously outline his theory of knowledge. Since 1960 he has published only a few articles, in which he rather obliquely articulates his ideas about film and ethnography, but he has never presented a detailed account of his epistemology (see Rouch 1974, 1978a, b, c).

Rouch's commentary about anthropological fieldwork and anthropological knowledge, like his films, is underdetermined. If we limit our analysis to what he has said, we miss Rouch's principal contributions to anthropology. If we examine Rouch's oeuvre directly, however, we discover that he is by all accounts a pioneering radical empiricist.

First, Rouch is an ethnographer, not a social theorist. He is unequivocal about this at the end of *La religion et la magie Songhay,* where he dismisses the search for explanatory "elementary structures," favoring instead the description of Songhay religion, which is "above all an original religion" (Rouch 1989, 321). Like Husserl, he wants to return to things themselves, to let things express themselves. Indeed, in *Religion* Rouch gives much space to Songhay exegesis, devoting many pages to Songhay definitions of religious concepts and to Songhay commentary on myths and rituals. Here he transfers Husserl's principles to the human arena; he lets the Songhay express their ideas in their own words. This textual strategy demonstrates Rouch's profound respect for Songhay ideas, practices, and wisdom, a respect that, when acknowledged by his Songhay hosts, led him deep into the often inexplicable worlds of Songhay sorcery and possession.

Second, as an ethnographer Rouch has privileged experience in his methodological scheme. He has worked steadily among the Songhay since 1942. He is the veteran of hundreds of possession rituals. He has committed much of his adult life to Niger and Mali, a commitment as much to his friends as to his work. For Rouch it is difficult to separate one's lived experience—one's implication in the life of others—from one's work. Discussing the initial fieldwork experience of Nadine Wanono among the Dogon, Rouch says: "I dwell on these first unpredictable moments [in the field] in which everything is decided, in which all can fall apart or all can succeed, and which depends upon a single look, a single gesture, a single word. This is something that no university can teach, with the exception of the fertile disorder of Henri Langlois or the secret poetry of Marcel Griaule" (Rouch 1987, 3). In the field one connects or is cast away. It may take years for us to understand *them*, but they usually understand *us*—the nature of our humanity—straightaway. Because Rouch understands this humanistic maxim, his ethnography devolved from the strict methods he inherited from Marcel Griaule and evolved from the texture of his relationships with Damoré Zika, Lam Ibrahim, Tallou Mouzourane, Mossi Bana, Wadi Godji, Daouda Sorko, and a score of others. Damoré Zika painted some of the most brilliant strokes in Rouch's filmic portraits of the Songhay. He conceived the idea of *Jaguar* after seeing himself for the first time in a film. He suggested that Rouch add the contrasting scenes at the end of *Les maîtres fous* so that we could see, for example, that the Hauka "general" was, in fact, just a private (Echard and Rouch 1988, interview 8).

Third, Rouch's work demonstrates his "negative capability." Rouch, like Keats and William James, is able to tolerate, and often to relish, the ambiguities, conflicts, and contradictions that experience presents to us. In *Les magiciens de Wanzerbe* and *Les maîtres fous* he does not attempt to explain or reduce the inexplicable; rather, he films images that challenge the rationality of our thought. Like the work of any good playwright or poet, Rouch's films do not represent theories of possession or magic, they embody them, leaving to the audience the opportunity to resolve ethical, cultural, political, or epistemological problems.

Fourth, Rouch uses his camera-being to describe sensually the world of the Songhay. Although limited by his medium, he has made films that are sensually evocative. From *Cimetière dans la falaise* to *Horendi*, Rouch's films have probed the relations of sound, vision, and action. In *Horendi* he demonstrates how movement—the possession dancer—directs the music of the possession orchestra. In *Les tambours d'avant* he makes sure to film the deities as Daouda Sorko douses them with perfume, for each family of Songhay deities has its favorite perfume, whose scent can sometimes trigger or lengthen possession episodes. As in Cézanne's paintings, some of the images in Rouch's films evoke the smells of the market and the textures of objects. Rouch's visual and acoustic sensuality—his embodiment as a filmmaker—gives his films a sense of ethnographic presence.

THE LIFE OF THE STORY

Radically empirical anthropologists force themselves to confront the vagaries of life as they unfold in experience. Stripped of the reductionist theories that molded their professional training in the academy, they open their being to the wonders of the world. Entering the tangle of social relations in which they are implicated, confronting the maze of the experiential world, radically empirical anthropologists are hard pressed to express themselves in "plain style."

Given the radically empirical "attitude," anthropologists mix their genres, sometimes employing narrative style, sometimes employing plain style, sometimes blurring the lines between fact and fiction. Michael Jackson expresses this point powerfully when he compares a radically empirical anthropological discourse to the game of cat's cradle: "Can our discourse be likened to these string figures, a game we play with words, the threat of the argument whose connection with reality is always oblique and tenuous, which cross to and fro, interlacing description with interpretation, instruction with entertainment, but always ambiguously placed between practical and antinomian ends? If so, truth is not binding. It is in the interstices as much as it is in structure, in fiction as much as in fact" (Jackson 1989, 187). Jackson could have been thinking of Rouch, whose films often blur the distinction between fact and fiction, documentary and story, self and other.

Rouch's lesson to us is *not* that ethnographic film is the answer to anthropology's representational and theoretical quandaries. After all, anthropologists have made a great many bad ethnographic films. Rather, Rouch's work illuminates one of Jackson's "paths toward a clearing." For Steven Feld (1989, 243), Rouch's films

> simultaneously enunciate the dedication to participation, involvement, long-term ethnographic commitment—with Songhay, Dogon, Parisians—and the processual, revelatory power of cinema to unleash and stimulate new ways of representing familiar scenes. It is a recognition of the parallel improvisatory and dramaturgical qualities of both everyday life and direct filming that signals the intersection of social and cinematic theory in Rouch's oeuvre. And it is from that recognition that his work so forcefully dissolves and obliterates the parochial distinctions between fact and story, documentary and fiction, knowledge and feeling, improvisation and composition, observation and participation.

Rouch stresses this view in one of the many interviews he has given over the years:

For me, as an ethnographer and filmmaker, there is almost no boundary between documentary film and films of fiction. The cinema, the art of the double, is already a transition from the real world to the imaginary world, and ethnography, the science of the thought systems of others, is a permanent crossing point from one conceptual universe to another; acrobatic gymnastics where losing one's footing is the least of the risks. (Rouch and Fulchignoni 1989, 299)

Perhaps our way to the future of anthropology is to follow Rouch's lead, lose our footing, and experience the exhilaration of crisscrossing ethnographic and epistemological boundaries. Perhaps our way to a future ethnographic practice is to learn anew how to dream, how to fall in love.

POSTFACE
The Work of the Griot

Ni bon bay za borey mana ni bay.
Know yourself before others get to know you.
—Songhay proverb

Me ra hari si danji wi.
One doesn't put out a fire with one mouthful of water.
—Songhay proverb

In the Songhay world there are many proverbs that speak to the concept of preparation. One must be ready to undertake any task. The more daunting the task, the more one must prepare. Sorcerers and possession priests must apprentice themselves to masters until they are "ready" to practice their crafts. In many cases an apprenticeship will last more than twenty years. Apprentices prepare themselves in two ways. First, they master skills and acquire specialized knowledge. For sorcerers and possssion priests, this means learning to find and identify plants and to prepare potions and incense, and memorizing hundreds of praise poems and incantations. Many apprentices quickly gain command of this esoteric knowledge but are not deemed ready to be practicing sorcerers or possession priests. For that they must apply themselves to the second, more difficult, arena of apprenticeship—the knowledge of self. If possession priests know that it takes many mouthfuls of water to douse a fire but have not yet mastered their destructive passions, they will never move forward along the path of the spirits. They will not be prepared to pass their incomplete knowledge on to the next generation.

Like sorcerers and possession priests, griots must be thoroughly prepared before they are ready to sing praise songs. They must know not only the history of the Songhay, but also the power of the "old words" they have committed to memory. The best griots, as the ancestors say, know themselves before others get to know them. They are masters of themselves who are capable of passing on from generation to generation great and powerful knowledge.

For the Songhay, ethnographers are griots. Like griots, they learn a body of cultural and historical knowledge. Unlike griots, they shape this knowledge into books and films. Songhay elders have been familiar with the power of the written word for centuries. Songhay familiarity with film dates to the colonial period in Niger (1922–60). There is therefore a place for ethnographers in the Songhay scheme of cultural things.

Which brings us back to the question of preparation. In the West, ethnographers prepare themselves by reading canonical texts, passing exams, debating abstract theories, and writing papers—mostly in plain style. Then they spend a year or two in a field setting, learn the field language (to some degree), interview informants, and return home to "write up" or "edit" the results. Sometimes ethnographers return to the field on second and third trips. This preparation results in articles, monographs, ethnographies, documentary shorts, and full-length ethnographic films. It results in expositions like chapter 12 of this book, which may be meaningful to us but are meaningless to most people in Songhay.

The Songhay elders I know have little respect for this kind of "one mouthful" ethnography. They say:

> Boro si molo kar farkey se.
>
> One does not play the lute to a donkey.

By the same token, one does not impart ethnographic knowledge to ethnographers who are ill prepared—who have yet to master rudimentary cultural skills, who have yet to master themselves.

So what do the Songhay elders expect of griots and ethnographers? They must possess a full knowledge of the past and the present. They must be eloquent and poetic. They must work many, many years to perfect their art. They must participate as fully as possible in Songhay social life. They must be committed to their craft. They must know themselves. And they must pass their knowledge on to the next generation so that Songhay will not lose its link to the past.

Through his ethnographic practice of "shared anthropology" Jean Rouch, in the view of Songhay elders, has become a griot. For fifty years he has told the story of the Songhay in articles, books, interviews, and films—so many films. For us he is the iconoclastic innovator of *cinéma vérité,* the model for a more radically empirical and artistic anthropology. For people in Niger, Rouch is a griot who he has told the Songhay story well, so well that his words and images have enabled the young to uncover their past and discover their future.

Griots in Songhay are much like the Dogon farmer who during funeral rites sows the seeds of future harvests so the dead may live again. Through their words and images, Songhay griots let the dead live again. For the Songhay elders *that* is the ethnographer's work, *that* is the ethnographer's legacy.

BIBLIOGRAPHY OF JEAN ROUCH

1943   Aperçu sur l'animisme Songhay. *Notes Africaines* 39:4–8.

1946   Culte des génies chez les Songhay. *Journal de la Société des Africanistes* 15:15–32.

1947   (In collaboration with Pierre Ponty and Jean Sauvy.) *Le petit Dan.* Paris: AMG.

Les pierres chantantes d'Ayorou. *Notes Africaines* 43:4–6.

Pierres tailles de grosses dimensions en pays Kouranko. *Notes Africaines* 43:7–8.

1948   "Banghawi": Chasse à l'hippopotame au harpon par les pêcheurs Sorko du Moyen Niger. *Bulletin d'IFAN* 10:361–77.

Vers une littérature africaine. *Présence Africaine* 6:144–46.

1949   Chevauchée des génies, culte de possession au Niger. *Plaisir de France*. Mimeographed.

Les gravures rupestres de Kourki. *Bulletin d'IFAN* 11:340–53.

La mort de Mungo Park. *Notes Africaines* 44:121–24.

Les rapides de Boussa. *Notes Africaines* 44:88–98.

"Surf riding" en côte d'Afrique. *Notes Africaines* 44:50–52.

1950   La danse: "Le monde noir." *Présence Africaine* 8:219–26.

Hypothèses sur la mort de Mungo Park. *Notes Africaines* 45:15–20.

Les magiciens de Wanzerbe. *Caliban* 15:1–7.

Les Sorkowa, pêcheurs itinérants du Moyen Niger. *Africa* 21:5–25.

Toponymie légendaire du "W" du Niger. *Notes Africaines* 45:50–52.

1951   Les pêcheurs du Niger: Techniques du pêche, organisation économique et problèmes de migrations. *IFAN* 72–79:17–20.

1952   Cinéma d'exploration et ethnographie. *Beaux-Arts* (Brussels), 1–7.

1953   *Contribution à l'histoire des Songhay.* Mémoires, 29. Dakar: IFAN.

Notes sur les migrations en Gold Coast. Niamey: IFAN.

Renaissance du film ethnographique. *Cinéma Educatif et Culturel* 5:23–25.

"Yenaandi": Rites de pluie chez les songhay. *Bulletin d'IFAN* 15:1655–19.

1954   *Le Niger en pirogue.* Paris: Fernand Nathan.

Projet d'enquête systématique sur les migrations en Afrique Occidentale. Bukawa: Colloque de Bukavu.

Les Songhay. Paris: Presses Universitaires de France.

1955   A propos des films ethnographiques français. *Positif,* 144–49. *Catalogue des films ethnographiques français.* Paris: UNESCO.

1956   Migrations au Ghana. *Journal de la Société des Africanistes* 26 (1–2): 33–196.

1957   Contribution à l'étude du site rupestre de Tessalit. *Notes Africaines* 52:72–77.

(With Edmond Bernus.) Notes sur les prostitués "Toutou" de Treichville et d'Adjame. *Etudes Eburnéennes* 5:231–44.

Rapport sur les migrations nigériennes vers la Basse Côte d'Ivoire. Niamey: IFAN.

1958   (With Edmond Bernus.) Les "marchés des voleurs" d'Abidjan. In *Mental disorders and mental meeting.* Bukawa: CCTA.

L'Africain devant le film ethnographique. *Cinéma et l'Afrique du Sud du Sahara* (Brussels), 92–94.

1959   Découverte de l'Afrique. *Exploration* (Paris), 15–88.

1960   Comment vivent ensemble. *Cinéma 60,* November–December, 51.

Je cherche la vérité des comportements et des mentalités. *Lettres Françaises,* February, 812.

Problèmes relatifs à l'étude des migrations traditionelles et des migrations actuelles en Afrique noire. *Bulletin d'IFAN,* Ser. B, 22 (3–4): 369–78.

Projet de création d'un centre de films africains. Niamey: IFAN.

La religion et la magie Songhay. Paris: Presses Universitaires de France.

1961   *Enregistrement sonore des traditions orales.* Accra: International Congress of Africanists.

1962   Awakening African cinema. *Courrier de l'UNESCO,* March, 11–15.

Cinéma-vérité, Rouch répond. *Contre Champ* 3.

Situation et tendances du cinéma en Afrique. Paris: UNESCO.

1963   Introduction à l'étude de la communauté de Bregbo. *Journal des Africanistes* 33:129–203.

1964   "Malettes cinématographiques" sur l'Afrique. Preface, *Courrier de UNESCO,* 1963.

Nouvelles techniques cinématographiques et cinéma d'enquête. Venice: Fondation Cini.

1965   Textes rituels Songhay. In *Textes sacrés d'Afrique noire,* ed. G. Dieterlen, 44–56. Paris: Gallimard.

1966   Anthropologie et impérialisme. *Temps Modernes* 193–94:299–300.

(With Monique Gessain and Monique Salzmann.) *Catalogue de 100 films d'intérêt—Analyse minutée de 100 films ethnographiques non français.* Paris: CNRS.

(With Monique Salzmann.) *Catalogue de films sur l'Afrique noire—Analyse et présentation de 600 films sur l'Afrique—Introduction au cinéma africain.* Paris: UNESCO.

De *Jaguar* à *Petit à petit. Cahiers du Cinéma* 200–201:58–59.

Le film ethnographique. In *Ethnologie générale: Collection de la Pléiade*, 429–71. Paris: Gallimard.

Les problèmes sonores du film ethnographique. In *La "Colonne sonore" dans le cinéma d'aujourd'hui.* Paris: UNESCO.

1971   Adventures d'un Nègre-blanc. *Image et Son* 249:55–83.

Dziga Vertov: Cinq regards sur Dziga Vertov. Paris: Champ Libre.

Ethnologie au service du rêve poétique. *Le Devoir* (Montréal), 18 September 1971.

La notion de personne en Afrique noire. *Colloques Internationaux de CNRS* 544. Published in English as On the vicissitudes of the self: The possessed dancer, the magician, the sorcerer, the filmmaker, and the ethnographer. *Studies in the Anthropology of Visual Communication* 5 (1): 2–8.

1974   The camera and the man. *Studies in the Anthropology of Visual Communication* 1 (1): 37–44.

1975   Le calendrier mythique chez les Songhay Zarma (Niger). In *Systèmes de pensée en Afrique noire.* Paris: CNRS.

En diable. In *Prophétism et thérapeutique (Albert Atcho et la communauté Bregbo)*, 11–26. Paris: Hermann.

Tradition orale dans la vallée du Niger: L'empire du Mali. In *Bamako 1: Colloque de 1975* and *Bamako 2: Colloque de 1976.* Paris: Fondation SCOA.

1978   On the vicissitudes of the self: The possessed dancer, the magician, the sorcerer, the filmmaker, and the ethnographer. *Studies in the Anthropology of Visual Communication* 5 (1): 2–8.

Le ranard fou et le maître pâle. In *Systèmes des signes: Textes réunis en hommage à Germaine Dieterlen*, 3–24. Paris: Hermann.

1979   Le caméra et l'homme. In *Pour une anthropologie visuelle*, ed. Claudine de France, 53–71. Paris: Mouton.

1989   *La religion et la magie Songhay.* 2d ed., corrected and expanded. Brussels: Université de Bruxelles.

1990   Le "dit" de Théodore Monod. Unpublished manuscript, Comité du Film Ethnographique, Paris.

Les cavaliers aux vautours: Les conquêtes des Zerma dans le Gurunsi, 1856–1900. *Journal des Africanistes* 60 (2): 5–36.

FILMOGRAPHY OF JEAN ROUCH

Compiled from Ruby (1989) with several additions and deletions, without annotation. CNRS stands for Centre National de Recherche Scientifique; CFE is for Comité du Film Ethnographique; ONF is Office Naitonal des Films; ORTF is Office de Radio-Télévision de France; IRSH is Institut de Recherches en Sciences Humaines (Université de Niamey); IFAN is Institut Français d'Afrique Noire.

1946   (With Pierre Ponty and Jean Sauvy.) *La chevelure magique* [the magic hair]. Black-and-white.

1946–47 (With Pierre Ponty and Jean Sauvy.) *Au pays des mages noirs* [In the land of the black magi]. Paris: Actualités Françaises. Black-and-white. Twelve (or fifteen?) minutes.

1948–49 *La circoncision* [Circumcision]. Paris: CNRS. Black-and-white. Fifteen minutes.

Hombori. Mali.

Initiation à la danse des possédés [Initition into the possession dance]. Paris: CNRS. Black-and-white. Twenty-two minutes. First prize, Festival Maudite de Biarritz, 1949.

Les magiciens de Wanzerbe [The magicians of Wanzerbe]. Paris: CNRS. Black-and-white. Thirty minutes.

1950   *La chasse à l'hippopotame* [The hippopotamus hunt]. Paris: CNRS. Thirty-six minutes.

1951–52 (With Roger Rosfelder.) *Bataille sur le grand fleuve* [Battle on the great river]. Dakar and Paris: IFAN. Thirty-five minutes.

(With Roger Rosfelder.) *Cimetière dans la falaise* [Cemetery in the cliff]. Paris: CNRS and Secretariat d'Etat à la Co-opération. Twenty minutes.

(With Roger Rosfelder.) *Les gens du mil* [The people of millet]. Forty-five minutes.

(With Roger Rosfelder.) *Yenaandi, ou Les hommes qui font la pluie* [Rain dance, or The men who make rain]. Dakar: IFAN. Twenty-seven minutes.

1953–54 *Les maîtres fous* [The crazy masters]. Paris: Films de la Pléiade. Thirty-three minutes. Prize for best short film, Venice Film Festival, 1957.

Mammy Water. (Editing and sound track completed in 1966.) Paris: Films de la Pléiade and CNRS. Twenty minutes.

1954   *Jaguar.* (Begun in 1954, released several times before completion in 1967.) Paris: Films de la Pléiade. Sixty (or ninety-one) minutes.

1955   *Les fils de l'eau* [The sons of water]. Paris: Films de la Pléiade. Seventy-five minutes. First prize for quality, National Center of French Cinematography.

1957   *Baby Ghana.* Paris: CNRS. Twelve minutes.

        La chasse au lion à l'arc [The lion hunters, English version]. (Begun in 1957 and completed in 1964.) Paris: Films de la Pléiade. Ninety minutes. Golden Lion award at the Venice Film Festival 1965.

        Moi, un noir [I, a black]. Paris: Films de la Pléiade. Eighty minutes. Delluc prize, 1959.

        Moro Naba. Paris: CNRS and IFAN. Twenty-seven minutes. Prize, Florence Film Festival, 1960.

1958   *La royale Goumbe.* Paris: CNRS/CFE.

        (With Gilbert Rouget.) *Sakpata.* (Released in 1963). Paris: CNRS/CFE. Twenty-five minutes.

1958–59 *La pyramide humaine* [The human pyramid]. (Released in 1961.) Paris: Films de la Pléiade. Eighty (or ninety?) minutes.

1960   (In collaboration with Edgar Morin.) *Chronique d'un été* [Chronicle of a summer]. Black-and-white. Seventy-five (or ninety?) minutes. Festival prizes Cannes, Venice, Mannheim, 1961.

        Hampi. Paris: CNRS/CFE. Twenty-five minutes. Festival prize Florence, 1962.

        La punition [The punishment]. (Released in 1962 for broadcast on French television.) Paris: Films de la Pléiade. Black-and-white. Sixty minutes.

1961   *Les ballets du Niger* [The ballets of Niger]. Black-and-white. Twenty minutes.

        (Rouch was adviser to Claude Jutra.) *Niger, jeune république* [Niger, young republic]. Quebec: ONF. Fifty-eight minutes.

1962   *Abidjan, port de pêche* [Abidjan, fishing port]. Paris: CNRS/CFE. Twenty-five minutes.

        Le cocotier [The coconut palm]. Paris: CNRS/CFE. Twenty-one minutes.

        Fêtes d'indépendance du Niger [Celebrations of the independence of Niger]. Niger: CNRS/CFE and IFAN. Twenty-one minutes.

        Le palmier à huile [The palm oil tree]. Paris: CNRS/CFE and IFAN. Twenty minutes.

        Les pêcheurs du Niger [The fishermen of the Niger]. Paris: CNRS/CFE.

        Rose et Landry [Rose and Landry]. Quebec: ONF and Canadian Film Board. Black-and-white. Twenty-three minutes. Two prizes Venice Film Festival, 1963.

        Urbanisme africain [African town planning].

1963   *Festival à Dakar* [Festival in Dakar]. Paris: CNRS/CFE.

Le mil [Millet]. Paris: CNRS/CFE. Twenty-seven minutes.

Monsieur Albert, prophète, ou Albert Atcho [Mr. Albert, prophet, or Albert Atcho]. Paris: Argos Films and CNRS. Twenty-seven or thirty-three) minutes.

1964   *L'Afrique et la recherche scientifique* [Africa and scientific research]. Paris: CNRS and UNESCO. Thirty-one minutes.

(Codirector Gilbert Rouget, with Germaine Dieterlen.) *Batteries Dogon, éléments pour une étude des rythmes, ou Tambour de pierre* [Dogon drums, elements of a study of rhythms, or Stone drums]. Paris: CNRS/CFE. Twenty-five minutes.

Les veuves de quinze ans [The fifteen-year-old widows]. Paris: Films de la Pléiade. Twenty-five minutes.

1965   *Alphabétisation des adultes au Mali* [Adult literacy in Mali].

Alpha noir [Black alpha]. Paris: CNRS/CFE. Ten minutes.

La Goumbe des jeunes noceurs [The Goumbe of the young revelers]. Paris: CNRS and Films de la Pléiade. Thirty minutes.

Jackville. Paris: CNRS/CFE. Twenty minutes.

Musique et danse des chasseurs Gow [Music and dances of the Gow hunters]. Paris; CNRS/CFE. Twenty minutes.

Tambours et violons des chasseurs Songhay [The drums and violins of the Songhay hunters].

1966   *Dongo horendi* [Festival for Dongo]. Paris: CNRS/CFE. Thirty minutes.

Dongo yenaandi, Gamkalle [Dongo's rain dance, Gamkalle]. Paris: CNRS/CFE. Ten minutes.

Gare du Nord. Paris: Films de Losange. Twenty minutes.

Koli Koli. Pairs: CNRS/CFE. Thirty minutes.

(With Germaine Dieterlen.) *Sigui 66: Année zero* [Year zero]. Paris: CNRS. Fifteen minutes. Double system sound.

1967   *Daouda Sorko.* Paris: CNRS/CFE. Fifteen (or twenty?) minutes.

Faran Maka's fonda [Faran Maka's path]. Ninety minutes. Double system sound. Not edited.

Royale Goumbe. Ten minutes. Double system sound. Not edited.

(Codirectors Gilbert Rouget and Germaine Dieterlen.) *Sigui no. 1: L'enclume de Yougou* [The anvil of Yougou]. Paris: CNRS/CFE. Thirty-five (or fifty?) minutes.

Yenaandi de Boukoki [Rain dance at Boukoki, Niamey, Niger]. Twenty-five minutes. Double system sound. Not edited.

Yenaandi de Gamkalle [Rain dance at Gamkalle, Niamey, Niger]. Forty-five minutes. Double system sound. Not edited.

Yenaandi de Gourbi Beri [Rain dance at Gourbi Beri, Niamey, Niger]. Ten minutes. Double system sound.

Yenaandi de Kirkissey [Rain dance at Kirkissey, Niger]. Ten minutes. Double system sound. Not edited.

Yenaandi de Kongou [Rain dance at Kongou, Niger]. Ten minutes. Double system sound. Not edited.

Yenaandi de Simiri [Rain dance at Simiri, Niger]. Ten minutes. Double system sound. No longer available.

1968   *Un lion nommé "l'Américain"* [A lion named "the American"]. Paris: CNRS/CFE. Twenty minutes.

Les pierres chantants d'Ayoru [The musical stones of Ayoru]. Paris: CNRS Audiovisuels/CFE. Ten (or twenty) minutes.

La révolution poétique: Mai '68 [The poetic revolution: May '68]. Forty (or fifty?) minutes. Double system sound. Not edited.

(With Germaine Dieterlen.) *Sigui no. 2: Les danseurs de Tyougou* [The dancers of Tyougou]. Paris: CNRS Audiovisuels/CFE. Fifty minutes.

Wanzerbe. Paris: CNRS/CFE. Thirty (or twenty?) minutes. Double system sound.

Yenaandi de Ganghel [Rain dance at Ganghel]. Paris: CNRS/CFE. Sixty (or thirty-five?) minutes.

1969   *Afrique sur Seine* [Africa on the Seine]. No running time.

L'imagination au pouvoir [The power of imagination]. No running time.

Petit à petit [Little by little]. Paris: Films de la Pléiade in collaboration with CNRS [Niamey and CFE]. Ninety-six minutes in 35 mm; 250 minutes in 16 mm (released in 16 mm—ninety-minute version).

(With Germaine Dieterlen.) *Sigui no. 3: La caverne de Bongo* [The Bongo cave]. Paris: CNRS Audiovisuels/CFE. Forty minutes.

Yenaandi de Karey Gorou [Rain dance at Karey Gorou]. Ten minutes. Double system sound. No longer available.

Yenaandi de Yantalla [Rain dance at Yantalla, Niamey, Niger]. Paris: CNRS/CFE. Forty minutes.

1970   (With Germaine Dieterlen.) *Sigui no. 4: Les clameurs d'Amani* [The clamor of Amani]. Paris: CNRS Audiovisuels/CFE. Fifty minutes.

Taway Nya—La mère [Mother of twins—mother]. Paris: CNRS/CFE. Twelve minutes. Double system sound.

1971   *Architectes d'Ayoru* [The architects of Ayoru]. Paris: CNRS/CFE. Thirty-five (or thirty?) minutes.

(With Gilbert Rouget.) *Porto Novo: La danse des reines* [Porto Novo: The dance of the queens]. Paris: CNRS/CFE. Thirty minutes.

Rapports mères-enfants en Afrique [Relations between mothers and infants in Africa]. Paris: ORTF. Twenty minutes.

(With Germaine Dieterlen.) *Sigui no. 5: La dune d'Idyeli* [The dune of Idyeli]. Paris: CNRS Audiovisuels/CFE. Forty (or fifty) minutes.

(Assisted by Lam Ibrahim Dia and Tallou Mouzourane.) *Les tambours d'avant: Turu et bitti* [The drums of yore: Turu and bitti]. (Produced in 1967–68 and released in 1971.) Paris: CNRS/CFE. Ten minutes.

Yenaandi de Simiri [Rain dance at Simiri]. Paris: CNRS/CFE. Thirty minutes.

1972   *L'enterrement du hogon* [The burial of the hogon]. Paris: CNRS/CFE. Thirty (or fifteen?) minutes.

(Codirector Germaine Dieterlen.) *Funérailles à Bongo: Le vieil Anai* [Funeral at Bongo: The old Anai]. (Released in 1979.) Paris: CNRS Audiovisuels/CFE. Seventy-five (or forty-five?) minutes.

Horendi. Paris: CNRS/CFE. Fifty (or ninety?) minutes.

(With Germaine Dieterlen.) *Sigui no. 6: Les pagnes de Yamé* [The wraparound skirts of Yamé]. Paris: CNRS Audiovisuels/CFE. Forty (or fifty?) minutes.

1973   *L'an 01* [The year 01]. Black-and-white. No running time.

Bukoki. Paris: CNRS/CFE. Twenty-five minutes.

Dongo hori [Dongo's festival]. Paris: CNRS/CFE. Twenty minutes.

La foot-girafe, ou L'alternative [The foot giraffe, or The alternative]. No running time.

Funérailles de femme à Bongo [A woman's funeral in Bongo]. Twenty minutes.

Rythme de travail [Work rhythms]. Paris: CNRS/CFE. Twelve minutes.

Sécheresse à Simiri [Drought at Simiri]. Paris: CNRS/CFE. Ten minutes.

Tanda singui (poser le hangar) [To sanctify the (possession) canopy]. Paris: CNRS/CFE. Twenty (or thirty) minutes.

V. V. Voyou. Paris: Société Commerciale de l'Ouest Africain. Thirty minutes.

1974   (Codirector Germaine Dieterlen.) *Ambara Dama*. Paris: CNRS Audiovisuels/CFE. Sixty minutes.

La 504 et les foudroyeurs [The Peugeot 504 and the lightning bolts]. Ten minutes.

Cocorico, Monsieur Poulet. Paris/Niamey: DALAROU (Damoré, Lam, Rouch), with technical assistance of CNRS/IRSH; CNRS/CFE; Musée de l'Homme. Ninety minutes.

Hommage à Marcel Mauss: Taro Okamoto [Homage to Marcel Mauss: Taro Okamoto]. Paris: CNRS/CFE. Fourteen minutes.

Pam kuso kar (Briser les poteries de Pam) [Breaking Pam's jars]. Paris: CNRS/CFE. Ten minutes.

(With Germaine Dieterlen.) *Sigui no. 7: L'auvent de la circoncision* [The circumcision shelter]. Paris: CNRS Audiovisuels/CFE. Fifteen minutes.

1975   *Babatu, les trois conseils* [Babatu, three pieces of advice]. Paris: CNRS/CFE. Ninety minutes.

   Initiation. Paris: CNRS/CFE. Forty-five minutes. Double system sound.

   Sécheresse à Simiri [Drought at Simiri]. Paris: CNRS/CFE. Ten minutes.

   Souna Kouma (la nostalgie de Souna) [Nostalgia for Souna]. Paris: CNRS/CFE.

   Toboy, tobaye, tobaye (lapin, petit lapin) [Rabbit, rabbit, little rabbit]. Paris: CNRS/CFE. Twelve minutes. Not available.

1976   *Faba tondi* [Rock of protection]. Twenty minutes.

   (Codirector Inoussa Ousseini.) *Médecine et médecins* [Medicine and doctors]. Paris and Niamey: CNRS Audiovisuels/CFE and IRSH. Fifteen minutes.

   Yenaandi: Sécheresse à Simiri [Rain dance: Drought at Simiri]. 120 minutes.

1977   *Ciné-portrait de Margaret Mead* [Cine-portrait of Margaret Mead]. Paris and New York: CFE and American Museum of Natural History. Thirty-five minutes.

   Fêtes des Gandyi Bi à Simiri [Black Spirit celebration at Simiri]. Paris: CNRS/CFE. Thirty minutes.

   (Coproducer Inoussa Ousseini.) *Le griot Badye* [Badye the bard]. Paris: CNRS/CFE. Fifteen minutes.

   Hommage à Marcel Mauss: Germaine Dieterlen [Homage to Marcel Mauss: Germaine Dieterlen]. Paris: CNRS/CFE. Twenty minutes.

   Hommage à Marcel Mauss: Paul Levy [Homage to Marcel Mauss: Paul Levy]. Paris: CNRS/CFE. Twenty minutes.

   Makwayela: Paris: CNRS/CFE. Twenty minutes.

   Yenaandi de Simiri [Rain dance at Simiri]. No running time. Double system sound.

1979   *Simiri Siddo Kuma.* Paris: CNRS/CFE. Thirty minutes.

   Yenaandi de Simiri accompagné de semailles [Rain dance at Simiri accompanied by seed planting]. No running time. Double system sound.

1980   *Capt'ain Omori.* No running time. Double system sound.

   (Codirected with the Group Cinema of the University of Leyden.) *Ciné-Mafia.* Thirty-five minutes.

1981   *Les cérémonies soixantenaires du Sigui* [The sixty-year cycle of Sigui ceremonies]. Paris: CNRS/CFE. Ninety minutes. Double system sound.

   (With Damoré, Lam, Tallou.) *Les deux chasseurs* [The two hunters]. Double system sound.

   (Codirectors Germaine Dieterlen and Luc de Heusch.) *Le renard pâle* [The pale fox].

1984   *Dionysos.*
1987   *Bac ou mariage.* Paris: CFE.
1990   *Liberté, égalité, fraternité, what's next?* Paris: ORTF. Ninety min-
        utes.

REFERENCES

PRINTED WORKS

Abitol, M. 1977. *Timbuktou et les Armas*. Paris: Maisonneuve.

Achebe, C. 1989. *Hopes and impediments: Selected essays*. New York: Doubleday.

Austin, J. 1962. *How to do things with words*. London: Oxford University Press.

Balakian, A. 1986. *Surrealism*. Chicago: University Chicago Press.

Banks, M. 1990. The seductive veracity of ethnographic film. *Society for Visual Anthropology Review* 6:16–21.

Barzun, J. 1983. *A stroll with William James*. Chicago: University of Chicago Press.

Bentham, J. 1931. *The theory of legislation*. London: International Library of Psychology.

Bergé, C. n.d. De l'autre côte du miroir. Unpublished manuscript, files of the author.

Bernus, E. 1960. Kong et sa région. *Etudes Eburnéennes* 8:239–324.

Bird, C. 1971. Oral art in the Mande. In *Papers on the Manding,* ed. C. T. Hodge, 15–27. Bloomington: Indiana University Press.

Breton, A. 1924. *Manifestes du Surréalisme*. Paris: Gallimard.

———. 1929. *Manifestes du Surréalisme*. Paris: Kra.

Broch, H. 1964 [1932]. *The sleepwalkers*. Trans. W. Muir and E. Muir. New York: Grosset and Dunlap.

Bousset, J. 1836. *Oeuvres complêts*. Paris: Lefevre.

Calame-Griaule, G. 1965. *Ethnologie et langage: La parole chez les Dogon*. Paris: Gallimard.

Camara, S. 1976. *Gens de la parole: Essai sur la condition et le rôle des griots dans la société Malinke*. Le Hague: Mouton.

Charbonnier, G. 1980. *Le monologue du peintre*. Paris: Guy Durier.

Clezio, P. 1972. *Jaguar. Télé-Ciné* 175:15–18.

Clifford, J. 1988. *The predicament of culture*. Cambridge: Harvard University Press.

Clifford, J., and G. Marcus, eds. 1986. *Writing culture.* Berkeley: University of California Press.

Cohen, A. 1969. *Custom and politics in urban Africa.* Berkeley: University of California Press.

Collet, J. 1967. Quand je fait un film c'est que ça m'amuse. *Telerama* 933.

Conrad, J. 1971 [1899]. *Heart of darkness.* New York: Norton.

Corbin, A. 1986. *The foul and the fragrant.* Cambridge: Harvard University Press.

DeBouzek, J. 1989. The ethnographic surrealism of Jean Rouch. *Visual Anthropology* 2 (3–4):301–17.

Delafosse, M. 1911. *Haut Senegal-Niger.* Paris: Maisonneuve.

Delahaye, M. 1961. La règle de Jean Rouch. *Cahiers du Cinema* 120.

Deleuze, G. 1989. *Cinema 2: The time image.* Minneapolis: University of Minnesota Press.

DeVos, G. 1982. *Les maîtres fous* et anthropologie américaine. In *Jean Rouch, un griot gaulois,* special issue of *CinemAction,* ed. R. Predal, 59–62. Paris: Harmattan.

Dewey, J. 1980a [1934]. *Art as experience.* New York: Perigee Books.

———. 1980b [1929]. *The quest for certainty.* New York: Perigee Books.

Diarra, A. F. 1974. Les relations entre les hommes et les femmes et les migrations Zarma. In *Modern migrations in western Africa,* ed. S. Amin, 226–38. London: Oxford University Press.

Dieterlen, G. 1941. *Les âmes des Dogons.* Paris: Institut d'Ethnologie.

———. 1982. *Le titre d'honneur des Arou.* Paris: Société des Africanistes.

Douglas, M. 1967. If the Dogon. . . . *Cahier d'Etudes Africaines* 7 (27): 659–72.

Dupire, M. 1960. Planteurs autochtones et étrangers en basse Côte d'Ivoire orientale. *Etudes Eburnéennes* 8:7–237.

Eaton, M., ed. 1979. *Anthropology-reality-cinema: The films of Jean Rouch.* London: British Film Institute.

Echard, N., and J. Rouch. 1988. Entretien avec Jean Rouch. A voix nu. Entretien d'hier à aujourd'hui. Ten-hour discussion broadcast in July 1988 on France Culture.

Edie, J. 1965. Notes on the philosophical anthropology of William James. In *An invitation to phenomenology,* ed. J. Edie, 110–33. Chicago: Quandrangle Books.

Eliot, T. S. 1942. *Four quartets.* New York: Harcourt, Brace and World.

es-Saadi, A. 1900. *Tarikh es-Soudan.* Trans. O. Houdas. Paris: Leroux.

Favret-Saada, J. 1981. *Deadly words: Witchcraft in the Bocage.* London: Cambridge University Press.

Feld, S., ed. 1974. *Studies in the Anthropology of Visual Communication* (first four issues).

———. 1982. *Sound and sentiment.* Philadelphia: University of Pennsylvania Press.

———. 1989. Themes in the cinema of Jean Rouch. *Visual Anthropology* 2 (3–4): 223–49.

Flaherty, F. 1960. *The odyssey of a filmmaker: The story of Robert Flaherty.* Urbana, Ill.: Beta Phi Mu.

Foucault, M. 1970. *The order of things: The archaeology of the human sciences.* New York: Random House.

Freeman, D. 1983. *Margaret Mead and Samoa.* Cambridge: Harvard University Press.

Fugelstad, F. 1975. Les Hauka: Une interprétation historique. *Cahiers d'Etudes Africaines* 58:203–16.

———. 1983. *A history of Niger, 1850–1960.* Cambridge: Cambridge University Press.

Gaggi, S. 1989. *Modern/postmodern: A study in twentieth century arts and ideas.* Philadelphia: University of Pennsylvania Press.

Gauthier G. 1972. Le cinéma en Afrique noire. *Image et Son* 149:3–5.

Geertz, C. 1973. *The interpretation of cultures.* New York: Free Press.

Ginsburg, F. 1991. Indigenous media: Faustian contract or global village? *Cultural Anthropology* 6 (1): 92–113.

Gleason, J. 1982. Out of water, onto the ground and into the cosmos: An analysis of the three phases of sacred initiatory dance among the Zarma (Songhay) of Niger. In *Spring: An annual of archetypal psychology and Jungian thought,* 3–12. Dallas: Spring Publications.

Gobineau, J. de 1967 [1953–55]. *Essai sur l'inégalité des races humaines.* Paris: Pierre Belfond.

Graff, G. 1979. *Literature against itself.* Chicago: University of Chicago Press.

Griaule, M. 1938. *Masques dogons.* Paris: Institut d'Ethnologie.

———. 1957. *Méthode de l'ethnographie.* Paris: Presses Universitaires de France.

———. 1965. *Conversations with Ogotemmêli.* London: Oxford University Press.

Griaule, M., and G. Dieterlen. 1965. *Le renard pâle.* Vol. 1, fasc. 1. *Le mythe cosmogonie: La création du monde.* Paris: Travaux et Mémoires de l'Institut d'Ethnologie.

Grob, J. 1962. Jean Rouch, ou L'ethnologie à l'art. *Image et Son* 149:3.

Hale, Thomas. 1990. *Scribe, griot, and novelist: Narrative interpreters of the Songhay empire.* Gainesville: University of Florida Press.

Hama, Boubou. 1988. *L'essence du verbe.* Niamey: Centre des Etudes Linguistiques, Historiques, et Traditions Orales.

Heller, E. 1988. *The importance of Nietzsche.* Chicago: University of Chicago Press.

Hiley, D. 1988. *Philosophy in question.* Chicago: University of Chicago Press.

Homiak, John. n.d. Images on the edge of the text: Ethnographic imaging and view of the anthropological self. Forthcoming in *Wide Angle.*

Howes, D. 1988a. On the odor of the soul: Spatial representation and olfactory classification in eastern Indonesia and western Melanesia. *Bijdragen tot de Tall-, Land- en Volkenkunde* 124:84–113.

———. 1988b. The shifting sensorium: A critique of the textual revolution in contemporary anthropological theory. Paper read at the Twelfth International Congress of Anthropological and Ethnological Sciences, Zagreb, Yugoslavia, 26 July 1988.

Howes, D., ed. 1990. *Les "cinq" sens*. Special issue of *Anthropologie et Sociétés* 14, 2.

Hunwick, J. 1985. *Shari'a in Songhay: Replies of al-Maghili to the questions of Askia al-Hajj Muhammad*. New York: Oxford University Press.

Husserl, E. 1960 [1931]. *Cartesian meditations*. The Hague: Marcus Nijhoff.

Ibn Battuta. 1966. *Textes et documents relatifs de l'histoire de l'Afrique*. Trans. R. Mauny. Dakar: Université de Dakar.

Ihde, D. 1976. *Listening and voice: Toward a phenomenology of sound*. Bloomington: Indiana University Press.

Jackson, M. 1989. *Paths toward a clearing*. Bloomington: Indiana University Press.

James, W. 1943. *Essays in radical empiricism*. New York: Longman, Green.

Kaba, L. 1984. The pen, the sword, and the crown: Islam and revolution in the Songhay reconsidered, 1463–1493. *Journal of African History* 25: 241–56.

Kane, S. 1982. Holiness ritual fire handling: Ethnographic and psychophysiological considerations. *Ethos* 10 (4): 369–84.

Kati, M. 1911. *Tarikh al Fattach*. Trans. M. Delafosse. Paris: Maisonneuve.

Kimba, I. 1981. *Guerres et sociétés*. Etudes Nigeriennes 46. Niamey: Université de Niamey.

Konaré Ba, A. 1977. *Sonni Ali Ber*. Etudes Nigeriennes 40. Niamey: Université de Niamey.

Kuenzli, R., ed. 1987. *Dada and Surrealist film*. New York: Willis, Locker and Owens.

Kundera, M. 1988. *The art of the novel*. New York: Grove.

Léca, N. n.d. Les Zerma. Unpublished manuscript. Institut de Recherches en Sciences Humaines, Niamey.

Leiris, M. 1958. *La langue secrète des Dogon de Sanga*. Paris: Institut d'Ethnologie.

———. 1981 [1934]. *Afrique fantôme*. Paris: Gallimard.

Lévi-Strauss, C. 1955. *Tristes tropiques*. Paris: Plon.

———. 1967. The sorcerer and his magic. In *Structural anthropology*. Garden City, N.Y.: Doubleday.

Lienhardt, G. 1961. *Divinity and experience: The religion of the Dinka*. London: Oxford University Press.

Lippard, L., ed. 1970. *Surrealists on art*. Englewood Cliffs, N.J.: Prentice-Hall.

Livingstone, D. 1872. *Livingstone's Africa*. Philadelphia: Hubbard Brothers.

MacCannell, D. 1978. *The tourist: A new theory of leisure*. New York: Schocken Books.

MacDougall, D. 1975. Beyond observational cinema. In *Principles of visual communication*, ed. P. Hockings, 109–24. The Hague: Mouton.

Malcomsen, S. 1989. How the West was lost: Writing at the end of the world. *Voice Literary Supplement*, April, 11–14.

Marcus, G. E. 1990. The modernist sensibility in recent ethnographic writing and the cinematic metaphor of montage. *Society for Visual Anthropology Review* 6:1–16.

Marcus, G. E., and M. M. J. Fischer. 1986. *Anthropology as cultural critique.* Chicago: University of Chicago Press.

Mauny, R. 1952. *Glossaire des expressions et termes locaux employés dans l'Ouest africain.* Dakar: IFAN.

Ministry of Foreign Affairs. 1981. *Jean Rouch: Une rétrospective.* Paris: Ministry of Foreign Affairs.

Montaigne, M. de. 1943. *Selected essays.* New York: Walter Black.

Morrissette, B. 1985. *Novel and film: Essays in two genres.* Chicago: University of Chicago Press.

Muller, J.-C. 1971. Review of *Les maîtres fous. American Anthropologist* 73:1471–73.

Nicholas, G. 1978. *Dynamique sociale et appréhension du monde au sein d'une société Hausa.* Paris: Institut d'Ethnologie.

Nietzsche, F. 1871. *The birth of tragedy out of the spirit of music.* Trans. F. Goffling. Garden City, N.Y.: Doubleday.

Olivier de Sardan, J.-P. 1976. *Quand nos pères étaient captifs.* Pairs: Nubia.

———. 1982. *Concepts et conceptions Sonay-Zerma.* Paris: Nubia.

———. 1984. *Les sociétés Sonay-Zerma.* Paris: Karthala.

Ong, W. 1967. *The presence of the word.* New Haven: Yale University Press.

Östör, A. 1990. Whither ethnographic film? *American Anthropologist* 92 (3): 715–23.

Painter, T. 1988. From warriors to migrants: Critical perspectives on early migrations among the Zarma of Niger. *Africa* 58 (1): 87–100.

Palau-Marti, M. 1957. *Les Dogon.* Paris: Presses Universitaires de France.

Panofsky, H. 1958. *The significance of labor migrations for the economic growth of Ghana.* M.S. thesis, Cornell University.

———. 1960. Les conséquences de migrations de travailleurs sur le bien-être économique du Ghana et de la république du Haute Volta. *Inter-Africa Institute Bulletin* 7 (4): 30–45.

Paulme, D. 1988 [1940]. *L'organisation sociale des Dogon.* Paris: J. M. Place.

Pierre, S. 1967. Le regard brulant du conteur. *Cahiers du Cinéma* 192:66–67.

Predal, R., ed. 1982. *Jean Rouch, un griot gaulois.* Special issue of *Cinem-Action* 17. Paris: Harmattan.

Price, S. 1990. *Primitive art in civilized places.* Chicago: University of Chicago Press.

Prothero, M. 1962. Migrant labor in West Africa. *Journal of Administration Overseas* 1 (3): 149–55.

Reverdy, P. 1970 [1918] Nord-Sud. In *Surrealists on art,* ed. L. Lippard, 16. Englewood Cliffs, N.J.: Prentice Hall.

Richman, M. 1990. Anthropology and modernism in France: From Durkheim to the Collège de Sociologie. In *Modernist anthropology,* ed. M. Manganaro, 183–215. Princeton: Princeton University Press.

Riesman, P. 1977. *Freedom in Fulani social life.* Chicago: University of Chicago Press.

Roberts, R., and M. Klein. 1980. The Bamana slave exodus in 1905 and the decline of slavery in the western Soudan. *Journal of African History* 21 (3): 375–95.

Rose, D. 1990. *Living the ethnographic life.* Newbury Park, Calif.: Sage.

Rotha, P., with the assistance of Basil Wright. 1980. Nanook of the North. *Studies in the Anthropology of Visual Communication* 6 (2): 33–60.

Rouch, Jane. 1981. *Nous irons plus au bals nègres.* Paris: Scarabee.

Rouch, Jean. 1953. *Contribution à l'histoire des Songhay.* Mémoires 29. Dakar: IFAN.

———. 1954a. *Le Niger en pirogue.* Paris: Fernand Nathan.

———. 1954b. *Les Songhay.* Paris: Presses Universitaires de France.

———. 1956. Migrations au Ghana. *Journal de la Société des Africanistes* 26 (1–2): 33–196.

———. 1957. *Rapport sur les migrations nigériennes vers la Basse Côte d'Ivoire.* Niamey: IFAN.

———. 1960. Problèmes relatifs à l'étude des migrations traditionelles et des migrations actuelles en Afrique noire. *Bulletin d'IFAN,* ser. B, 22 (3–4): 369–78.

———. 1974. The camera and the man. *Studies in the Anthropology of Visual Communication* 1 (1): 37–44.

———. 1978a. Jean Rouch talks about his films to John Marshall and John W. Adams. *American Anthropologist* 80 (4): 1005–20.

———. 1978b. On the vicissitudes of the self: The possessed dancer, the magician, the sorcerer, the filmmaker, and the ethnographer. *Studies in the Anthropology of Visual Communication* 5 (1): 2–8.

———. 1978c. Le renard fou et le maître pâle. In *Systèmes des signes: Textes réunis en hommage à Germaine Dieterlen,* 3–24. Paris: Hermann.

———. 1987. Preface. In *Ciné-rituel des femmes Dogon,* by N. Wanono. Paris: CNRS.

———. 1989 [1960]. *La religion et la magie Songhay.* 2d ed., corrected and expanded. Brussels: Université de Bruxelles.

———. 1990a. Les cavaliers aux vautours: Les conquêtes des Zerma dans le Gurunsi, 1856–1900. *Journal des Africanistes* 60 (2): 5–36.

———. 1990b. Le "dit" de Théodore Monod. Unpublished manuscript, Comité du Film Ethnographique, Paris.

Rouch, J., and E. Fulchignoni. 1989. Conversation between Jean Rouch and Professor Enrico Fulchignoni. *Visual Anthropology* 2:265–301.

Ruby, J. 1975. Is an ethnographic film a filmic ethnography? *Studies in the Anthropology of Visual Communication* 2 (2): 104–11.

———. 1989. A Filmography of Jean Rouch, 1946–1980. *Visual Anthropology* 2 (3–4): 333–67.

———. n.d. Speaking for, speaking about, speaking with, or speaking alongside—the documentary dilemma. Unpublished manuscript, files of the author.

Saad, E. 1983. *Social history of Timbuktu*. Cambridge: Cambridge University Press.

Sadoul, G. 1967. Du folklore à l'ethnographie moderne. *Lettres Françaises* 1188:6–7.

————. 1990. *Dictionnaire des cinéastes*. New ed. Paris: Seuil.

Said, E. 1978. *Orientalism*. New York: Random House.

Schildkrout, E. 1978. *The people of Zongo*. Cambridge: Cambridge University Press.

Schmoll, P. 1991. The search for health in a world of dis-ease: Affliction management among the Hausa of central Niger. Ph.D. diss., University of Chicago.

Schutz, A. 1962. *Collected papers I: The problem of social reality*. The Hague: Marcus Nijhoff.

————. 1967. *The phenomenology of the social world*. Trans. G. Walsh and F. Lenhert. Evanston, Ill.: Northwestern University Press.

Schwartz, T. 1983. Anthropology: A quaint science. *American Anthropologist* 85 (4): 919–29.

Searle, J. 1968. *Speech acts*. Cambridge: Cambridge University Press.

Seeger, A. 1981. *Nature and society in central Brazil*. Cambridge: Harvard University Press.

Sidikou, A. 1974. *Sédentairité et mobilité entre Niger et Zagret*. Etudes Nigeriennes 34. Niamey: Université de Niamey.

Stoller, P. 1984. Horrific comedy: Cultural resistance and the Hauka movement in Niger. *Ethos* 11:165–67.

————. 1989a. *Fusion of the worlds: An ethnography of possession among the Songhay of Niger*. Chicago: University of Chicago Press.

————. 1989b. *The taste of ethnographic things: The senses in anthropology*. Philadelphia: University of Pennsylvania Press.

Stoller, P., and C. Olkes. 1987. *In sorcery's shadow: A memoir of apprenticeship among the Songhay of Niger*. Chicago: University of Chicago Press.

Tambiah, S. 1968. The magical power of words. *Man*, n.s., 3:175–203.

Tedlock, D. 1983. *The spoken word and the work of interpretation*. Philadelphia: University of Pennsylvania Press.

Torgovnick, M. 1990. *Gone primitive: Savage intellects, modern lives*. Chicago: University of Chicago Press.

Tyler, S. 1987. *The unspeakable: Discourse, dialogue and rhetoric in the postmodern world*. Madison: University of Wisconsin Press.

Urvoy, Y. 1935. *Les populations du Soudan central (Colonie du Niger)*. Paris: Larose.

van Beek, W. E. A. 1991. Dogon restudied: A field evaluation of the work of Marcel Griaule. *Current Anthropology* 32 (2): 135–67.

Vansina, J. 1985. *Oral tradition as history*. Madison: University of Wisconsin Press.

Vertov, D. 1985. *Kino-eye: The writings of Dziga Vertov*. Ed. A. Michelson, trans. K. O'Brien. Berkeley: University of California Press.

Wanono, N. 1987. *Ciné-rituel des femmes Dogon*. Paris: CNRS.

Watta, O. 1985. "The human thesis: A quest for meaning in African epic."
Ph.D. diss., State University of New York, Buffalo.

Watzlawick, P. 1977. *How real is real? Confusion, disinformation, communication.* New York: Vintage.

Yacouba, Depuis. 1911. *Les Gow, ou Les chasseurs du Niger.* Paris: Leroux.

Yakir, Dan. 1978. Ciné-transe: The vision of Jean Rouch. *Film Quarterly* 31 (3): 1–10.

Zaner, R. 1970. *The way of phenomenology.* Indianapolis: Bobbs-Merrill.

FILMS

Adair, P. 1960. *The holy ghost people.* New York: McGraw-Hill. Sixty minutes.

Dali, S., and L. Buñuel. 1929. *Un chien andalou.* Paris.

Flaherty, R. 1922. *Nanook of the North.* New York.

———. 1925. *Moana.* New York.

Flaherty, R. 1934. *Man of Aran.* New York.

Rouch, J. 1946. *Au pays des mages noirs.* Actualités Françaises. Black-and-white. Twelve (or fifteen?) minutes.

———. 1948–49a. *La circoncision.* Paris: CNRS. Black-and-white. Fifteen minutes.

———. 1948–49b. *Initiation à la danse des possédés.* Paris: CNRS. Black-and-white. Twenty-two minutes.

———. 1948–49c. *Les magiciens de Wanzerbe.* Paris: CNRS. Black-and-white. Thirty minutes.

———. 1951–52a. *Bataille sur le grand fleuve.* Dakar: IFAN. Thirty-five minutes.

———. 1951–52b. *Cimetière dans la falaise.* Paris: CNRS. Twenty minutes.

———. 1951–52c. *Yenaandi, ou Les hommes qui font la pluie.* Paris: CNRS. Twenty-seven minutes.

———. 1953–54. *Les maîtres fous.* Paris: Films de la Pléiade. Thirty-three minutes.

———. 1954–67. *Jaguar.* Paris: Films de la Pléiade. Sixty (or ninety-one) minutes.

———. 1957a. *Baby Ghana.* Paris: CNRS. Twelve minutes.

———. 1957b. *Moi, un noir.* Paris: Films de la Pléiade. Eighty minutes.

———. 1957–64. *La chasse au lion à l'arc* [The lion hunters]. Paris: Films de la Pléiade. Ninety minutes.

———. 1958–59. *La pyramide humaine.* Paris: Films de la Pléiade. Eighty (or ninety?) minutes.

———. 1967a. *Daouda sorko.* Paris: CNRS/CFE. Fifteen (or twenty?) minutes.

———. 1967b. *Sigui no. 1: L'enclume de Yougou.* Paris: CNRS. Thirty-five (or fifty?) minutes.

———. 1968. *Sigui no. 2: Les danseurs de Tyougou.* Paris: CNRS Audiovisuels/CFE. Fifty minutes.

————. 1969a. *Petit à petit*. Paris: Films de la Pléiade. Ninety minutes.

————. 1969b. *Sigui no. 3: La caverne de Bongo*. Paris: CNRS Audiovisuels/ CFE. Forty minutes.

————. 1970. *Sigui no. 4: Les clameurs d'Amani*. Paris: CNRS Audiovisuels/ CFE. Fifty minutes.

————. 1971a. *Porto Novo: La danse des reines*. Paris: CNRS/CFE. Thirty minutes.

————. 1971b. *Sigui no. 5: La dune d'Idyeli*. Paris: CNRS Audiovisuels/CFE. Forty (or fifty) minutes.

————. 1971c. *Les tambours d'avant: Turu et bitti*. Paris: CNRS/CFE. Ten minutes.

————. 1972. *Sigui no. 6: Les pagnes de Yamé*. Paris: CNRS Audiovisuels/ CFE. Fifty (or ninety?) minutes.

————. 1974a. *Cocorico, Monsieur Poulet*. Paris/Niamey: DALAROU. Ninety minutes.

————. 1974b. *Pam kuso kar (Briser les Poteries de Pam)*. Paris: CNRS/CFE. Ten minutes.

————. 1974c. *Sigui no. 7: L'auvent de la circoncision*. Paris: CNRS Audiovisuels/CFE. Fifteen minutes.

————. 1975. *Babatu, les trois conseils*. Paris: CNRS/CFE. Ninety minutes.

Vertov, D. 1922–25. *Kino-Pravda: Film newspaper*. Moscow.

INDEX

245